The War on Christmas

Battles in Faith, Tradition, and Religious Expression

Bodie Hodge
General Editor

First printing: October 2013

Master Books®, P.O. Box 726, Green Forest, AR 72638

Master Books® is a division of the New Leaf Publishing Group, Inc.

ISBN: 978-0-89051-790-1

Library of Congress Number: 2013948497

Cover Design: Left Coast Design

Interior Design: Diana Bogardus

Unless otherwise noted, Scripture quotations are from the New King James Version of the Bible.

Please consider requesting that a copy of this volume be purchased by your local library system.

Printed in the United States of America

Please visit our website for other great titles:

www.masterbooks.net

For information regarding author interviews,

please contact the publicity department at (870) 438-5288

Photo Credits: T-top, B-bottom, L-left, R-right, C-Center, BK-Background

Creation Museum: pg 110, pg 140, pg 142

Wikimedia Commons: pg 8, pg 33, pg 35, pg 92, pg 97, pg 101, pgs 102-103, pg 131 — Images from Wikimedia Commons are used under the CC-BY-SA-3.0 license or the GNU Free Documentation License, Version 1.3.

flickr: pg 53 Tom Taylor, Greenville S.C., pg 117 dianabog (Diana Bogardus)

istockphoto.com: pg 19, pg 39, pg 113, pg 114, pg 116, pg 120, pg 139 T

Dreamstime.com: pg 43, pg 91, pg 112

NASA: pg 81 T, pgs 82-83

Shutterstock.com: pg 7, pg 9, pg 11, pg 12, pg 15, pg 16, pg 17, pg 20, pg 21, pg 23, pg 25, pg 26, pg 27, pg 28, pg 29, pg 30, pg 31, pg 36, pg 38, pg 40, pg 44, pg 47, pg 50, pg 51, pg 52, pg 55, pg 56, pg 57, pg 58, pg 61, pg62, pg 63, pg 67, pg 68, pg 69 (2), pg 71, pg 72, pg 76, pg 81 B, pg 84, pgs 86-87, pg 89, pg 95, pg 98, pg 104, pg 105, pg 106, pg 108, pg 111, pg 121, pg 122, pg 123, pg 125, pg 126, pg 129, pg 133, pg 134, pg 135, pg 137, pg 139 B,

Master Books®
A Division of New Leaf Publishing Group
www.masterbooks.net

TABLE OF CONTENTS

INTRODUCTION

Christmas. Who would attack Christmas? Hard to believe, isn't it? But Christmas is under attack. I would like to give some background as to why this beautiful holiday has caused such controversy.

Many years ago, much of the Western World was heavily Christianized and many people believed in God's Word as the authority. Then there was a subtle attack. It was so subtle that most Christians missed it. It was this idea that man could determine truth about origins apart from the Bible. When the Bible is left out, God is left out. So man, by default, becomes that authority. This is known as the religion of humanism, when man is elevated to a position of authority above God.

Since then, we have seen God and His Word attacked in every area as humanists demand the removal of God and His Word from every area of life. They do this to favor their own religion, which treats man as supreme above God. We have seen:

1. Christian-based public schools and universities (Harvard, Yale, Princeton, etc.) become humanistic;

2. The Bible removed from schools;

3. Prayer removed from schools;

4. Creation removed from schools;

5. The Pledge of Allegiance removed from use;

6. Attacks on the U.S. motto "In God We Trust";

7. Removal of 10 Commandments from public places;

8. Attempts to force acceptance of the sin of homosexual behavior upon Christian institutions and churches.

With these types of attacks, did we really believe that Christmas would be left alone? We now see conflicts surrounding Christmas in the form of refusals to say "Merry Christmas" but instead "Happy Holidays," the forced removal of Nativity scenes in public (and even some private) places, writing *X-mas* instead of *Christmas*, and even claims that Christmas was originally pagan!

Yes, there is a war on Christmas, and Christians need to know about this holiday and how to defend it, if they choose to celebrate it. This book is intended to provide some answers concerning a host of issues and misconceptions surrounding Christmas, and will look extensively at the very first Christmas. We want to proclaim the authority of the Bible from the very first verse of Scripture. God is the authority and this false religion of humanism needs to go.

If we as Christians do not know what we are celebrating, how can we share this good news of Christ with unbelievers? I pray this book is informative, equipping, and a blessing to you and your family all year long.

What
About

Happy Holidays!

Christmas?

CHAPTER 1

Christmas
and a
Humble Christ

Black Friday! What do you think of when you hear those words? Spectacular deals for Christmas? The (un)official beginning of the Christmas season? The worst day ever for anyone in retail or food service? Regardless of what pops into your head when you hear those words, the phrase bears a special meaning — at least in the Western World. It reminds us we need to start buying gifts for our family and friends.

The Christmas season is wrought with traveling, family get-togethers, office parties, breaks from school, and insane deals on flat-screen televisions. And let's not forget Santa Claus, hanging the stockings, decorating the tree, eating copious amounts of delicious food, and opening presents. Does this describe your Christmas?

Unfortunately, this probably describes the majority of people in America (and around the world). But what's the real reason for Christmas? Most people could probably answer this question by stating "the birth of Christ." But are we truly celebrating the birth of Christ? Sure, the wise men brought Him gifts, but they also worshipped Him. While we give gifts to each other, ask yourself what gift you are bringing to Him. The wise men knew the significance of Christ, so they brought Him gifts and worshipped Him.

But the true gift of Christmas is Christ — the Son of God, who became a man and willingly sacrificed Himself for the atonement of our sins to save us from a justly deserved eternal punishment. We are blessed exceedingly by this gift but only seem to celebrate it once a year, although we should be celebrating year-round. Do we truly understand who Jesus is and what He did? We'll be taking a closer look at this. In the meantime, forget about all the secular Christmas hype, focus on what you are giving to Christ, and worship Him.

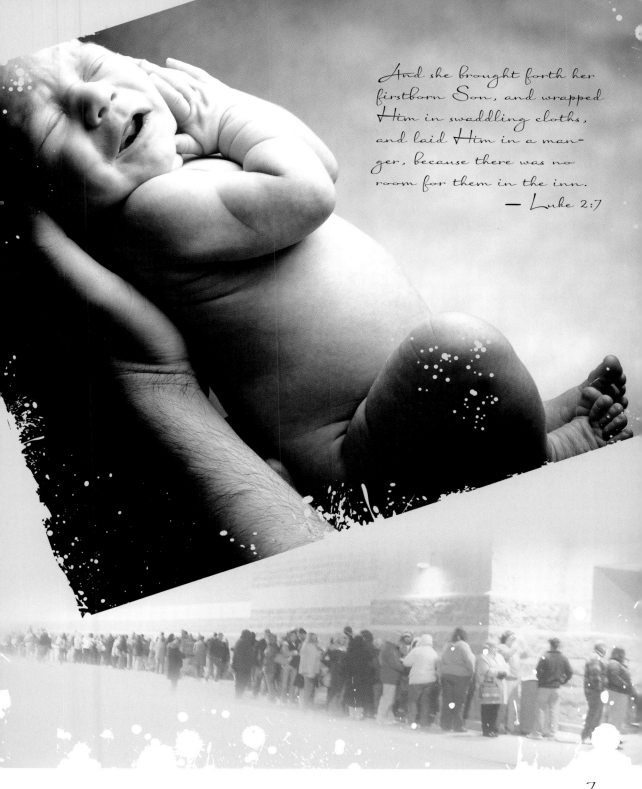

And she brought forth her firstborn Son, and wrapped Him in swaddling cloths, and laid Him in a manger, because there was no room for them in the inn.

— Luke 2:7

Nativity scene on the 2001 Christkindlmarket in downtown Chicago. Christkindlmarket is a Christmas market held annually at Daley Plaza in Chicago, Illinois, United States. The festival is part of the Magnificent Mile Lights Festival and attracts more than 1 million visitors each year.

WHY DID CHRIST COME IN SUCH A HUMBLE AND LOWLY WAY?

After a supernatural conception, Christ was born through natural means. He was carried in the womb and was born as a helpless, vulnerable, powerless, and dependent newborn (of course, God supervised everything so He was never at risk). He didn't come to earth as a conquering angel or a mighty emperor. His parents were poor and probably had little livestock of their own (Luke 2:24; Leviticus 12:8), not to mention they were from Nazareth, an area not held in high regard, even Nathanael said, *"Can anything good come out of Nazareth?"* (John 1:46).

It's difficult to think of something more humble, vulnerable, and lowly than a newborn. God could have entered into this world as the Angel of the Lord, but He chose a much more humble way. Christ's incarnation was a reflection of God's character and heart. He was the utmost example to us of how to approach and present ourselves before the Father (Luke 18:17).

Proverbs 29:23 tells us that *"the humble in spirit will retain honor."* We know that Christ was the most humble of all who have lived on earth, even though He was and is also God, but for our sake He humbled Himself. And because of His humble state, He was given the highest honor:

. . . who, although He existed in the form of God, did not regard equality with God a thing to be grasped, but emptied Himself, taking the form of a bond-servant, and being made in the likeness of men. Being found in appearance as a man, He humbled Himself by becoming obedient to the point of death, even death on a cross. For this reason also, God highly exalted Him, and bestowed on Him the name which is above every name (Philippians 2:6–9; NASB).

According to Isaiah 57:15, God dwells *"with the contrite and lowly of spirit in order to revive the spirit of the lowly and to re-*

Many of the characters of Greek mythology are based on real historical figures who were raised up to god-like status. One example here is "Hellen," the alleged mythological patriarch and god of the Aeolians (or Elisians). Hellen (Ἕλλην) is likely a variant of Elishah.[3] Even in other cultures, ancestors were often deified; for example, in Germanic and Norse mythologies there is Tiras (Tyras, Tiwaz, Tyr), who was the king of the gods and also happens to be one of Noah's grandsons (Genesis 10:2).

So it makes sense that Cronus/Kronos (Κρόνος), a variant of Cethimas/Kittem, could have been raised up to god-like status. Considering that Noah and his early descendants were living such long lives, it should

the New Testament came from "Tarsus," a variant of Tarshish, though Paul was a Jew who was born and living in this portion of Greece (which gave him citizenship in the Roman Empire; Acts 22:28-29). There were also the "Taurus" mountains in Turkey, and "Tanais" is the old name for the Don River flowing into the Black Sea.

Eliseans was the old name of the ancient Greek tribe now called the Aeolians. Cethimus inhabited the island Cethima, from which the name of the island Cyprus was derived. The name of Cyprus in Hebrew is *Kittiy*, from Kittim. (Josephus, a Jewish historian about 2,000 years ago, elaborated on these relationships in more detail.)

be obvious why many of these ancestors were raised up to be "god-like." Not only did they live long lives, but they were obviously the oldest people around and would seem to be the people (gods, demigods) that started civilization.

Noah would have been roughly 500 years older than anyone else and his sons approximately 100 years older. We know this was because of the Flood, but the true message would quickly be changed to fit the pagan ideas. Thus it is interesting that this pagan festival was likely born as a result of a suppressed view of a biblical character.

Interestingly, this name varia-

tion is strikingly similar to biblical Kittim/Chittim from whom Cyprus, Kition (now Larnaka, and Josephus gave the name Cethimus 2,000 years ago) get their names. These are all places near Greece, Cyprus, and Eastern Turkey, where Javan's descendants came from. Kittim's descendants settled in parts of Eastern Turkey, and Greece and Cyprus. Many old names still bear resemblance to variations of Kittim's name in that region of the world. Kittim was the son of Javan, the son of Japheth (likely where the god *Jupiter* comes from), the son of Noah. When Kittim and his family left Babel they settled in these regions.

Like many of the Norse gods, they went back to people in history who were raised up to a god-like status. Considering that Japheth, Javan, and Kittim, etc. often outlived their offspring with the declining long ages they lived (sometimes 300 to 500 years old), it makes sense why such people were idolized and raised up to god-like status. Many pagan cultures have ancestor worship going back to such people who have been "deified" such as Shinto, Norse, Saxon, and Germanic tribes, as well as Greeks and Romans, etc.

Whether Christmas happens to occur at the same time (or close to the same time) as a pagan

Paganism flourishing today at Christmas

holiday is irrelevant. There is nothing inherently wrong with celebrating a Christian holiday at the same time the pagans celebrate. Do Christians refuse to take communion if it falls on a predominantly pagan holiday like Halloween? Absolutely not. On Halloween, some celebrate Reformation Day, because of what Martin Luther did. Many would contend that Easter is based on ancient pagan holidays, as well, but even if the timing is close to these spring holidays, we remember it because Christ's Resurrection occurred around that time.

What should be of greater concern to Christians is the extent to which we have adopted some of the pagan practices during Christmastime. Some have gone overboard on this, and we should be cautious of making Christmas about mythical images like Santa, Charlie Brown, Rudolph, etc., rather than the birth of Christ and why He came to save those who were lost.

The Church has often failed during Christmastime because we simply talk about the birth of Christ without talking about *why* He came. What is important is that we understand the implication of the omnipotent Son of God leaving His heavenly throne to empty Himself! Why would the Creator of the universe choose to do this, knowing He would be raised by sinful parents in a sinful world to be rejected and to die a horrible death? Unbelievable as it is, it was to pay the penalty for the sin of humankind (Romans 3:23, 6:23) so that we — undeserving, hateful sinners, doomed to die — could instead live with Him in paradise for eternity. Now that is worth celebrating!

(Endnotes)

1. This is not be confused with a Sol Invictus, a day of worship to a Roman state-supported sun god. This began around A.D. 274, well after other dates previously mentioned for Christmas.

2. We use "god(s)" in lower case to refer to the "gods" of mythologies; it is not giving an endorsement of these as "gods." There is only one God, the triune God of Scripture. Note the sixth planet is named for Saturn.

3. Set spellings of names were not necessarily common until recent times. Various languages often had variant spellings of the same name — even same language cultures often had variant spellings. We even see this in the Bible with Jeconiah or Jehoiachin; Xerxes and Ahasuerus.

21

CHAPTER 5

When was Jesus Born?

This is a great question. When we turn to the Scriptures (Luke 1:26–37), it says: *Now in the* **sixth month** *the angel Gabriel was sent by God to a city of Galilee named Nazareth, to a virgin betrothed to a man whose name was Joseph, of the house of David. The virgin's name was Mary. And having come in, the angel said to her, "Rejoice, highly favored one, the Lord is with you; blessed are you among women!"*

But when she saw him, she was troubled at his saying, and considered what manner of greeting this was. Then the angel said to her, "Do not be afraid, Mary, for you have found favor with God. And behold, you will conceive in your womb and bring forth a Son, and shall call His name Jesus. He will be great, and will be called the Son of the Highest; and the Lord God will give Him the throne of His father David. And He will reign over the house of Jacob forever, and of His kingdom there will be no end."

Then Mary said to the angel, "How can this be, since I do not know a man?"

And the angel answered and said to her, "The Holy Spirit will come upon you, and the power of the Highest will overshadow you; therefore, also, that Holy One who is to be born will be called the Son of God. Now indeed, Elizabeth your relative has also conceived a son in her old age; and this is now the **sixth month** *for her who was called barren. For with God nothing will be impossible"* (emphasis added).

Here we learn approximately when John was conceived, relative to when the Holy Spirit came upon Mary for the conception of Christ. John would have been conceived around six months before Jesus. If we assume John's conception was the previous year's final month or perhaps the first month of the year, we can do some rough calculations. By assuming this, Elizabeth, John's mother, could have been in her sixth month during the sixth month of the Jewish year.

In Witness Whereof the said ...
... caused this Certificate to be ...
... thorized officer ...

23

This meeting with Gabriel was presumably close to the time when the Holy Spirit would come upon Mary. In fact, it could have been almost immediate, as verse 28 indicates *"the Lord is with you,"* but it was likely soon after, as verse 35 says *"will come upon you."*

In the Jewish calendar, there are 12 months of roughly 30 days each with a leap month every so often to get them back to about 365 days.

Jewish calendar equivalents

MONTH	NAME	SCRIPTURE REFERENCE	MODERN GREGORIAN CALENDAR EQUIVALENT
First	Nisan	Esther 3:7	March–April
Second	Iyar (Iyyar)	N/A	April–May
Third	Sivan	Esther 8:9	May–June
Fourth	Tammuz	N/A	June–July
Fifth	Ab (Av)	N/A	July–August
Sixth	Elul	Nehemiah 6:15	August–September
Seventh	Tishri	N/A	September–October
Eighth	Marchesvan (Heshvan)	N/A	October–November
Ninth	Chislev (Kislev)	Nehemiah 1:1; Zechariah 7:1	November–December
Tenth	Tebet (Tevet)	Esther 2:16	December–January
Eleventh	Sheni (Shevat)	N/A	January–February
Twelfth	Adar	Esther 3:7, 9:1	February–March
Leap month (intercalary)	Adar Sheni (second Adar)	N/A	February–March on leap years

This would have put John the Baptist at about six months in the womb around August/September. Assuming about nine months for pregnancy, John would have been born about November/December by the modern calendar, based on the assumptions we used.

If the Holy Spirit did come upon Mary in the sixth month (Elul) or around August/September, then Jesus should have been born about nine months later, which would place His birth around May/June. Since John the Baptist was still in the womb of Elizabeth when he leapt for joy in Jesus' presence (Luke 1:39-42), this means that the conception had to take place within the next three months or so of the visit by Gabriel — before John was born. Regardless, by this reckoning, the birth of Christ isn't even close to Christmas on the modern calendar.

Be still, and know that I am God;
I will be exalted among the nations,
I will be exalted in the earth!
— *Psalm 46:10*

OTHER NEW YEAR'S DAYS ON THE JEWISH CALENDAR?

We need to exercise some caution since we were using some assumptions (e.g., no leap month and the date of the Jewish New Year. Esther 3:7 points out that Nisan is the first month of the Jewish calendar, and that is still acknowledged today. In Judaism, however, there are other "new year's" days as well. The most popular is called Rosh Hashanah, literally meaning "head of the year."

Rosh Hashanah is celebrated on the first of Tishri, which is normally the 7th month (Leviticus 23:24) and is the start of the civil year. If this were the reference point for the news when the angel Gabriel met Mary, then the 6th month from this would have been the 12th month on the normal Jewish calendar (or February/March), and if this were the case, then Jesus would have been born nine months later in November/December. So it is not without biblical merit that December may have been the date of Christ's birth if we use Rosh Hashanah as the start of the new year.

Around A.D. 220 Julius Africanus, an early Christian writer, reckoned that Jesus was conceived on March 25.[1] Hence, nine months later — about December 25 — Jesus was born. Other Christians have made cases for the December Christmastime as well. Ultimately, we can't know exactly when He was born.

To clarify some points, we, nor other Christians, do not "worship" a pagan holiday or any holiday. We "worship" God on the day that is set aside as Christmas. We take time to "remember" (not worship) the birth of Christ on that day. This is important, because we often get wrapped up in the wrong things, and sometimes we need to step back and remember: *Be still, and know that I am God; I will be exalted among the nations, I will be exalted in the earth* (Psalm 46:10).

ZACHARIAS AND THE FEAST OF TABERNACLES

Some have cleverly reckoned that *if* we can find out the time when Zacharias (John the Baptist's father) was serving at the temple, then we can find approximate dates for both John the Baptist's and Jesus' births (since they should be about six months apart). Logically, this is a sound argument, and it has potential.

If we jump back to Temple service in the time of David the King, he was preparing for aspects of the Temple for Solomon would build (as the Lord would not permit David to build it). But David did make preparations and even began the divisions of priests to work the temple at allotted schedules (1 Chronicles 28:13).

These divisions for service were broken down previously in Chronicles (1 Chronicles 24:1–19). They were of the order of Aaron and his four sons (Nadab, Abihu, Eleazar, and Ithamar). Of course, two of Aaron's sons had died without children (Nadab and Abihu). So all 24 divisions came from Eleazar and Ithamar, and since Eleazar has more children, they accordingly had more divisions.

Each division had to work the temple over the course of a week from a Sabbath to Sabbath (2 Chronicles 23:8). Then it is

And the order of service is listed below:

Name/Division

1 Jehoiarib
2 Jedaiah
3 Harim
4 Seorim
5 Malchijah
6 Mijamin
7 Hakkoz
8 Abijah
9 Jeshua
10 Shecaniah
11 Eliashib
12 Jakim
13 Huppah
14 Jeshebeab
15 Bilgah
16 Immer
17 Hezir
18 Happizzez
19 Pethahiah
20 Jehezekel
21 Jachin
22 Gamul
23 Delaiah
24 Maaziah

assumed that service began on the first Sabbath on the first month of the Jewish calendar (Nisan or March/April), hence Zacharias who was in the eighth order of Abijah or Abia (Luke 1:5) would have been around May/June, and six month later Jesus would have been conceived around November/December, and accordingly was born about nine months later in August/September. On top of this, we do know that shepherds were outside with their flocks at night so it may have been a bit warmer, too, so this makes sense.

OBJECTIONS TO SERVICE RECKONING Although this sounds good at first, but we still need to exercise some caution unless there is more information presented. What stuck out was the assumption that the priestly order of service began at the *first month*. The Bible was silent on this, and for good reasons. It makes more sense that temple service began when the temple was complete [initially during the reign of Solomon]: *And in the eleventh year, in the month of Bul, which is the eighth month, the house was finished in all its details and according to all its plans. So he was seven years in building it* (1 Kings 6:38).

It seems unlikely that service to the temple would be put off for several months, but instead began in the month of Bul, which is the eighth month. But as the Old Testament reveals, many Israelites fell short of God's expectation and services surely fell short. Recall Hezekiah having to renovate the temple and get the Levites back on track in 2 Chronicles 29.

Notice another problem — the month of Bul does not appear on the current Jewish calendar. In fact, the Bible refers to other months in the time of Moses up to the captivity. (Prior to Moses, in the days of Noah the months were simply given as numbers, not names, so this development is most likely a post-Flood development.) Moses was aware of the system of months with names as he later mentioned the month of **Abib** in Exodus 13:4, 23:15, 34:18, and Deuteronomy 16:1. Other months were also mentioned later than Moses such as **Ziv** in 1 Kings 6:1 and 6:37; **Ethanim** in 1 Kings 8:2; and, of course, **Bul** in 1 Kings 6:38.

These four months mentioned correspond to the ancient Canaanite months and refer to agriculturally significant months for their etymology.[2] For example, Abib means *"the month when barley shoots into an ear,"* and so on. This Canaanite influence is to be expected considering that Abraham moved and lived among the Canaanites as did his descendants for many years, prior to moving to Egypt and Moses bringing them back to the land of Canaan, which was the Promised Land.

Furthermore, the Jewish calendar that we are familiar with (and uses Nisan as the first month) is virtually identical to the Babylonian calendar, and rightly so. The Jews borrowed that calendar when they were in captivity in Babylon. This is why references to that calendar do not appear in the Bible until Esther and Nehemiah, which

were after the captivity (Nisan - Esther 3:7, Sivan - Esther 8:9, Elul - Nehemiah 6:15, Tebet - Esther 2:16, Adar - Esther 3:7, and Adar - Esther 9:1). So the question really is, how could they begin their service in the month of Nisan when that calendar was not in use among the Israelites yet?

Fast-forwarding in time, after the captivity Ezra 6:18 records the reassignment of the priestly divisions. But there was a problem. Not all the divisions returned for service. Dr. John Gill points out in his commentary on 1 Chronicles 24:7:

. . . . the Jews say only four of these courses returned from the Babylonish captivity, which were those of Jedaiah, Harim, Pashur, and Immer; though Pashur is not among these here; yet they say each of these four had six lots, and that the names and the order of the other courses were retained and continued under them.[3]

We know that Zacharias in Luke 1:5 was of Abijah (or at least performed the duties of that service time), so that specific lineage had to have been reassigned. In fact, there is no reason to assume that all 24 divisions were not reassigned since they did this in accordance with the Law of Moses. In keeping with this ordinance, they would have likely kept with the same ordering of the priestly lineage's names.

After the captivity though, the temple needed renovating, etc. Ezra records that the Temple had been completed and ready for service on the third day of the month of Adar (Ezra 6:15). Again, it makes sense that the priestly duties began at this time, with the first division. Because the Bible doesn't give an absolute beginning to the onset of the priestly duties, it may not be wise to assume a date, especially since God knew there would be different completion dates and accordingly different dates to begin service.

It is possible, I suppose, if someone wanted to work out the calculation based on this latest date of initial service, that they may be closer to John's and, likewise, Jesus' birth. But one must also consider Herod's Temple, of which Zacharias was working. According to John 2:20, it was built about 46 years before Jesus' proclamation that He would *raise up the temple in three days.*

When was its exact commission date? Did they start over with the first division of priests? The Bible simply does not tell us. So at this point we can still not be certain of the date of Christ's birth. But we can say that Jesus was born closer to the late evening/night, for an angel informed the shepherds of Christ's birth *at night.*

(Endnotes)

1   Sextus Julius Africanus, Chronographiai, a.d. 221.

2   Jack Finegan, *Handbook of Biblical Chronology, Revised Edition* (Peabody, MA: Hendickson Publishers, 1998), p. 18–64.

3   John Gill, *Exposition of the Entire Bible:* Commentary Note on Luke 1:5 (1748-1763).

CHAPTER 6

Timeline
of Events
Surrounding
Christ's Birth

Skeptics often dismiss the accounts of Matthew 2 and Luke 2 by claiming they do not line up, and therefore the accounts should be discarded. Sometimes they go so far as to say that few are even aware of these issues.

But is this really a problem? When we take a closer look, this claim is simply reduced to dust. The following is a plausible timeline that makes sense and works well with the information given in the Scriptures.[1]

CIRCA 4 B.C.[2]

a. Because of the Roman census, Joseph and Mary travel to Bethlehem from their hometown of Nazareth. Jesus was likely born in the lower room where animals often stay, not the guest room (*kataluma*), and subsequently laid in a manger (Luke 1:26–27, 2:4–7).

b. The shepherds visited following the angelic announcement (Luke 2:8–12, 20).

c. The angels worshiped the Christ (Luke 2:13–14).

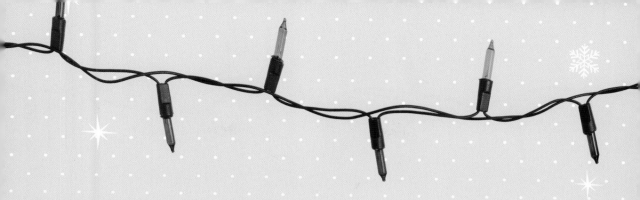

EIGHT DAYS LATER

Jesus was circumcised. This probably did not occur in Jerusalem but a local synagogue or perhaps a priest came to them, as was the case for John the Baptist (Luke 1:59, 2:21; Leviticus 12:3).

Jesus was given His name (Luke 2:21).

AT LEAST 41 DAYS AFTER HIS BIRTH

The Law stipulated a woman wait 40 days following the birth of a son to finish her purification (Leviticus 12:1–8). So Mary and Joseph went to the temple in Jerusalem to offer a sacrifice of two doves or pigeons, which signified they were poor (Luke 2:22–24). This suggests the magi had not visited yet to offer their expensive gifts; otherwise, Joseph and Mary could have afforded the lamb and dove required by the Law for those with adequate means.

At the temple, Simeon held Jesus, blessed God and the family, and prophesied in the Holy Spirit about Jesus (Luke 2:25–35).

Anna, a prophetess, saw the Christ at the temple (Luke 2:36–38).

SOON AFTER THE 41ST DAY

The family returned to Bethlehem — not Nazareth, as some have suggested. After all, they were still in Bethlehem when the wise men later visited and they apparently planned to return there following the flight to Egypt. [3] As such, it is unlikely they would have packed up everything to go to Jerusalem for offering sacrifices. So they would have returned to Bethlehem where they left their belongings (Matthew 2:5–9).

They were now staying in a house (*oikian*) — perhaps the same one, but probably not in the stall area since the guest room (*kataluma*) may have been available at this time.

WITHIN THE YEAR[4]

Alerted by the so-called Christmas star, an unknown number of magi from the East (perhaps Persia[5]) made their way to Herod's palace in Jerusalem to inquire of the Christ child (Matthew 2:1–4).

Contrary to popular opinion, the star was not a typical event in the heavens (e.g., supernova, planetary alignment, comet, etc.) Instead, it was truly a miraculous and special star (Matthew 2:2, 7, 9–11).

Jewish chief priests and scribes informed Herod that, according to Micah 5:2, Bethlehem was to be the birthplace of the Messiah (Matthew 2:4–6).

These magi followed the star, which moved ahead of them, bringing expensive gifts of gold, frankincense, and myrrh to Jesus — who was now a young child living in a house[6] (Matthew 2:9–11).

They worshiped the Christ Child (Matthew 2:11).

Jesus is called a "young Child" (*paidion*, Matthew 2) instead of babe (*brephos*, Luke 2:16) at the time that the magi arrived. *Brephos* specifically refers to a baby, whether born or unborn, while *paidion* refers to an immature child, possibly an infant (Matthew 2:11), so we should not be dogmatic about His age.

They returned to their homeland via a different route after being divinely warned in a dream not to go back to Herod (Matthew 2:12).

Soon after the wise men left, Herod realized that they were not going to return and he ordered the killing of all boys in and around the region of Bethlehem who were two years of age and under (Matthew 2:16). Herod knew the approximate timing of the appearing of the star (Matthew 2:7), which may be the time that Christ was born. With this information, Herod, who was paranoid about the crown and did not want anyone taking over, would have made sure to kill the child. So he may have at least doubled the time from when the star first appeared to the wise men, thinking this would guarantee that the child would be killed, even if the information was off.

An angel warned Joseph to flee to Egypt to protect his family. This trip would ultimately fulfill a prophecy (Hosea 11:1). Perhaps the new gifts helped finance that trip (Matthew 2:13–15).

LATE 4 B.C. TO EARLY 3 B.C.

Herod died in 4 B.C. in Jericho and was buried in Herodion approximately 25 miles away. Reports are that the procession traveled with the body one mile per day. So it was likely 3 B.C. when he was buried.[7] Herod's son Archelaus took over (Matthew 2:22).

Herod's tomb in Herodion (Herodyon, Herodium)
Elef Millim project

EARLY 3 B.C.

An angel informed Joseph that they could move back since Herod had died (Matthew 2:15, 19).

Since Joseph and Mary had completed the laws and commands (*nomos* in Greek) of the Lord, they returned to the land of Israel from Egypt and settled in Nazareth of Galilee, which became the hometown of Jesus and was where Joseph and Mary lived prior to going to Bethlehem for the census[8] (Matthew 2:22; Luke 2:39).

Jesus would be called a Nazarene, fulfilling a spoken prophecy (Matthew 2:23).

The timeline makes sense when the Gospels of Luke and Matthew are carefully analyzed. Any alleged contradiction of the timeline at the time of Christ's entrance into the world simply vanishes in light of the chronology given. When it comes to the Scriptures, they can be trusted. Sometimes we just need to take some time to carefully study them.

And the
Child grew
and became
strong in
spirit, filled
with wisdom;
and the grace
of God was
upon Him.
—Luke 2:40

36

(Endnotes)

1 We should not be dogmatic about the specific details here. This article is designed to show that the details of the biblical account are not contradictory but entirely consistent.

2 Ussher believed Jesus was born near the beginning of 4 B.C. since the king, Herod the Great, died near the end of that year, and Jesus was born during his reign. James Ussher, translated by Larry and Marion Pierce, *The Annals of the World* (Green Forest, AR: Master Books, 2003), p. 779.

3 Some respected chronologists place the visit of the magi, the flight to Egypt, Herod's death, and the return from Egypt prior to Mary's sacrifices on the 40th day at the temple. See Dr. Floyd Jones, *Chronology of the Old Testament* (Green Forest, AR: Master Books, 2005), p. 214–216. Though this is possible, there are some problems. For example, Matthew 2:21–22 states: "Then he arose, took the young Child and His mother, and came into the land of Israel. But when he heard that Archelaus was reigning over Judea instead of his father Herod, he was afraid to go there. And being warned by God in a dream, he turned aside into the region of Galilee." Why would Joseph take Mary and Jesus to the temple *in Jerusalem* when they feared Archelaus (Herod's son) who was ruling in Jerusalem? Why would they go to Judea after being instructed by an angel to go to Galilee?

4 Ussher places the visit of the magi prior to the 40th day (*The Annals of the World,* p. 779). Some churches celebrate the Epiphany on January 6 (12 days after Christmas) in honor of the visit of the magi. This is the origin of the "12 days of Christmas" tradition. However, it makes more sense that Joseph and Mary were still poor. Furthermore, they were likely still living with relatives during the census period and potentially in the same animal-housing portion of the place where Jesus was born and laid in a manger. It was not until later that they were living in a house when the wise men visited.

5 The magi may have been familiar with the promises of the coming Messiah due to Daniel's influence and/or the Jewish holdovers from the Babylonian captivity. The Hebrew scrolls (e.g., Numbers 24:17) would have been highly revered among magi. Keep in mind that magi and wise men were together among the elite in Babylon in those days. Daniel 2:48 states that Daniel was elevated above all of them.

6 Some may propose that Joseph, Mary, and Jesus were in Nazareth already and the star then altered the magi's journey from Bethlehem to Nazareth. However, if this were the case, then there would have been no reason for the angel to warn Joseph to flee to Egypt to avoid the coming massacre by Herod. Had they moved to Nazareth immediately after doing business in Jerusalem and did not return to Bethlehem where they had been staying, they would have had to arrive back in Bethlehem for the visit from the magi. So it still makes more sense to have them go back to Bethlehem after the sacrifices.

7 Josephus, *Antiquity of the Jews*, Book 17, chapter 8 [Herod's death — his last will — burial. 4, 3 B.C.] and *Wars of the Jews,* Book 1, chapter 33 [The golden eagle cut to pieces — Herod's barbarity — attempts to kill himself — commands Antipater to be slain — survives him by five days. 4 B.C.] *The Revised Works of Josephus*). See also Ussher, *The Annals of the World,* p. 781.

8 Luke 2:39 indicates that when they had completed all that was required of them by the Lord, they returned and settled in Galilee where they had originally come from. This would have been upon their return from Egypt to complete what had been stated by the Lord through the angels. They had completed the temple rituals given by Moses, and they had now just completed the instructions given by an angel to leave and return. Their decision to go to Galilee was prompted by an angel due to Herod's son Archelaus taking the reign in Judea because Galilee was out of his jurisdiction (Matthew 2:22).

CHAPTER 7

Making the Christmas Sermon
Relevant for Today's Culture

If you think that the average "Christmas message" doesn't move non-believers, you're not alone. This might help some pastors reach more.

I heard several sermons on the birth of Jesus. Now, in our Western culture that is rapidly losing its once-Christian worldview, Christians and Christian leaders need to use this time more than ever to challenge non-Christians. But will they give the vital message people need to hear at this time of history?

I was thrilled to be able to bring a friend who has struggled with the Christian faith for his entire life to church one Christmas season. Just before we arrived, he asked me a question that had been troubling him. I was fascinated to note that he didn't ask about Jesus and the manger, or about the shepherds or the angels who proclaimed the birth of Jesus on earth — instead, he asked, "Why do many Christians use organ transplants to prolong their life or try to prolong the lives of their children when they're born with problems and God had deemed it was their time to die?" He continued, "Why wouldn't a Christian accept their death that came from God? Shouldn't they just accept it if they are true Christians and want to go to heaven instead of trying to survive on this earth?"

Now, why would he ask questions like that? The answer is that the culture is increasingly losing the true meaning of Christmas because the education system and the media continues to indoctrinate people to reject the Bible as absolute truth. Instead, the Christian faith and the Bible is attacked, ridiculed, and condemned as a "book of stories" because so-called science has supposedly proved it cannot be true — particularly its history in Genesis.

I'm sure my friend wasn't expecting an answer. After all, such questions as the ones he asked have been leveled at Christians for years. (Sadly, many Christians don't know how to answer such questions,

The last enemy that will be destroyed is death.
— I Corinthians 15:26

because they, like him, don't believe the true history of the world from Genesis — which explains the origin and meaning of death.)

I was sure the sermon we were about to hear would be from a pastor who assumed people believed the Bible. I thought he would remind them of the babe in a manger and why He came to earth. I realized that my friend needed answers, so he would know that he could trust the Bible before he even heard the sermon. I was pleased he had asked me what was on his heart, a question that was one of things stopping him from considering the Christian faith.

My friend had viewed death, suffering, and dying as something God must be responsible for — which was the crux of the issue. He did not understand that death was an enemy (1 Corinthians 15:26), an intrusion due to sin. Death wasn't something that God made and declared *very good* in Genesis 1:31, but a result of sin. I explained that God created a *perfect* world, and because the first man Adam sinned, death entered the world as the punishment for sin. I had to explain that the earth was not millions of years old as he had been indoctrinated to believe, and thus there was not death, disease, and bloodshed for millions of years before man's existence.

I continued: When man sinned, God as a righteous and holy Creator had to judge sin with death. It was as if He withdrew some of His sustaining power to *no longer* uphold the universe in a perfect state to cause man to experience a taste of what happens without God. Thus, God is permitting things like disease and suffering, to happen, but He isn't the one to blame for this — man is. Then it was like a light bulb came on in my friend's head. With this new view of God, the Bible started to make sense to him.

Sadly, there are many people within the Church who accept the supposed millions of years, instead of the truth as given in Genesis. Because of this, they don't have valid answers for people like my friend, but instead would ignore his questions and relate the story of the babe in the manger in the hope my friend would start believing this.

Many people struggle with accepting the truth of Jesus and the Bible because they have the wrong view of history. They, like my friend, have been indoctrinated to reject the Bible as a true account of history and the meaning of life. This is a major stumbling block for so many people to believing God's Word and being saved.

Knowing that many non-Christians view God like this and also knowing that they only set foot in church about once a year, I'm praying that Christian leaders will take advantage of this opportunity and address issues like *death and suffering, and how we know the Bible is true, dinosaurs,* and so on, that are relevant issues for where the culture is today, while speaking during this Christmas season. This could make such a difference in the lives of many who have a faulty view of God, and thus challenge them concerning the truth of the Bible.

And I will put enmity between you and the woman, and between your seed and her Seed; He shall bruise your head, and you shalt bruise His heel.

—Genesis 3:15

FOUNDATION OF CHRISTMAS

In one sermon that I heard, the minister said "Let's turn in the Bible to the foundation of Christmas." Then he said to go to Luke chapter 2. I immediately thought to myself, *That's not the foundation of Christmas. That **was** the first Christmas.*

The foundation of Christmas goes back much further. It starts in the first book of the Bible — Genesis. The initial reference to the birth of Jesus is in Genesis 3:15.

And I will put enmity between you and the woman, and between your seed and her Seed; He shall bruise your head, and you shalt bruise His heel (Genesis 3:15).

This first prophecy pointing to the virgin birth of Jesus (seed of a woman) came immediately after Adam and Eve sinned. Though they were sentenced to die, God in His mercy gave a promise of redemption through the one who would be born of a virgin as Isaiah further elaborates — Jesus Christ (Isaiah 7:14).

In fact, many references to Jesus' birth have their foundation in Genesis, such as Jesus being a descendant of Isaac (Genesis 26:4) and Jacob (Genesis 28:13–14). Ultimately, the foundation of Jesus' birth goes back to Genesis. This is where a Christmas sermon should

start — particularly in a culture that has been brainwashed to believe that part of the Bible cannot possibly be true. Why would these people listen to a sermon about Bethlehem, the stable, the shepherds, and the wise men if they already think the book it all comes from cannot be trusted.

Genesis is where we first learn about the *bad news* of Adam's sin that allowed death to enter into the creation. In today's culture, people continually preach the *good news* of Jesus but fail to teach the bad news in Genesis. This is why many don't listen to the good news because they failed to understand the bad

43

news in Genesis.

We need to teach people to understand *why* they need Jesus before they'll understand their need to receive Jesus. They need a proper foundation — they need to be taken back to Genesis and first of all be taught that modern science has not disproved this historical document but actually confirms it. Then they need to be taught the foundational truths of Genesis that enable one to understand what the babe in a manger is all about.

WHY JESUS HAD TO BE BORN Back in Genesis, the bad news of Adam's sin was punishable by death (Genesis 2:17). Romans 6:23 confirms that the wages of sin is death. Adam and Eve sinned, so something had to die to cover that sin. This is why God killed animals to cover Adam and Eve's sin (Genesis 3:21). Although we don't know what animals were sacrificed, we have often pictured it as a lamb foreshadowing the Gospel. Jesus, the Lamb of God, was the final sacrifice to cover peoples' sins on the Cross.

The Israelites followed this pattern by presenting sin offerings to cover their sins by sacrificing an animal life for their disobedience to God. But an animal can't take away the sin of a man, as humans are not related to any other creature — man was made in the image of God.

God is a God of grace. When someone rightly decrees punishment to someone for their crime, then, out of love, takes that punishment upon themselves; that's grace and mercy. This is why our Creator, in the person of Jesus Christ, had to come into the world — He became a human (but remained God) so He could pay the ultimate penalty for our sin.

the last Adam

God sentenced man to death because of our sin. He showed His love for us by exercising grace and took the punishment upon Himself. Jesus, being God, came into the world just like any other person — by being born. Yet Jesus lived a perfect life so that He could be the final sacrifice to cover all peoples' sins. This is why Jesus was born and why Jesus had to die. This is why Jesus is called *the last Adam* (1 Corinthians 15:45) — He in effect became a "new Adam," a "perfect Adam," so He could die for the descendants of Adam and offer them a free gift of salvation.

The Bible says the greatest act of love is when one lays down his life for his friends (John 15:13). The God of the Bible displays this kind of love.

WAS JESUS REALLY BORN OF A VIRGIN? Isaiah also predicted that a virgin would bear a child and this would be a sign.

Then he said, "Hear now, O house of David! Is it a small thing for you to weary men, but will you weary my God also? Therefore the Lord Himself will give you a sign: Behold, the virgin shall conceive and bear a Son, and shall call His name Immanuel (Isaiah 7:13–14).

These prophecies were manifested in Mary, a virgin. She delivered a baby boy who was called Immanuel — meaning "God with us." Besides, Joseph couldn't be the father of Jesus! The genealogy of Joseph in Matthew 1:1–16 yields that Jeconiah (variation of Jehoiachin) was a direct ancestor of Joseph.

Why is this significant? Please read the curse given to Jehoiachin from Jeremiah: *Thus says the LORD: 'Write this man down as childless, A man who shall not prosper in his days; For none of his descendants shall prosper, Sitting on the throne of David, And ruling anymore in Judah'"* (Jeremiah 22:30).

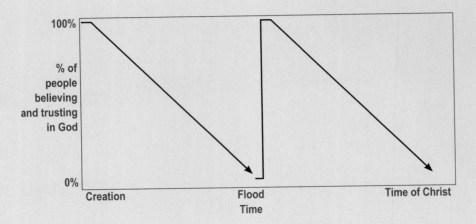

% of people believing and trusting in God

100%

0%

Creation   Flood   Time of Christ
Time

Jesus, sitting forever on the throne of David, could not have been Jehoiachin's descendant since no descendant of Jeconiah, thus descendant of Joseph, could inherit the throne of David. Therefore, Mary had to be a virgin. Isaiah confirms that Jesus will reign on the throne of David.

Of the increase of His government and peace there will be no end, Upon the throne of David and over His kingdom, to order it and establish it with judgment and justice from that time forward, even forever. The zeal of the Lord of hosts will perform this (Isaiah 9:7).

SIGNIFICANCE OF BABY JESUS Jesus' entrance into the world was fascinating! Fulfilling prophecy, having gifts brought from afar, having local shepherd men honor him, having a king attempt to assassinate him (Jeremiah 31:15 and Matthew 2:16–18) and fleeing to Egypt in the middle of the night (Matthew 2:13–15) were a few miracles that hint at the importance of this child.

For unto us a Child is born, unto us a Son is given; and the government will be upon His shoulder. And His name will be called Wonderful, Counselor, Mighty God, Everlasting Father, Prince of Peace (Isaiah 9:6).

God, the Son, left His sanctuary to be made lesser in the form of a human. He left behind heavenly perfection to live as one of us. This child restored the broken relationship, due to Adam's sin in Genesis 3, between man and God.

For there is born to you this day in the city of David a Savior, who is Christ the Lord (Luke 2:11).

Jesus came to earth at a very significant point in earth history, too. Let's consider the past and get the big picture of this significance. (See the graph.)

In Genesis, when Adam and Eve were the only people on earth, 100 percent of the people believed and trusted in God

(albeit they become sinners). As time progressed, people stopped believing and trusting in God.

In Genesis at the time of Noah, his family was the only ones on earth that still believed and trusted in God enough to enter the ark. So the percentage was rather low considering the population had continued to grow.

After God sent the Flood, Noah's family was the only one on earth, so the percentage was again nearly 100 percent of people believing and trusting in God.

As time progressed, God kept calling the Israelites back to Him. Ultimately, though, as the population of the earth re-grew, the overall percentage began to drop. Just before Jesus' birth the bulk of the world's people were not believing or trusting in God.

Even the Pharisees, Jewish leaders in the time of Jesus, were not trusting in God but following traditions and not what God was actually saying in the Bible — otherwise they would have been expecting the Messiah.

The wise men knew, and John the Baptist, who prepared many in Israel for Jesus, knew. This is still a very low percentage of people believing and trusting in God when Jesus was born. Jesus came when few believed and trusted in God.

When Jesus came to earth it was a low point in earth history, so His timing was very significant, but the mission was completed perfectly and we now have the opportunity to return to God as a free gift in Jesus Christ.

So hopefully the next Christmas sermon you hear will incorporate some of the answers that people need in today's culture. When you answer questions people have about the trustworthiness of the Bible they will be more open to the gospel itself, which is also found in the pages of the Bible.

Confusion

······ *and* ······

Happy Holidays!

Misconceptions

Chapter 8

Misconceptions
Surrounding
Christmas

—

An Introduction

Answers in Genesis is a ministry devoted to biblical authority. This means that we believe the Bible is the inspired, inerrant, and authoritative Word of God. The Bible can be trusted from the very first verse, and it must be the basis for our thinking.

One of the keys to taking a stand on the Word of God is making sure we understand what is actually stated in the Bible. Too often we allow other sources to influence our thinking about certain Bible passages. Christians must learn to be serious students of the Word. We need to pay close attention to the text itself rather than allowing our culture and traditions to determine our understanding.

Many of us have been led to believe that the Bible proclaims some things it really doesn't. This is often the result of well-intentioned but inaccurate teaching in Sunday school, sermons, songs, portrayals of biblical accounts in film and television, or even our own misinterpretation of the Bible.

Nowhere are these misconceptions more apparent than in our understanding of the birth of Christ. The little drummer boy, Santa Claus, Frosty the Snowman, and Rudolph the Red-nosed Reindeer have nothing to do with that night over 2,000 years ago when the Lord Jesus Christ was born, yet they have become part of our culture's portrayal of Christmas. When we, as Christians, are careless with our reading of the text, it is easy to become guilty of embellishing the accounts.

While these misconceptions are usually unintentional, we must still be careful not to add or subtract from God's Word. We pray that the lessons here will help you pay closer attention as you read and study His Word, and that you will come to a deeper and more accurate understanding of the Bible.

A new born King to see,
pa rum pum pum pum

CHAPTER 9

The X Stands for Christ

THE X STANDS FOR CHRIST

We've all seen the signs wishing people a Merry Xmas. What does the X stand for in Xmas? How can some claim that the X stands for Christ, while others say that this is another attempt at removing Christ from the culture? Which view is correct? In a sense, both are.

Christ is a title given to the Lord Jesus to signify that He is the Messiah. In Greek, this word is Christos (χριστος). Since the first Greek letter of this title (the letter *chi*) looks like an x in English, some have used it as an abbreviation for Christ.[1] Many have claimed that this practice dates back to the first century, and there is solid evidence that shows this was practiced in the 16th century, perhaps as a cost-saving measure for those using the printing press. However, those using the abbreviation would still pronounce the X as Christ.

There is no question that many use the X today for the very purpose of eliminating Christ from the holiday that bears His title. Some may even do this in ignorance. Secularists have been working hard to remove any mention of God, Jesus, and Christianity from our culture. Should we expect anything less from those who don't know the Lord?

So what is a Christian to do? Can we use the abbreviation or must we always write out Christmas? I believe one needs to follow his or her own conscience, guided by the Holy Spirit, on this issue — as with every other. It is not sinful to use abbreviations, but it would definitely be wrong for a Christian to use it because he or she is ashamed of Jesus Christ (Luke 9:26). As such, one must examine his or her reasons for whatever decision they reach.

(Endnotes)

1 The chi-rho abbreviation, formed by a combination of the first two letters in Christ (looks like a blending of x and p), was common in the early Church, and was eventually adopted as an official symbol by Constantine.

53

CHAPTER 10

We Three Kings

Nativity scenes around the world display them. Songs and poems have been written about them. They are featured in movies, plays, and Sunday school skits. They are some of the most recognizable figures in our culture as nearly everyone has seen images of three wise men riding on camels and following a star. Some have even gone so far as to name these guys.

What do we really know about these men, now known as Gaspar, Melchior, and Balthasar? Does the biblical account of the magi support the traditional story surrounding these enigmatic characters? This section will examine many of the details given in Scripture concerning the magi. Who were they? How did they learn about the King of the Jews? How many were there? When and where did they see the Lord Jesus Christ?

MAGI, KINGS, OR WISE MEN? The Greek word μαγοι (mágoi) is translated as "wise men" in the NKJV, KJV, and ESV, while the NASB and NIV use the word "magi." Originally, the word often referred to a class of Persian wise men, and possibly priests, who were interpreters of special signs, particularly in astrology (see Daniel 2:1–18). Eventually, the word was used variously to refer to one who possessed supernatural knowledge and ability, a magician, or even a deceiver or seducer.[1] There is little to no New Testament basis for identifying them as kings.[2]

The Book of Matthew contains the account of the wise men:

Now after Jesus was born in Bethlehem of Judea in the days of Herod the king, behold, wise men from the East came to Jerusalem, saying "Where is He who has been born King of the Jews? For we have seen His star in the East and have come to worship Him" (Matthew 2:1–2).

The original meaning of *mágoi* is likely in view here — wise men who interpreted special signs. There are at least three reasons for this identification.

55

First, they acknowledged that they were interested in signs in the heavens. Second, the Bible states that they were from "the East," which would be in the direction of Babylon and ancient Persia.[3] Third, of all the peoples of "the East," the Babylonians, had many opportunities to learn of the Jewish Scriptures, which contain multiple promises of the coming Messiah. Daniel was an influential government official in Babylon about 600 years earlier, and he foretold the coming of the Messiah (Daniel 9:24–26). Also, tens of thousands of Jews lived in Babylon during the time of the exile (605–536 B.C.), and they maintained a large presence there for the following centuries.

HOW DID THEY LEARN OF THE KING OF THE JEWS?

The third reason above provides a plausible solution to this question. Since the magi presumably had access to the Hebrew Scriptures, they could have known about the promises of the coming Messiah. Some scholars believe that the Book of Numbers informed the magi of the child who would be preceded by a star. *I see Him, but not now; I behold Him, but not near; a Star shall come out of Jacob; a Scepter shall rise out of Israel* (Numbers 24:17). Perhaps they were told in a dream about the Messiah's birth. After all, God warned them in a dream not to return to Herod

after they had seen the baby Jesus and presented their gifts to Him (Matthew 2:12).

While these are both plausible suggestions, we do not have enough information about the magi to know for sure. However, we can be sure that they fully expected to behold a child who was "born King of the Jews." This is probably why they traveled first to Jerusalem, the most likely location for the birth of a Jewish king.

HOW MANY MAGI CAME TO SEE JESUS?

Although the popular Christmas hymn and traditions tell us that three wise men visited Christ, the Bible does not give us the number of wise men. Matthew wrote the following concerning the magi's visit:

When they heard the king, they departed; and behold, the star which they had seen in the East went before them, till it came and stood over where the young Child was. When they saw the star, they rejoiced with exceedingly great joy. And when they had come into the house, they saw the young Child with Mary His mother, and fell down and worshiped Him. And when they had opened their treasures, they presented gifts to Him: gold, frankincense, and myrrh (Matthew 2:9–11).

The traditional view that three wise men journeyed to see Christ is likely based on the fact that three gifts were given. However, since the Bible does not tell us the number of magi, we can only speculate. We know there were at least two magi, and there may have been many more.

WHEN AND WHERE DID THEY SEE THE LORD JESUS CHRIST?

The traditional view presented in films, such as The Nativity Story, is that the wise men saw Jesus on the night of His birth, but this is highly unlikely. Matthew 2:1 reveals that the magi came to Jerusalem and subsequently visited with Herod after Jesus had been born.

The angelic announcement of Christ's birth to the shepherds was at night, which means that Jesus was born at night. In Luke 2:11, the angel told the shepherds, *For there is born to you this day in the city of David a Savior, who is Christ the Lord.* The Greek word translated as "this day" is σέμερον (*sēmeron*) and it means "the same day as the day of discourse" (i.e., today).[4] Since the Jewish day began at sundown (roughly 6:00 p.m.), then the angelic use of *sēmeron* indicates that Christ was born at night since that day would have started at sundown.

So it is highly implausible that the wise men would arrive in Jerusalem at night and immediately obtain an audience with Herod. The king then gathered *all the chief priests and scribes of the people* (Matthew 2:4) so he could determine where the Messiah was to be born. The experts told Herod that the Messiah needed to be born in Bethlehem, which was

predicted in Micah 5:2. So the wise men departed and made their approximately six-mile journey to Bethlehem. If we assume that the wise men met with Herod during the day after Jesus was born, then the earliest they could have visited Jesus would be the next night.

As we study the Bible to gain an accurate understanding of these events, may we, like the wise men, worship the Savior Jesus Christ.

"Glory to God in the highest,
And on earth peace, goodwill toward men!

—Luke 2:14

GOD GIVES GRACE If all have sinned and deserve judgment, why is anyone alive today? Not even Noah deserved to be saved from the Flood. *But Noah found grace in the eyes of the* LORD (Genesis 6:8).

Grace is an undeserved gift. We cannot earn God's saving grace by doing good works like serving in a soup kitchen, going to church, or trying to keep the Ten Commandments.

God has given everyone grace by showing Himself in creation and man's conscience (Acts 14:16–17; Romans 1:18–22, 2:14–16). Because everyone is dead in sin, sinners need the Lord's saving grace (Ephesians 2:1–10). The God of grace made one way of salvation that He revealed in His Word — the Bible.

ENTER GOD'S ONE WAY OF SALVATION. God made one way to save Noah from the Flood. Noah believed God. His faith proved genuine by his obedience in building and entering the ark (Hebrews 11:7). Still by grace through faith alone, God saves sinners today who flee His wrath against sin by turning to His one way of salvation. The Christmas account unfolds God's salvation plan.

Like Noah, Mary *found favor [grace] with God* (Luke 1:30). Like all other sinners, Mary needed God's grace. She realized this and sang praise to God her Savior (Luke 1:47).

Angels announced Jesus' birth to shepherds, calling Him *Savior, who is Christ the Lord* (Luke 2:11). These titles have

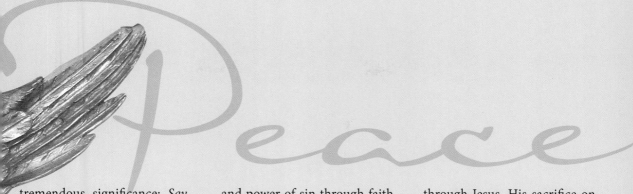
tremendous significance: *Savior* shows Jesus came to save sinners, *Christ* shows His position as the promised Messiah, and *Lord* shows His power as God in the flesh.

Jesus lived a perfect life, teaching and doing miracles that showed He was the Son of God. As the perfect sacrifice, Jesus took the punishment for sin — death — by dying on the Cross in the believer's place. He proved His victory over sin and death by rising from the dead.

God made Jesus the one way of salvation (Acts 4:12). As Noah believed God by entering the ark, sinners believe God's one way of salvation by entering into Jesus, the door of salvation (John 10:9). God saves repentant sinners from the penalty and power of sin through faith in Jesus as Savior and Lord.

Noah's salvation from the Flood through the ark pictures the believer's salvation through Jesus (1 Peter 3:18–22). Just as the waters of judgment fell on the ark instead of Noah, God's wrath against sin fell on Christ at the Cross instead of the believer (John 3:36).

Sinners must not postpone turning to Jesus. As God finally closed the door of the ark and sent the Flood, the Lord promised to again send His wrath, a surprise to people living as those in Noah's day — unprepared, unrepentant, unregenerate (Genesis 7:16–17; 2 Peter 3:1–13).

So this Christmas, remember that peace on earth comes only through Jesus. His sacrifice on the Cross made peace between God and believing sinners (Colossians 1:20; Romans 5:1). One day, after judgment, His peace will reign forever. Enter into Jesus, the ark of salvation!

I am the door. If anyone enters by Me, he will be saved, and will go in and out and find pasture.

— John 10:9

CHAPTER 14

What is the Significance of the Name "JESUS"?

THE NAME JESUS Why did the angel tell Mary and Joseph to name the baby "Jesus"? Is there some holy significance to this particular sequence of letters or sounds? No, these letters and sounds are different in every language into which the name of Jesus is translated. The name of Jesus is not *phonologically* unique; it was a fairly common Jewish name and is still used today, though not in English. For example, Jesús is a fairly common name in many Hispanic countries.

"Jesus" is an English rendering of the Greek name *Iēsous*, which is a translation of the ancient Hebrew *Yehoshua*. This name is formed from Hebrew roots signifying "Jehovah is salvation" and is translated in our English Old Testament as "Joshua." The Greek version of this name also refers to Joshua once in the New Testament (Hebrews 4:8).

The name of Jesus is significant because of who it represents — it means "God our Savior." Jesus Christ is *Immanuel,* "God with us" (Matthew 1:23). He came to earth as a man in order to die in our place and become our Savior. This is why the angel said, *You shall call His name JESUS, for He will save His people from their sins* (Matthew 1:21).

The name of Jesus reminds us about the amazing humility of the Son of God when He came as a man to die. As His followers, we must strive to show the same selfless humility that Jesus demonstrated while on earth:

Let this mind be in you which was also in Christ Jesus, who, being in the form of God, did not consider it robbery to be equal with God, but made Himself of no reputation, taking the form of a bondservant, and coming in the likeness of men. And being found in appearance as a man, He humbled Himself and became obedient to the point of death, even the death of the cross (Philippians 2:5–8).

However, Jesus is not just a name of unmatched humility; it is also a name of infinite

God
Jesus
★Christ
King of Kings
Gift of God★
Alpha & Omega
The Lamb of God
★ Redeemer, Deliverer ★
Glory of Israel, Bread of Life
Anointed of God, Beloved of God
Son of God, Word, Teacher of God
Son of Man, Eternal Life, Word of Life
Root of Jesse, Servant, Witness, Holy One
Mediator, Advocate, Passover, Shepherd, Master
★ Image of God, Prophet, Truth, Way, Redeemer
Jehovah, Nazarene, Messiah, Ruler, Son of David★
Lord of Hosts, Messenger of the Covenant, Truth, Judge
Wonderful, Counselor, Mighty God, Everlasting, Prince of Peace
★Friend of Sinners, Finisher of Faith
Emmanuel

exaltation. His name is glorified far above every other name: *Therefore God also has highly exalted Him and given Him the name which is above every name, that at the name of Jesus every knee should bow, of those in heaven, and of those on earth, and of those under the earth, and that every tongue should confess that Jesus Christ is Lord, to the glory of God the Father* (Philippians 2:9–11; cf. Acts 4:12).

WHY ARE THE GENEALOGIES OF CHRIST IMPORTANT?

In our modern culture — especially in America — many families have little sense of heritage. We may have some family traditions, but most Americans don't even know the names of their great, great grandparents or care where they lived or what they did, etc. Modern genealogy is primarily reserved for hobbyists. In contrast, genealogies were a deeply integral part of Jewish society at the time of Jesus. Land was inherited based on family lines, and those who could not prove their ancestry in Israel were considered outsiders.

Because of this difference, modern readers usually skip right over the genealogies in Scripture. The "begats" may not be fascinating reading, but don't disregard them. God had reasons for inspiring every part of the Bible — even the genealogies of Christ.

Imagine accurately tracing your ancestry back 4,000 years. As incredible as it sounds, the biblical lineage of Jesus does just that. His genealogy is recorded all the way back to the first man, Adam. This is not an insignificant detail; it is a crucial fulfillment of prophecy. Adam's sin brought judgment and death into the world, but a Savior was promised — the Seed of the woman who would strike the head of the serpent (Genesis 3:15). Jesus Christ is the "Last Adam" (1 Corinthians 15:45), the promised Seed of the woman, which Paul summarized: *Therefore, as through one man's offense judgment came to all men, resulting in condemnation, even so through one Man's righteous act the free gift came to all men, resulting in justification of life* (Romans 5:18).

Jesus is the Savior who was promised throughout history.

The genealogies in Matthew and Luke show Him as the descendant of Abraham, Isaac, Jacob, and eventually David — men to whom these prophecies were made. God promised Abraham that all nations would be blessed through his offspring, which was ultimately fulfilled in Jesus Christ (Galatians 3:7–9, 16).

By reading these genealogies, we see that Jesus was a direct descendant of King David. This is also a fulfillment of many Old Testament promises, which today's passage demonstrates. The promised Messiah would be the descendant of David (2 Samuel 7:12–14) and would one day rule on David's throne (Isaiah 9:6–7).

Jesus Christ has fulfilled these and will eventually fulfill every messianic prophecy in Scripture. He is the promised Messiah — the descendant of Abraham and David — our Savior who gave His life to redeem us from our sins.

Now Jesus Himself began His ministry at about thirty years of age, being (as was supposed) the son of Joseph, the son of Heli, the son of Matthat, the son of Levi, the son of Melchi, the son of Janna, the son of Joseph, the son of Mattathiah, the son of Amos, the son of Nahum, the son of Esli, the son of Naggai, the son of Maath, the son of Mattathiah, the son of Semei, the son of Joseph, the son of Judah, the son of Joannas, the son of Rhesa, the son of Zerubbabel, the son of Shealtiel, the son of Neri, the son of Melchi, the son of Addi, the son of Cosam, the son of Elmodam, the son of Er, the son of Jose, the son of Eliezer, the son of Jorim, the son of Matthat, the son of Levi, the son of Simeon, the son of Judah, the son of Joseph, the son of Jonan, the son of Eliakim, the son of Melea, the son of Menan, the son of Mattathah, the son of Nathan, the son of David, the son of Jesse, the son of Obed, the son of Boaz, the son of Salmon, the son of Nahshon, the son of Amminadab, the son of Ram, the son of Hezron, the son of Perez, the son of Judah, the son of Jacob, the son of Isaac, the son of Abraham, the son of Terah, the son of Nahor, the son of Serug, the son of Reu, the son of Peleg, the son of Eber, the son of Shelah, the son of Cainan, the son of Arphaxad, the son of Shem, the son of Noah, the son of Lamech, the son of Methuselah, the son of Enoch, the son of Jared, the son of Mahalalel, the son of Cainan, the son of Enosh, the son of Seth, the son of Adam, the son of God.

Luke 3:23-38

How Christmas

Happy Holidays!

Came To Be

CHAPTER 15

What
was the
Christmas Star?

The Apostle Matthew records that the birth of Jesus was accompanied by an extraordinary celestial event: a star that led the magi[1] (the "wise men") to Jesus. This star *went before them, till it came and stood over where the young Child was* (Matthew 2:9). What was this star? How did it lead the magi to the Lord? There have been many speculations.

COMMON EXPLANATIONS

The star mentioned in Matthew is not necessarily what we normally think of as a star. That is, it was not necessarily an enormous mass of hydrogen and helium gas powered by nuclear fusion. The Greek word translated *star* is *aster (αστηρ)*, which is where we get the word *astronomy*. In the biblical conception of the word, a star is any luminous point of light in our night sky. This would certainly include our modern definition of a star, but it would also include the planets, supernovae, comets, or anything else that resembles a point of light. But which of these explanations best describes the Christmas star?

A supernova (an exploding star) fits the popular Christmas card conception of the star. When a star in our galaxy explodes, it shines very brightly for several months. These beautiful events are quite rare and outshine all the other stars in the galaxy. It seems fitting that such a spectacular event would announce the birth of the King of kings — the God-man who would outshine all others. However, a supernova does not fit the biblical text. The Christmas star must not have been so obvious, for it went unnoticed by Israel's King Herod (Matthew 2:7). He had to ask the magi when the star had appeared, but everyone would have seen a bright supernova.

Nor could the Christmas star have been a bright comet. Like a supernova, everyone would have noticed a comet. Comets were often considered to be omens of change in the ancient

Some have thought the Christmas Star might
have been a supernova, like the one seen here
in M83, a spiral galaxy.

world. Herod would not have needed to ask the magi when a comet had appeared. Moreover, neither a comet nor a supernova moves in such a way as to come and stand over a location on earth as the Christmas star did (Matthew 2:9). Perhaps the Christmas star was something more subtle: a sign that would amaze the magi but would not be noticed by Herod.

A CONJUNCTION? This leads us to the theory that the Christmas star was a *conjunction* of planets. A conjunction is when a planet passes closely by a star or by another planet. Such an event would have been very meaningful to the magi, who were knowledgeable of ancient astronomy, but would likely have gone unnoticed by others. There were several interesting conjunctions around the time of Christ's birth. Two of these were triple conjunctions; this is when a planet passes a star (or another planet), then backs up, passes it again, then reverses direction and passes the star/planet a third time. Such events are quite rare.

Nonetheless, there was a triple conjunction of Jupiter and Saturn beginning in the year 7 B.C. Also, there was a triple conjunction of Jupiter and the bright star Regulus beginning in the year 3 B.C. Of course, we do not know the exact year of Christ's birth, but both of these events are close to the estimated time. Advocates of such conjunction theories point out that the

> *The heavens declare the glory of God;*
> *And the firmament shows*
> *His handiwork.*
>
> — *Psalm 19:1*

planets and stars involved had important religious significance in the ancient world. Jupiter was often considered the king of the gods, and Regulus was considered the "king star." Did such a conjunction announce the birth of the King of kings? However, the Bible describes the Christmas star as a single star — not a conjunction of two or more stars. Neither of the above conjunctions was close enough to appear as a single star.

But there was one (and *only* one) extraordinary conjunction around the time of Christ's birth that could be called a "star." In the year 2 B.C., Jupiter and Venus moved so close to each other that they briefly appeared to merge into a single bright star. Such an event is extremely rare and may have been perceived as highly significant to the magi. Although this event would have been really spectacular, it does not fully match the description of the Christmas star. A careful reading of the biblical text indicates that the magi saw the star on at least two occasions: when they arrived at Jerusalem (Matthew 2:2) and after meeting with Herod (Matthew 2:9). But the merging of Jupiter and Venus happened only once — on the evening of June 17.

Although each of the above events is truly spectacular and may have been fitting to announce the birth of the King of kings, none of them seems to fully satisfy the details of the straightforward reading of Matthew 2. None of the above

speculations fully explain how the star *went ahead of* the magi nor how it *stood over where the child was*. Indeed, no known natural phenomenon would be able to stand over Bethlehem since all natural stars continually move due to the rotation of the earth.[2] They appear to rise in the east and set in the west, or circle around the celestial poles. However, the Bible does not say that this star was a natural phenomenon.

NATURAL LAW Of course, God can use natural law to accomplish His will. In fact, the laws of nature are really just descriptions of the way that God normally upholds the universe and accomplishes His will. But God is not bound by natural law; He is free to act in other ways if He so chooses. The Bible records a number of occasions where God acted in a seemingly unusual way to accomplish an extraordinary purpose.

The virgin birth itself was a supernatural event; it cannot be explained within the context of known natural laws. For that matter, God previously used apparently supernatural signs in the heavens as a guide. In Exodus 13:21, we find that God guided the Israelites with a cloud by day and a pillar of fire by night. It should not be surprising that a supernatural sign in the heavens would accompany the birth of the Son of God. The star that led the magi seems to be one of those incredible acts of God — specially designed and created for a unique purpose.[3] Let us examine what this star did according to Matthew 2.

PURPOSE OF THE STAR
First, the star alerted the magi to the birth of Christ, prompting them to make the long trek to Jerusalem. These magi were *"from the East"* according to verse 1; they are generally thought to be from Persia, which is east of Jerusalem. If so, they may have had some knowledge of the Scriptures since the prophet Daniel had also lived in that region centuries earlier. Perhaps the magi were expecting a new star to announce the birth of Christ from reading Numbers 24:17, which describes a star coming

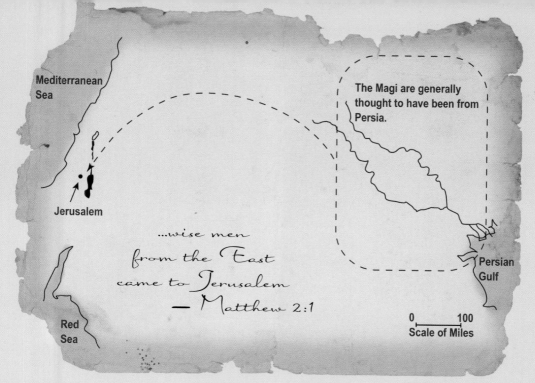

Mediterranean
Sea

The Magi are generally
thought to have been from
Persia.

Jerusalem

...wise men
from the East
came to Jerusalem
— Matthew 2:1

Persian
Gulf

Red
Sea

0   100
Scale of Miles

from Jacob and a King ("Scepter")[4] from Israel.[5]

Curiously, the magi seem to have been the only ones who saw the star — or at least the only ones who understood its meaning. Recall that King Herod had to ask the magi when the star had appeared (Matthew 2:7). If the magi alone saw the star, this further supports the notion that the Christmas star was a supernatural manifestation from God rather than a common star, which would

have been visible to all. The fact that the magi referred to it as "His star" further supports the unique nature of the star.[6]

The position of the star when the magi first saw it is disputed. The Bible says that they "saw His star in the east" (Matthew 2:2). Does this mean that the star was in the eastward heavens when they first saw it, or does it mean that the magi were "in the East" (i.e., Persia) when they saw the star?[7] If the star was in the east, why did the magi travel

west? Recall that the Bible does not say that the star guided the magi to Jerusalem (though it may have); we only know for certain that it went before them on the journey from Jerusalem to the house of Christ. It is possible that the star initially acted only as a sign, rather than as a guide. The magi may have headed to Jerusalem only because this would have seemed a logical place to begin their search for the King of the Jews.

But there is another interesting possibility. The Greek phrase translated *in the east (εv αvατoλη)* can also be translated *at its rising*. The expression can be used to refer to the east since all normal stars rise in the east (due to earth's rotation). But the Christmas star may have been a supernatural exception — rising in the *west* over Bethlehem (which from the distance of Persia would have been indistinguishable from Jerusalem). The wise men would have recognized such a unique rising. Perhaps they took it as a sign that the prophecy of Numbers 24:17 was fulfilled since the star quite literally rose from Israel.

CLEARING UP MISCONCEPTIONS
Contrary to what is commonly believed, the magi did not arrive at the manger on the night of Christ's birth; rather, they found the young Jesus and His mother living in a house (Matthew 2:11). This could have been nearly two years after Christ's birth (see chapter 6), since Herod — afraid that his own position as king was threatened — tried to have Jesus eliminated by killing all male children under the age of two (Matthew 2:16).

It seems that the star was not visible at the time the magi reached Jerusalem but then reappeared when they began their (much shorter) journey from Jerusalem to the Bethlehem region, approximately 6 miles (10 km) away. This view is supported by the fact that first, the magi had to ask King Herod where the King of the Jews was born, which means the star wasn't guiding them at that time (Matthew 2:2). And second, they rejoiced exceedingly when they saw the star (again) as they began their journey to Bethlehem (Matthew 2:10).

After the magi had met with Herod, the star went on before them to the Bethlehem region[8] and stood over the location of Jesus. It seems to have led them to the very house that Jesus was in — not just the city. The magi already knew that Christ was in the Bethlehem region. This they had learned from Herod, who had learned it from the priests and scribes (Matthew 2:4–5, 8). For a normal star, it would be impossible to determine which house is directly beneath it. The

physical temple (John 2:20–22).

When Jesus arrived in Jerusalem, there was a big crowd of people shouting, *"Hosanna! 'Blessed is He who comes in the name of the Lord!' The King of Israel!"* (John 12:13). They expected Him to be their earthly king, but that was not the purpose of His coming. Many of these same people likely shouted for His crucifixion when Jesus was on trial a few days later.

Not even the disciples completely understood everything that was said and done until Jesus was glorified (John 12:16), although Jesus was preparing them for their future ministries. He said that the Holy Spirit would be sent to them so that they would recall all that was said after everything was accomplished (John 14:26).

The shepherds recognized that there was something special about Jesus when they saw Him that day, as they were *glorifying and praising God for all the things that they had heard and seen, as it was told them* (Luke 2:20). They likely did not fully understand what was to come, but they took the angels at their word and spread the good news about Christ Jesus the Messiah.

Moreover, Simeon understood that Jesus was destined to affect many hearts and also indicated to Mary that her Son would suffer (Luke 2:34–35). No details were given, so it is hard to know whether Simeon or Mary fully understood what that meant.

God knew what He was doing all along; before Jesus was born, He knew people would not understand. There was a reason God's wisdom remained hidden: God's plan for Jesus Christ needed to come to pass before this mystery was to be revealed to everyone.

CHAPTER 19

Uncovering *the* Real Nativity

CHRISTMAS TRADITION

Christmas is a favorite time of the year for many of us. It's a season full of joyful celebration and family traditions. It's a time of hustle and bustle and last-minute shopping in search of the ideal gift. The average home might be adorned inside and out with swags of evergreen garland and large wreaths tied with velvety red bows.

Inside, a toasty fire crackles beneath a row of overfilled stockings, and the air is filled with the wafting scent of cinnamon and apple cider. And in some homes, somewhere under the Christmas tree, beneath twinkling lights and billowing tinsel, nestled behind mountains of brightly wrapped boxes and bows, you might find a little nativity set.

It's a familiar scene. The average nativity shows Mary and Joseph positioned in the center of the rustic setting, surrounded by cattle, sheep, and donkeys — all facing the newborn king. The shepherds stand over to one side . . . all lined up in a semi-circular row. Across from them are three wisemen with their gifts of gold, frankincense, and myrrh. All this takes place in a stable. After all, the Bible says Mary laid the baby Jesus in a manger, and mangers are found in barns and stables, right? In fact, didn't we read that the innkeeper had no room for them in the inn, so he reluctantly let them stay out back in his stable?

But wait . . . does the Bible really fill in all these details? Or have we added tradition upon tradition until the glittery scene before us hardly resembles the real historical event — the night of our Savior's birth.

105

ARCHAEOLOGY AND THE BIBLE

During His earthly ministry, Jesus said that if His followers would neglect to praise Him, the very *stones would . . . cry out* (Luke 19:40). And that's exactly what they've done.

The science of archaeology was born in the early 19th century, not all that long ago. Many wondered if this emerging science would support the biblical account as real history, or reveal the text to be nothing more than wishful thinking, an elaborate fairy tale, or a diabolical hoax. However, since that time,

more than 25,000 biblical sites have been discovered. Scripture has been confirmed by archaeology in tens of thousands of details. In fact, even when archaeologists were sure they would find something to discredit some portion of Scripture they only ended up doing the opposite.

So what does the Bible and archaeology have to say about the birth of Jesus? As it turns out, plenty. Before we begin, quiz yourself to see if you can separate biblical truth from holiday tradition: True or False?

1. Mary was in labor when she got into town, so Joseph had to take whatever lodging he could get.

2. The Bible uses the Greek word kataluma — translated "inn." Kataluma means "small hotel."

3. The Bible says that Mary and Joseph spent the night in a stable.

4. The innkeeper told Mary and Joseph there was no room for them in the inn.

5. The innkeeper's wife brought water and towels

to Mary and assisted in Jesus' birth.

6. The Bible says there were three wise men.

7. The wise men were present the night of Christ's birth.

Believe it or not, all of these statements are false. (See end of this chapter for explanation.)

BACK TO THE BIBLE Most people think of Answers in Genesis as a creation vs. evolution ministry, but our purpose and mission is to uphold the authority of Scripture.

God's Word is the final authority on all matters about which it speaks — not just the moral and spiritual matters, but also its teachings that bear on history and archaeology — indeed all sciences. Therefore, the Bible informs and guides our interpretation of archaeology and, at the same time, archaeology bolsters our faith in the accuracy and infallibility of God's Word.

For centuries, the traditional "Christmas story" has been told and retold many times in books, sermons, plays, and movies — so much so that the line between tradition and biblical reality is often blurred to the point that our minds tend to fill in details that aren't really in the biblical text.

For example, this may surprise you, but the Bible actually makes no mention of an innkeeper in Bethlehem. There probably wasn't really an inn the way we think of an inn — like a little hotel, of sorts. Mary and Joseph might not have stayed in a stable — at least not the way we think of a stable. And not only do we suspect that there were not three wise men, they probably weren't present the night Jesus was born.

In 1 Thessalonians 5:21, we are instructed to *Test all things, hold fast what is good.* For this reason, then, we are investigating and rethinking some of the holiday traditions that have been assigned to the biblical text.

We want to be like the Berean Christians who *received the word with all readiness, and searched the scriptures daily, whether those things were so* (Acts 17:11). Our goal is not to attack long-held traditions, but to gently set them aside for the sake of the truth and get back to what the Bible really says.

NO ROOM IN THE INN Let's take a look at the account of Christ's birth as written in the Gospel of Luke: *And it came to pass in those days that a decree went out from Caesar Augustus that all the world should be registered. . . . So all went to be registered, everyone to his own city.*

Joseph also went up from Galilee, out of the city of Nazareth, into Judea, to the city of David, which is called Bethlehem, because he was of the house and lineage of David, to be registered with Mary, his betrothed wife, who was with child. So it was, that while they were there, the *days were completed for her to be delivered. And she brought forth her firstborn Son, and wrapped Him in swaddling cloths, and laid Him in a manger, because there was no room for them in the inn* (Luke 2:1–7).

Already we have an image in our minds based on traditions that we grew up with. It might go something like this: Joseph gets into town late and there's a "no vacancy" sign hanging outside the little inn. He desperately pounds on the door and pleads with the innkeeper, who eventually takes pity on the weary couple and sends them around back to the stable. The innkeeper's compassionate wife quickly scrounges around for some clean water and blankets . . . and just in time, too, because Mary is already in labor.

But wait. Does the Bible actually say that? Lets take a closer look at the text. In verses 3 and 4 we see that Joseph is traveling to the home of his family.

So all went to be registered, everyone to his own city.

Joseph also went up from Galilee, out of the city of Nazareth, into Judea, to the city of David, which is called Bethlehem, because he was of the house and lineage of David.

In the Hebrew culture, it would have been customary for Joseph to stay in the home of his rela-

And she brought forth her firstborn Son, and wrapped Him in swaddling cloths, and laid Him in a manger, because there was no room for them in the inn.

— Luke 2:7

tives, in the guest room, not in a local inn. Some might argue that Joseph probably headed to an inn rather than to his family because he was afraid he might be shunned, considering Mary's condition outside of wedlock. But there is more to this picture than meets the eye.

Did Mary give birth the night they arrived in Bethlehem? Well, verse 6 says: *So it was, that while they were there, the days were completed for her to be delivered.*

This text seems to indicate that they were there for a while before Mary gave birth. If Joseph could find nothing more than a stable that first night, it seems he could have found something better before Mary had her baby. Verse 7 says: *And she brought forth her firstborn Son, and wrapped Him in swaddling cloths, and laid Him in a manger, because there was no room for them in the inn.*

"Inn." Doesn't that refer to a hotel, or something like one? Actually, the Greek word translated here as "inn" is the word kataluma, which usually refers to a "guest room." The word kataluma only occurs two other times in Scripture — both of those are translated "guest room," and they refer to the upper room where Jesus gave instructions to His disciples regarding the Last Supper: *"Where is the guest room [the kataluma] in which I may eat the Passover with My disciples?"* (Mark 14:14; see also Luke 22:11).

You may recall that Luke does refer to an "inn" and an "innkeeper" in the parable of the Good Samaritan, but there, instead of the word kataluma, Luke uses the word pandocheion which means "an inn, a public house for the reception of strangers." So when you read "inn," think "guest room." Now that certainly paints a different picture, doesn't it? She laid Him in a manger, because there was no room for them in the guest room.

THE GUEST ROOM (KATALUMA)

We'll probably never be able to dig up first-century Bethlehem. It's been built over many times and is considered a holy site by some groups since it is the town of King David and the birthplace of our Lord. But

archaeologists have recently uncovered and reconstructed other first-century towns that are probably very similar to the Bethlehem of Jesus' day.

These reconstructions give us a better picture of the homes that occupied the hillsides of Judea at the time of Jesus' birth. Some of these homes were multiple stories tall, and some were only one. A multiple-story home was often built into the side of a hill. The lower portion of the house was sometimes built around a cave or carved out by hand. The lower portion of a peasant home is most likely where the family lived. There was usually a raised platform at the back of the room that many archaeologists believe is the place where the family prepared and ate their meals, visited together, and then rolled out their mats to sleep. The upper portion of the house is often where the guest room — the kataluma — was located. In the case of a single-story home, the kataluma may have been as simple as a corner of the main living area that was set aside for guests. This model was based on a multiple story version of a first-century Hebrew home.

THE MANGER Mary laid the baby Jesus in a manger. Doesn't that automatically mean they were in a stable? Over the last several centuries that is the only explanation that seemed to make any sense, but first-century Bethlehem was not like the farm communities that have been developed since that time. When we read "manger," we tend to project our current understanding of where a manger should be located onto the biblical text.

Now many archaeologists believe that the lowest level of the common peasant home was where animals were brought in at night. This would have protected the animals from thieves and may have provided extra warmth to the family on cold desert nights. There was often a manger, a feeding trough for animals, which was carved into the floor or built into the wall of the main living area. This is not surprising because, even as recently as modern times, many Middle Eastern homes have lower levels with mangers built into them.

With this biblical, historical, and archaeological understanding in mind, let's re-evaluate the arrival of Mary and Joseph. Joseph and Mary were probably welcomed into the home of relatives. But due to the census, many people were returning to Bethlehem, including Joseph's other out-of-town relatives. Because the traditional guest room, the *kataluma,* was already taken, Mary laid the baby Jesus in a man-

ger. Under the circumstances, a built-in stone manger would be unusual and humble, but a perfectly suitable place to serve as a temporary crib to lay the newborn Son of God.

WHAT ABOUT THE WISE MEN?

Let us reiterate this important topic. So where were the wise men the night of Christ's birth? And where did we get the idea that there were three of them? From a faraway land, the wise men followed an unusual star from the East, in search of the newborn king that they might worship him (Numbers 24:17). Naturally, they went to the palace of King Herod in Judea. Surely he would know the

whereabouts of his successor. But the king knew nothing about the matter! Herod called together the chief priests and teachers of the law who told him of an ancient prophecy that revealed the birthplace of the child who would be king (Micah 5:2). So this scheming, paranoid ruler sent the wise men to Bethlehem, and urged them to return with news of the Christ child's specific location. The wise men did not return to Herod because they were warned in a dream that he was determined to kill the child king.

And the Word became flesh and dwelt among us, and we beheld His glory, the glory as of the only begotten of the Father, full of grace and truth.

— John 1:14

woman (actually a virgin): the baby who was born in Bethlehem — the last Adam. The first Adam gave life to all his descendants. The last Adam, Jesus Christ, the baby of Bethlehem, communicates "life" and "light" to all people, and gives eternal life to those who receive Him and believe on His name — to become the sons of God (John 1:1–14).

This is the message of the baby born in Bethlehem. It starts with the creation of a perfect world, and then, because of our sin in Adam, leads to our need of a Savior — which is why Jesus stepped into history 2,000 years ago.

Today, we talk about "keeping Christ in Christmas," but do we communicate clearly enough about why this is so important?

If we discount the story of creation, we remove the need for Christmas. And sadly, generations of young people are being educated in schools and by the media with evolutionary ideas about our origins. The erosion of Christianity in society is directly linked to the attack on the history of Genesis and the increasing indoctrination in a false history: that man is a result of millions of years of evolutionary processes.

The message of the two Adams is what life is all about. But if we want people to understand this message, we need to ensure that we show them that the history in Genesis is true, for otherwise they will not understand or listen to what is said about the Babe of Bethlehem.

CHAPTER 21

Winter Time
Worship: Santa Claus
or
Jesus?

As I drive through my neighborhood in December, I am confronted with giants dancing on my neighbors' lawns. A 6-foot-tall Scooby-Doo in a red knit cap sways in the breeze. An inflatable carousel that wouldn't fit in my living room spins a snowman, a reindeer, and an elf in an endless circuit. Santa can be seen in plastic light-up form, inflated fabric, plywood silhouette, and various other renditions — including catching a bass on a large fishing pole. Oh! Look! That yard has a manger scene surrounded by reindeer and candy canes and soldiers and snowmen and . . . you get the point.

If you brought someone from Russia to my neighborhood, what would they infer from the inflated and illuminated army? I sincerely doubt that it would convey the message of the Creator entering His creation to redeem it from the curse of sin. The manger scenes might raise a question, and the lit cross with the message "A Savior Is Born" would surely draw the visitor's attention (that's my yard). But these are certainly lost among the troop formations. So is this season about celebrating dancing snowmen and blinking lights or a Savior and the hope He brings?

Sadly, our culture has shifted its focus to the dazzling lights and away from a dazzling Savior. Commercialism has swallowed whatever Christmas used to be before it was this. Battles are fought over the very name of the holiday, and Santa Claus is embraced more freely than the infant Jesus.[1] Santa is an icon in modern culture, and his image is used to sell everything from soda to sports cars. How is a Christian to view Santa in light of the true meaning of Christmas?

SANTA'S ORIGINS As with many things in our culture, Santa has his beginnings in a Christian past. As the legends have it, the concept of Santa is rooted in the real Nicholas, Bishop of Myra, dating to the

fourth century. Nicholas inherited a large amount of money and used much of his fortune to help the poor. Nicholas gave freely to meet the needs of people around him, fulfilling the commands of Christ to aid the poor.

After his death, the Catholic Church recognized him as a saint — hence the common American usage of St. Nick as a substitute for Santa. The red clothing is likely founded in the red robes worn by bishops. The white beard and other trappings (e.g., reindeer, sleighs, elves, etc.) are likely adopted from various cultural influences being mingled together over the centuries. If you study the celebration of Santa (a.k.a. St. Nick, Kris Kringle, Father Christmas,

and Sinterklauss) around the world, the similarities are obvious, as shoes are substituted for stockings and the North Pole for the mountains of Lapland.

SANTA ABUSE The mythical Santa is clearly founded in a man who honored Christ with his life and his possessions. Nicholas gave freely of his riches to benefit those who were less fortunate than himself. This is clearly a fundamental Christian principle, as we see care for the poor proclaimed throughout Scripture (e.g., James 2:1–17).

Is that the same idea we see in the Santa celebrated today? The popular song extols children to stop shouting, pouting, and crying in order to earn Santa's favor and his gifts. This is clearly not the attitude that we see in the biblically motivated actions of the original St. Nick — and a far cry from a biblical attitude of raising children in the fear and admonition of the Lord.

I have personally overheard mothers using gifts from Santa to manipulate their children into behaving in a way that pleases the parent at the time. Such manipulation is entirely unbiblical. As Christians, we should discipline our children for sinful behavior because it is an offense against God, not because it is inconvenient or embarrassing for us. Using gifts from a mythical figure can only serve to promote a form of moralism that is alien to the gospel of Jesus Christ. If our actions are done to earn rewards for ourselves, are we not acting selfishly? This is not an attitude we should seek to instill in our children.

Our motivation for being obedient to God's commands should be out of an attitude of gratitude for the grace He has shown us. The gospel speaks of God's work in forgiving us of our sins — not because of the righteous acts which we have done, but because of what Christ did on the Cross for us (Titus 3:4–7). Nothing that we can do can make us righteous before God or make us deserving of His good gifts.

For by grace you have been saved through faith, and that not of yourselves; it is the gift of God, not of works, lest anyone should boast. For we are His workmanship, created in Christ Jesus for good works, which God prepared beforehand that we should walk in them (Ephesians 2:8–10).

Does the promotion of Santa lead to an exaltation of Christ? Since the two bring competing messages, I would suggest the answer is no. As Christ continues to be marginalized by society, our goal should be to magnify Him in our homes that our children would be impressed

with His kindness to us shown on the Cross. This is the message the original St. Nicholas would have communicated.

MOMMY, IS THERE REALLY A SANTA?

A Christian parent must thoughtfully consider that Scripture is full of commands against deceiving others (e.g., Exodus 20:16; Psalm 101:7; Ephesians 4:25; 1 Peter 2:1–3). Persistently proclaiming the existence of a man in a sleigh with flying reindeer as fact can only lead to deceit. Please understand that I am not saying there is no place for imagination, but the level of emphasis on Santa appears to cross the line. The active teaching of Santa as a real person who performs real miracles to reward children for acting a certain way, in full knowledge that he is a myth, can only be described as deceit.

Any parent who teaches their children much of what is popular about Santa knows that they will eventually learn that it was all a lie. Lying is a sin and cannot be justified on biblical grounds. Have we bowed to cultural pressures to have our children conform to the ways of the world, or do we celebrate Santa so that Christ can be exalted? Rather than dealing with the root of sin against God, who is the definition of "good," the "goodness" promoted by Santa finds its roots in the humanistic philosophy of behavior modification.

As children grow, they will undoubtedly begin to hear others speaking of the mythical nature of Santa. They will ask and will expect an answer from the parents they have trusted. Since some may not wish to totally skirt the issue of Santa Claus (and it is difficult to do anyway), consider how it is possible to allow children to learn about the real St. Nicholas — and maybe even share in some of the fun of make-believe — while remaining honest with your children.

GLORY ROBBER?

If Santa has taken the glory from Christ in your family's celebration of Christmas, maybe it is time to seriously consider changing the emphasis. I understand that these are matters of conscience in many ways and that sincere followers of Christ will come to different conclusions. What

Santa Claus is a pagan corruption of a real person, St. Nicholas, who lived around A.D. 300

I would ask is that you examine your decisions in light of what Scripture teaches. If our conscience convicts us of sin in our hearts, we can bring that to God in repentance and know that He will freely forgive us because of what Christ has done.

This is the message which we have heard from Him and declare to you, that God is light and in Him is no darkness at all. If we say that we have fellowship with Him, and walk in darkness, we lie and do not practice the truth.

But if we walk in the light as He is in the light, we have fellowship with one another, and the blood of Jesus Christ His Son cleanses us from all sin.

If we say that we have no sin, we deceive ourselves, and the truth is not in us. If we confess our sins, He is faithful and just to forgive us our sins and to cleanse us from all unrighteousness. If we say that we have not sinned, we make Him a liar, and His word is not in us (1 John 1:5–10).

Rather than offering a plat-

form to chastise those with views contrary to this writing, I hope you will think and pray about how to bring Christ the worship He is due during this season when we recognize His incarnation. Let us all make the Word of God the authority in our decisions about celebrating this, and every, holiday — giving God the glory He alone deserves.

(Endnotes)

1   My purpose in this chapter is not to discuss the cultural shift to *holiday* and away from *Christmas*.

CHAPTER 22

From Creation *to* Bethlehem

In December, many Christians celebrate a holiday called Christmas. During this season, there is particular emphasis on an event that occurred around 2,000 years ago in the town of Bethlehem in Judea (today called Israel).

Christmas commemorates the birth of a baby — an event recorded in the Bible in such New Testament passages as Luke 2:1–20 and prophesied about in Old Testament passages such as Isaiah 7:14. The name given to this baby was Jesus. During Christmas time, many churches display nativity scenes. These exhibits show the newborn Jesus in a stable surrounded by various animals, shepherds, and Mary and Joseph. Such nativity scenes traditionally have also been displayed in public places (shopping centers, public schools, parks, etc.) in much of our Western world.

At Christmas, people sing special songs known as "carols." The words of many of these carols outline the events surrounding the birth of Jesus.

Because of the influence of Christianity and the birth of baby Jesus, history is divided into two basic divisions — A.D. (Anno Domini, Latin for "in the year of the Lord," Jesus) and B.C. ("before Christ"). As evidenced by the fact that Western calendars and historians count the number of years from this time, this was a very significant event even apart from religious aspects.

CHRISTMAS IS CHANGING

In much of the Western world today, nativity scenes are no longer displayed in public places. Such displays are now banned from many public parks and schools. Whereas Christmas carols used to be sung in public (i.e., government) schools, many times such songs have been replaced by ones that do not mention anything about Jesus and His birth.

Furthermore, more and more people are now calibrating their calendars with B.C.E. (Before

Nativity in the Wilkes–Barre, Pennsylvania public square.

Christmas in the Park

the Common Era) and C.E. (Common Era), rather than "before Christ" and "in the year of our Lord (Jesus)." The year-counts are the same, but the name of Christ has been removed.

In public schools in America, teachers and students are being urged or required by administrators and lawyers fearful of lawsuits to use phrases like "Happy Holidays" instead of "Merry Christmas" or "Happy Christmas." Many advertising pieces during the Christmas season now delete the "Christ" part of the word Christmas.

Why was the birth of the baby Jesus considered so significant in the first place? And why is Christmas being viewed dif-

HOLLY TRINITY
AND THE
GHOSTS
OF YORK

BEN SAWYER

1646:
THE MAGIC WAR ENDS

In the beginning, the city of York was old.

In truth, it had always been old. Long before the Saxons, the Vikings and the Romans had brought their names and their buildings and their ideas to this corner of northern England, the land itself had always been ancient. People had lived their lives and died their deaths here for as long as anyone could remember, and even longer still before that. Once, in a forgotten past, people came to this place and decided. This is where we shall live, where we shall raise our children and bury our dead. And it will be defended. They erected stone walls to guard their bodies and stone churches to guard their souls, and the shape of the city that had always been there emerged through different generations' need for a place to call home.

The country had been torn apart by Civil War, and the old city had seen its share of conflict, both open and secret. But a long siege had finally broken, and now York found itself serving new masters in Parliament. The city slowly came to life as the sun's rays spread out across the ramshackle collection of buildings, the rivers that flowed between them and the vast and gleaming Minster that sat at the heart of the settlement. It finally touched the edge of the city, the fortified Roman walls that stood tall and broad circling the outskirts, on which two figures were silently watching the dawn.

One was a young man, wrapped in a tattered cloak of coarse wool. A thicket of brown stubble sat in the middle of his scruffy hair, where the tonsure was growing out, a last trace of a calling long-since dissolved but not entirely gone. The other was a girl some fifteen years old, clad in a simple brown dress with a white cap covering her hair. Her eyes were downcast and her hands clasped in front of her.

"She is gone then?" the man enquired.

The girl nodded in confirmation.

"But she will return?"

"She will, sir," said the girl softly.

A melancholy smile formed on the man's face as he made his decision. "Then I shall wait."

"As you will, sir," said the girl. "It's just that…"

"What is it?" The man's voice was warm and kind. "Speak, child."

"It may be many years, sir." The girl's gaze returned to her feet.

The man nodded. He spoke with resolve. "Then I shall wait forever."

"As you say, sir," said the girl.

"I shall rise each day at dawn," the man said, passion building in his voice. "And pray that this day is the one that will return her to me. To us. Will you join my vigil, child?"

"I shall, sir," said the girl.

"Then let us pray now."

The sunlight continued to bleed from the horizon, and glinted off the sliver of metal clutched in the girl's left hand. Her arm rose and fell so swiftly nobody would have seen it. The man flinched, and looked down, puzzled. He touched his hand to his side and his fingers came away bloody. He turned to the girl and reached out to her, his fingers catching the edge of her cap as his legs collapsed beneath him. The last thing he saw was a long mane of copper-coloured hair flowing down around her shoulders.

"The herder dies after telling his tale," the girl said as she watched the blood leave his body. "But I'll let her know you were asking after her."

2

CHAPTER 1

Mira Chaudhri knew nothing of this quiet little murder from her home city's distant past. York's history accumulated events large and small, and by the twenty-first century, there had been far too many sunrises for that one to stick. Only two people remembered, and through them, Mira would come to learn of this and worse.

The ancient Minster that had seen that sunrise in 1646 still stood in Mira's day, and it also remembered, after a fashion. Tucked away in a small side street across from it was a second-hand book shop, and behind the counter was Mira. It was a Wednesday in late summer, and it had been a slow one.

As a rule, there were very few fast days. The shop's clientele was a sedate lot, mainly retirees of an academic bent and students who had the good grace to be sober, possibly out of fear of the narrow building's treacherous staircases. She had worked here for just over a year, which was maybe not what her grandparents had in mind when they came to this country all those years ago. ("But as long as you're *happy* that's the main thing," her mother frequently said, clearly implying that it wasn't.) Getting to grips with the place had not been a challenge. Mira's simple daily routine was regarded with a degree of envy among the city's retail sector, whenever they gathered to vent their spleen about the damnable *public*.

The sound of feet descending the stairs jolted her upright. Her colleague Tony was returning from an expedition to the three floors above. What the shop lacked in ground space it made up for in height.

"How's upstairs looking?" she asked.

"Not many in today. Just the Red Queen." It was impossible to resist melodrama when using those three words.

"Again?" Mira said in amazement. "How long's she been up there?"

"Don't know. Never saw her come in," Tony shrugged. "Looks like she's been busy though."

"I'll check on her," groaned Mira, clambering from behind the desk and navigating a zig-zagging path between the tables, shelves and stacks of books that lay between her and the stairs. She made her way up the narrow, uneven staircase to the first floor, home to their history books and, for the moment, the strange regular customer Tony had taken to calling the Red Queen. Although customer was maybe not the right word, since that implied occasionally buying something.

Mira poked a head round the door. The rooms in the shop were all high ceilinged, with each wall covered in book-cases of aged battered wood from top to bottom. In the centre of the room, a set of steps provided for reaching the top shelves was currently in use as a makeshift chair.

The first thing people noticed about the Red Queen was her hair, a bushy, unruly mop of auburn curls. With her face buried in a book as it was now, any other features were hard to make out. The second thing people noticed was the long topcoat of deep purple wool, which she seemed to wear in all weathers. From beneath the folds of the coat poked out a pair of buckled knee-high boots of battered leather, their original crimson colour visible in places through a patchwork of scuffs and scratches. A long, black umbrella with a curved handle of gnarled, pale wood sat propped beside her. On this day, however, none of these things was the most noticeable element. It was the stack of books that stood some four feet high beside her improvised throne, as she proceeded to read the room. Mira didn't look, but just knew that if she turned to her left, her eyes would be greeted with an empty shelf. The Red Queen was flicking through a book on York's Victorian industrial pioneers, the hint of a smile visible beneath the dangling hair.

"Excuse me?" Mira said.

The Red Queen looked up, pushing back a handful of hair, and dismissed an escaped curl from her forehead with a snort of upward breath. Her pale grey eyes looked at Mira with an expression of indulgent amusement.

"Can I help you with anything?" Mira asked.

The Red Queen glanced around the room as if weighing up its merits before committing.

"No," she finally said in a husky Yorkshire brogue. "No, I think we're good here."

"Well, I'll be downstairs if you need anything," Mira added.

The woman opened and closed her left hand in a sarcastic wave that sent Mira packing to the upper floors. She stopped halfway up the stairwell, and leaned back against the wall. This, she had to admit, was the problem with having the easiest job in the city. While her friends all had battle scars from their constant struggle with the *public*, she never had any trouble, which was apt to make a person timid. As inoffensive as the Red Queen would be elsewhere, in this place she felt like an intimidatingly serious obstacle, one that Mira had no clue how to deal with. She had long suspected she was settling into a comfortable rut, and days like this proved it.

Mira busied herself on the second floor for as long as seemed reasonable, and then headed back down. When she returned to the history room, the Red Queen was nowhere to be seen, but the stack of books remained. Mira looked to her left and saw the empty shelf, just as she'd imagined it. She wearily started putting the books back in their proper place.

The task took her to the brink of closing time. She returned to the ground floor to see Tony hanging up the phone and looking sheepish.

"What's up?" she asked, then adopted a mock scolding tone. "Have you been talking to journalists again?"

Grace, the shop's owner, had recently impressed upon them the importance of not talking to any reporters who might visit, but refused to be drawn on why the shop might suddenly be of interest to the media. Mira and Tony had spent an afternoon concocting wild theories, and when the press failed to turn up, had written it off as Grace's latest bout of eccentricity, albeit a harmless one. It had certainly been less disruptive than her brief passion for poetry recitals. Nevertheless, a sign politely reminding all employees to maintain media silence was still tacked to the noticeboard above the desk, between an advert for a yoga group and a plea for information about a scary-looking man who had, thankfully in Mira's view, gone missing.

"No, nothing like that," Tony sighed, polishing the lenses of his glasses nervously. "But we've got a problem. The good news is Chris is finally coming round to fix the lights, but he's coming tonight and he can't promise when he's going to arrive. Apparently, we're at the bottom of a very long list of jobs."

"So someone's going to have to stay here and let him in." Mira completed his thought.

"I was wondering if you'd mind staying? You know I'd be happy to do it normally, but..."

"Go." Mira smiled. Tony was weeks away from fatherhood and tended to get anxious about anything that kept him away from home. Especially something unplanned. "I'll take care of it. Did she buy anything?"

Mira punctuated her question with an upwards gesture.

"I suppose not," Tony replied. "I never saw her leave."

Mira waited alone in the shop, as time ticked by with no sign of the electrician. Soon the sun had faded, and the reasons for his services became apparent, as the shop was draped in eerie darkness. The only illumination came from a skylight at the top of the staircase, the glow of the moon catching the heaped shelves. Mira's phone pitched in. A cold light bounced between her reading glasses and the copy of *Mansfield Park* she had selected to keep her company. Mira had never been in the shop this late before, and it was not the cheeriest of environments.

She was considering calling it a night when she heard a crash from upstairs. Rolling her eyes at the thought of one more pile of books to clear up, Mira picked her way through the cluttered room and peered up the gloomy stairwell, the light from above casting inky shadows. She fancied for a moment that she could hear singing.

It is a well-known fact among travel companies and tour guides that York has more ghost stories than any other city in Europe. None of them take place in second-hand book shops and none of them were believed by Mira Chaudhri.

Mira crept up the stairs, which creaked in a ludicrously ominous fashion beneath her feet as she made her way to the first floor. She was about to ask if anyone was there when she caught sight of something moving quickly out of the corner of her eye. Mira dropped her phone in shock, plunging everything into darkness. She heard the sound of breaking glass, followed by a sharp, annoyed cry. She could make out the light of her phone where it lay face down on the floor, and felt her way across the carpet for it. As she stood, a torch flashed into life and Mira found herself looking into the irritated face of the Red Queen.

"What are you doing here?" they both asked at once, shining their respective lights in each other's eyes.

"Never mind, just hold this for a mo," the woman said, thrusting something into Mira's hand before crouching to scan the floor with her torch.

"The shop's closed. Quite a while ago, actually." Mira tried to gather up some authority. "I'm going to have to ask you to... what is this thing?"

She shone her phone on the object in her hand. It was a slim, ornate brass cylinder about six inches in length. The jagged edge of glass at one end suggested this was the housing of a tube, like a light, the broken pieces of which were now scattered over the carpet.

"It's bloody well knackered, that's what it is," the Red Queen snapped, as she picked through shards of glass and sent her torchlight dancing across the floor. Finally, she snatched up a metal disc the size of a coin and scrutinised it thoroughly.

"No, this is no good. Damn it. Thanks a lot, I'm never gonna get another one of those. What the scut did you think you were…?"

A loud creak from the floor above silenced the Red Queen, who directed her torch's beam up the staircase.

"I thought I heard something moving about earlier," Mira whispered.

"Yeah, that were me."

"Oh, yes, right," Mira replied as another creak echoed down the stairs. "So… what's that?"

"That's not me," said the Red Queen.

"Who is that up there?" Mira called, her voice trembling. This earned her a cuff across the shoulder. She thought she could make out something moving in the shadows.

"Look, um, the shop's shut so can you…?"

The singing Mira thought she heard earlier returned, muffled and yet somehow familiar. She looked to the Red Queen, who glared into the darkness.

"Go home."

Mira felt put out to realise that she'd just been given an order, and resolved to take charge of the situation.

"I'm going to phone the police," she said loudly. She lowered her phone to tap the screen and the light suddenly picked out something she'd not seen before. A thin, translucent tube was snaking its way between the banisters, glowing a brilliant white from within when the light caught it. It dangled from overhead like some weird vine. Mira leaned in to get a closer look, when suddenly it lashed forward, slashing through the air at her face. She felt a sting on her left cheek and scurried back, startled.

"Run!" shouted the Red Queen and pushed her downwards.

As she stumbled towards the far wall, Mira's foot slipped on the frayed carpet, and she fell down the bottom flight, landing flat on her back in the front room and sending a pile of books scattering. As Mira mentally checked that she hadn't seriously hurt herself, she heard the singing grow louder, but with a harsh gurgling quality overwhelming the melody. An odour of dampness assailed her, until the shop stank like the bottom of a river. She looked up the stairs into the shadows, which writhed as if they were alive. Mira was about to add concussion to her self-diagnosis when a shape peeled off from the blackness and rushed towards her. As it passed over her, the smell became stronger still and the singing reached a crescendo. And then it was gone.

In the silence, Mira had a moment to concentrate on her throbbing head and scraped back, then a boot thumped to the ground inches from her right ear, snapping the arm of her glasses, which had fallen off in the tumble. The Red Queen jumped over the prone Mira and stormed through the bookshop door into the street.

Shaking, Mira got to her feet. Her face stung where the *thing* had touched her. She rubbed her cheek and saw spots of blood on her fingers. A burst of furious shouts erupted outside, then screaming that choked off as abruptly as it had begun. Mira stumbled to the door and lurched into the cool air, to see the Red Queen kneeling beside a large shape on the deserted cobbled street. Her foot struck a small object, and she looked down to see a screwdriver. As she drew closer, more objects caught her eye – some pliers, a length of fuse wire and finally an open tool box lying on its side, having spilt its contents into the night. Mira realised with mounting horror what the Red Queen had found.

The body lay stretched out on the pavement, and Mira's fears were proven all too correct when she saw him. It was Chris Morley, Grace's handyman on call, the man she had been waiting for. His thin, lined face was contorted in a twisted expression of terror, but it was his neck that Mira's eyes were drawn to. The skin around his throat was a vivid purple and covered in blisters, and a broken shape bulged painfully under his collar.

"Oh my God," she gasped.

"Come on, where are you?" said the Red Queen frantically, looking up and down the street.

"I… I…" Mira breathed heavily and tried to remember what she was supposed to do. "I should… I… Going to call the police…" She slumped against a shop window and felt her legs wobble.

"Don't be so bloody idle-headed. What can...?" shouted the Red Queen, before breaking off, rubbing her forehead vigorously. "No, wait. You're right. You stay here, and I'll go and... find a... constable."

Mira was suddenly pulled back to the world by the odd choice of words, and looked to where the Red Queen had been standing, only to find herself alone with the body. Her eyes combed the street, but the strange woman was nowhere to be seen. She took a step towards where Chris lay, her eyes fixed on the corpse, but then jumped with fright as she realised the Red Queen was stood in front of her, the umbrella resting on her shoulder. Mira was sure she had left, and tried to remember which direction she had gone, but found she could not.

"Forgot me brolly," the Red Queen said sheepishly.

Mira glanced away from her to the body for a second, and when she looked up, she was once again alone. This time the Red Queen had disappeared entirely. Mira took another trembling step towards Chris and looked into his dead eyes as Plan A popped back into her mind. *Police. Focus. Police. Ring. Phone. Phone? Pocket. Calm. Dead. Calm.* She gripped her phone tightly to stop her hand from shaking and made her finger tap the screen. As she waited for an answer, a burst of noise erupted from a nearby bar as a band struck up the second half of their set, and she was obliged to stagger back to the shop so she could hear.

Which meant she did not see a short, slender figure emerge from a doorway and stroll to where Chris lay, walking around the body as if tracing a chalk outline on the pavement with her feet.

"Three down," she said. "Three to go."

1866: AGE OF INDUSTRY

Thomas Cooke placed his hand upon the lever, and more power rushed through the machine. Smoke billowed from the chimney that rose up beside his seat, and the clattering, puttering engine propelled his invention down the street on its three great wheels, the armatures connecting them thrusting smoothly back and forth beneath the heavy wooden body of the vehicle. He lovingly tapped the gauges on the front of the boiler and sighed contentedly to himself, proudly surveying the city from on high. People heard him coming from some distance and dashed aside, which Thomas took as a sign that he was correct in all his beliefs. It was only when the woman with the auburn hair strolled across the road that his reverie was shattered. He pulled hard on the brake lever and brought the machine juddering to a halt.

"What the scut is that?" shouted the woman.

Thomas would have been shocked by her language, but was distracted by her defensive posture. He had an absurd impression that she intended to engage the machine in fisticuffs.

"This, madam, is my steam-powered vehicle and I will thank you to pay attention to where you are going!"

The woman stared at Thomas, clearly baffled. "It's what now again?"

"It is a steam-powered vehicle of my own design, and you had better get used to it!" Thomas huffed. "I know what you lot think! You'd have me employing some urchin to walk ahead of me with a red flag! Well, I won't, do you hear me? I won't!"

"Well, that's... good, I suppose. I see you're a man of principle," the woman replied. "Sorry, this may sound like a daft question, but what year is this?"

Thomas laughed. "I suppose it must seem like the future has come rather suddenly, mustn't it? I have created a wonder of science, even if I do say so myself. And there will be more one day, many more, you mark my words!"

"Won't that be nice," she said. "Sorry, I do need to ask…"

"Fifteen miles per hour!" Thomas was warming to his theme. "Oh yes, fifteen! And these backward-looking cretins want a man walking in front with a flag! The absurdity of it!"

"Yeah, what year…"

"You can tell them from me," Thomas continued, ignoring her as he restarted the engine. "That if they won't have it on the roads, I shall turn it into a boat! Let them try and stop me then!"

The wheels slowly resumed turning as the machine rattled away, gradually gathering speed. The woman stood in the middle of the street and watched it go. Her eyes rose to the skyline and she turned on the spot, until finally she caught a glimpse of the familiar outline of the Minster.

"I take it there's been some changes since last time…"

CHAPTER 2

Streets in York were traditionally called Gates. The actual gates that stood at four points around the city walls were traditionally called Bars. The actual bars were traditionally plentiful. Caroline had been told that joke as soon as she moved to the city. Even after all this time, it still seemed like a deliberately confusing arrangement.

Petergate was noisy as the night drew in, but Caroline had grown skilled at filtering things out when she had to concentrate. She walked briskly towards the band of yellow and black striped tape stretching across the street. A young, fresh-faced constable moved quickly to intercept her as she reached the rudimentary barrier.

"I'm sorry, miss. You can't come down here..." he said, waving his hands dramatically.

"That's DI James, you pillock," boomed a paunchy, middle-aged detective with the face of a bulldog and a deep Welsh accent.

The constable apologised hurriedly, before dashing off in pursuit of his duty.

"Thanks Greg," Caroline said. "He's keen."

"First day," Greg replied.

"Wonderful place to start," Caroline sighed. "Shall we?"

The two detectives moved to the centre of the cordoned off area, where the body lay. A man of late middle years in battered overalls grimaced up at them from the pavement, his throat painfully crushed.

"Our man again," Greg said, shaking his head.

"Looks like it," Caroline replied. "Who called us?"

Greg pointed towards an ambulance that was blocking the

pedestrian street with its bulk. "A Ms Mira Chaudhri. Works in the book shop on the corner. She was waiting for this chap to come and fix the lights. He doesn't show, she finds this. Not been questioned yet."

"So that'll be my job, then?"

"The words 'a woman's touch' never passed my lips."

"Piss off, Greg." Caroline smiled as she crossed to the ambulance. The first thing she saw as she moved around to the rear of the vehicle was the familiar orange of a shock blanket topped by a short, choppy mess of black hair. She circled to face the figure sat on the vehicle's back step, a frightened-looking Asian woman in her early twenties. Her thick fringe flopped above faraway eyes and a small dressing had been applied to her left cheek. Caroline thought about the L-shaped scar just under her own right eye, a vivid white mark that stood out boldly against her dark skin.

"Hello, Ms Chaudhri," she said with all the sympathy that had been uncomfortably thrust into her job description. "I'm DI James – Caroline. I know this must be very upsetting for you, but we do need to ask you some questions."

Ms Chaudhri nodded without blinking, and Caroline already knew this was not the time to be doing this. Nevertheless, she pressed on, and listened to the fragmented story that came forth. Mira shakily described her encounter with the strange woman in the shop, and how she had found the body in the street.

"Is someone coming to get you?" Caroline asked, and was rewarded with another weak nod that left her even more certain there was nothing more to be done here. "Well, I'll wait with you until…"

"Mira!" came a shout from down the street as a tall young white man with a head of scruffy brown curls and the dress sense of a first-year student barrelled towards them. The eager constable headed in his direction and Caroline feared he might rugby tackle the intruder.

"Down boy," Caroline shouted at the officer. "Hello, sir. I'm DI Caroline James. Are you here to take her home?"

"Yes, yes, I am. Is she okay?"

"She'll be fine, sir. She's had a shock but she's not hurt. Can I take your name?" Caroline said.

"Yes, yes, of course," he said with the air of someone who might need a moment to think about the task. "Sam. Sam Nesbitt."

"Well, Mr Nesbitt, we've taken her statement. We'll need to go over it again, but that can wait until she's had a chance to rest. If you could get her to call us tomorrow, and if you could give your addresses to one of the officers, you can take her home."

"Thank you... inspector?" Sam said, unsure how to address her, then furiously shook her hand before rushing over to Mira. He tried to help her up, but she brushed him away.

"Don't fuss," she whispered.

Caroline watched them talk to one of the constables before leaving, then returned to where Greg was kneeling beside the body.

"Her boyfriend taking her home?" he asked.

"He's not her boyfriend," Caroline replied.

"How d'you know that?"

"Because I'm a sodding detective," she said. "Shall we make a start?"

Caroline was correct in guessing that Sam Nesbitt was not Mira's boyfriend, although she had been wrong to assume they lived at different addresses. Mira and Sam had become friends during their time at university, and now shared a flat at Rowntree Wharf, a converted former warehouse that jutted into one of the two rivers that flowed through the city, looking like a moored steamship crossed with a fortress. After more than a year together, they had settled into the kind of easy-going, platonic domesticity that Sam's friend Nathan saw as a sure sign of two people who fancied the pants off of each other.

Mira sat on the sofa, her feet curled up under her. The shock blanket lay draped across the back of the seat. She had only realised she was still clutching it when they'd got in. Sam stood in the kitchen half of their all-purpose living space, a kettle beginning to bubble in front of him. The noise was comforting, and Mira felt the horrors of the evening subsiding as she settled into the safe confines of her home.

"Tea on the way." Sam smiled warmly as he stated the obvious. "How're you doing?"

"Better, thanks," Mira said. "Good to be home."

"Do you want to talk about it?" he asked, sitting down on the threadbare armchair that faced her.

"I honestly don't know what I want." Mira shook her head. "He was just... and then he was... I don't know. I can't believe it, I really can't. It doesn't feel real somehow."

Her head throbbed and the mark on her cheek itched. She rubbed the dressing absent-mindedly, and sniffed at the collar of her shirt, where a strange smell lingered.

"I feel like..." A click signalled that the kettle had completed its task. "I feel like tea. Yeah, that's about all I can cope with right now."

"Okay, well, that I can provide." Sam got to his feet, as Mira slouched further down the sofa.

"What would I do without you?" she murmured.

Sam paused for a moment, before briskly returning to his duty and preparing two cups. When he returned, Mira was fast asleep on the sofa. He gently draped the shock blanket over her, then settled down to watch over his friend. She twitched and moaned in her sleep, as she dreamed of distant singing.

CHAPTER 3

Mira studied her face in the compact mirror as she waited at the police station, satisfying herself that the mark on her cheek had been concealed. When she'd first removed the dressing, she'd half expected a lurid scar, but was relieved to see a faint scratch that was easily foundationed into oblivion.

That morning, she'd woken up past midday. She'd been struggling with getting up recently, but this was a new low. Mira and Sam's flat looked out over a dirty stretch of river where geese nested, and she was used to being woken by their loud cries. However, they'd been oddly silent lately. Instead, she had been roused by a phone call from Grace, who was keen to make sure she was alright and insisted that she not come in for a few days.

"I know it would be terribly traumatic for you to be here after something so awful, and I'm sure Tony will be fine on his own," she had gabbled in a mother-hennish manner. Mira wasn't so sure Tony would agree under his present circumstances, but was still grateful not to have to return to the shop just yet. Revisiting yesterday's events in other ways was not something she could get out of, however, so now she waited.

A door opened and two figures emerged – one was an older, heavy set white man with thinning hair. The other was a black woman with a noticeable scar on her cheek, wearing a severe charcoal suit. It took Mira a few seconds to recognise her as the detective she had spoken to through a haze of shock the night before. The man, who spoke with a Welsh accent and studied warmth, introduced them as DS Greg Unwin and DI Caroline James. They took her to a small, plain room with three simple, hard chairs arranged around a table and invited her to tell her story once again. Which she did, as well as she could.

"Did you see anyone else?" Caroline asked.

"There was…" For a moment, Mira felt she could smell the damp stench of whatever had been on the stairs and hear its distant singing. The mark on her cheek tingled. "I think there was someone else. Yes, yes, there was someone else there. But I didn't see who it was, what they looked like."

Caroline nodded calmly, and she and Greg exchanged a loaded glance. From a jacket pocket, she produced two photographs and placed them on the table in front of her. The first showed a middle-aged woman with ash blonde hair, the second a grinning teenage boy in square-edged glasses.

"Do you recognise either of these people?" Greg asked.

Mira shook her head.

"Both of these people were murdered in the last week," Caroline explained. "The circumstances were very similar to Mr Morley's death. We believe they were all killed by the same person. Are you sure you don't recognise either of them? Are you aware of anything that might connect them to Mr Morley?"

"I remember now, I saw her picture in the paper." Mira fought back a surge of panic. "But I'd never met her, I don't know…"

Greg picked up the photographs from the table. "Thank you, Ms Chaudhri, you've been very helpful. If we need to speak to you again, we'll let you know."

And that was that. As soon as Mira left the police station, she reached for the mirror, half expecting the mark on her cheek to have grown or burned through her make-up. Her hands shook and she breathed heavily, but everything was as it had been.

No, not everything. Not by a long way. Not by three people. Three people and a thing. She closed her eyes and tried not to see the tendril snaking its way around the banister, not to see the great black shape rushing through the air before her face. *There had been a man there, that was all. It was dark, and you were scared, and your mind played tricks on you. That's all.* She blinked. Behind her eyes, the tendril lashed and the mark on her cheek burned.

Mira stood alone in the police station car park, feeling the first drops of rain fall on her, and tried to decide what she wanted to do. She definitely intended to take up Grace's offer of some time off, but didn't feel like going home. And she felt sure that she and the police had done all they could for each other. She put her left foot forward, and started walking. And she didn't stop until she saw the boots.

The fountain that sat in the middle of the city centre had not been switched on for years. It had always struck Mira as a sad place, like an empty space where life had once been, disregarded by everyone who passed. Mira had been drifting aimlessly for a while and found herself staring at the smooth panels of the angular marble structure, which were beaded with raindrops in the absence of any water from the fountain itself. The sight of a familiar pair of crimson boots, kicking through the puddles, snapped her out of her distracted mood. The Red Queen was marching in a circle, spinning her open umbrella above her head and attracting no more attention than the lifeless fountain. Her expression was frustrated and deep in thought.

Suddenly, she stopped sharply and dropped her umbrella to the pavement with a clatter. She leaned heavily on a bench and breathed in hard for a moment, but quickly recovered, although her mood had not improved. She scooped up her brolly and strode away. Mira followed close behind, thinking that this was when a normal person would call the police. But she wasn't feeling normal today.

The Red Queen walked down Goodramgate until she disappeared through an iron gate set into a stone wall between a comic shop and a Chinese restaurant. Mira had passed by this gate many times and had never given it much thought. A sign fixed to the wall read 'Holy Trinity Historic Church'. Mira stepped through and found herself on a small patch of grass where rows of trees stood, their foliage hanging low and dominating what little space there was. As she walked up the straight stone path that ran between them, the arched entrance of the church emerged from behind the greenery. Beside the door sat a bronze bell in a metal frame, surmounted by a wooden sign reading 'Ring for Peace'. It was as if someone had dropped a piece of a quiet country village into the middle of the city. Only the smells wafting from the kitchens at the rear of the restaurant confirmed the building's actual whereabouts. The Red Queen was nowhere to be seen, but the door to the church stood open. Mira cautiously stepped through the shadowy arch into the building, half expecting the woman to lunge out of the shadows at her, it having been the basis of their relationship so far. But she was alone.

The interior took her by surprise. Where she expected to see rows of pews there were cubicles of dark wood, each large enough to accommodate five or six parishioners, their walls standing nearly as high as her shoulder and organised in a grid that covered virtually the whole of the church. The roof was supported by stone columns that rose from the network of boxes, their upper bodies splaying out across the ceiling. Thin black candelabra holding white candles jutted upwards at every conceivable point and a pulpit stood in the heart of this strange hive. The church was not large, but its layout made Mira feel small, as if she had strayed into the depths of a forest.

She padded quietly down an aisle between two sets of boxes, noting other areas of the church that lay to one side with lower, sunken floors made of irregular stones. They seemed more primitive – as if the further she strayed into the building, the older it got. Ahead of her, a simple stone tomb sat at the church's lowest point, while to her right was a small side chapel. She stepped down into it, noting an altar that was little more than a crude stone slab split down the centre. Beside it was a hole in the wall through which she could glimpse the church's newer and more elaborate main altar, a miniature cathedral of black wood looming in front of the boxes. In these simple surroundings, the gap in the wall felt like a window into another time. Her eyes drifted back to the stone before her, but when she gazed through the opening again, she saw the Red Queen.

Mira ducked, pressing herself hard against the stone altar, and held her breath. She was sure that nobody had been standing there when she came in, and was suddenly aware that she was in a strange, spooky place with someone who might have strangled three people. She understood that the fountain really had been the point when a normal person would have followed the script and *called the bloody police, like you should have.* She heard the sound of the woman's boots against the uneven floor and crept from her hiding place, peering over the top of the boxes. She could just see a mop of hair moving down the central aisle before it disappeared. The sound of a door being opened was followed by a creaking and a dull thud.

Mira scuttled from her hiding place, moving as quietly as possible to the front of the church. She peered down the central aisle, but there was no one, just the ceiling-high leaded window that made up most of the rear wall. The boxes on either side were canted like a rollercoaster across the uneven floor. The door to one was standing open.

Mira rushed over to the open box and leant inside. A pillar terminated in the corner, and in the floor next to its base was a trapdoor. Without thinking, Mira pulled it open and peered inside, but saw nothing. She clambered through the opening into a small space underneath, barely four feet across and not even that tall, enclosed on all sides by solid stone.

"Curiouser and curiouser," she said, then added, "I really just said that out loud, didn't I?"

Mira climbed out of the hole and decided it was way past time she went home.

Mira hung her coat on the wall of the flat's tiny vestibule, and smiled at the familiar sound of an acoustic guitar coming from behind the living room door. Sam was shambolically working his way through the chorus of 'The Long Hot Summer'. She found him seated on the sofa, pages of sheet music sprayed across the coffee table in front of him.

"One of us was supposed to cook tonight, and I honestly can't remember which," she said.

"You've got a pretty solid excuse for not doing it, so I'm going to go with it being your turn," Sam replied. He put his guitar aside and began tapping at his phone. "Takeaway?"

"That'll be good." She flopped down heavily beside him.

"You okay?" he asked. "How was it?"

"I've never been questioned by the police before," Mira said. "Never mind that, I've never known anyone get… well. I don't really know what to make of it all. I keep thinking I'm okay, then I freak out, then it feels normal again, but it's not, it's really not. I can't get my head round this, I really can't."

She looked at the concern on his face. "Can you be normal at me for a bit? I could do with it."

"Sure." He smiled, trying to think of something. "Did I tell you we've got a gig on Saturday?"

"No, you didn't, that's great," she said. "Anywhere good?"

"Vaults again. Bit last minute, but should be alright. But Nathan's on another of his obscure nineties punk binges."

"Ouch." Mira felt the weight of the world beginning to wash away.

"That was my reaction," Sam laughed. "So we'll be exercising our power of veto on the set list tomorrow."

"Good, those are always the best rehearsals." Mira grinned back at him.

"What are you in the mood for?" Sam asked, indicating the takeaway app on his phone.

"Whatever's going," Mira sighed. "Just not that Amber Palace place again."

"I quite liked it."

"Well, I could feel my grandmother spinning in her grave, Englishman, so power of veto."

"Motion carried," Sam said. "Chinese? Oh, Grace dropped those round."

He pointed to the table, where Mira's glasses lay, the broken arm wrapped in a bandage of tape. Mira picked them up with a smile, which faded when she noticed a tiny scratch towards the lower edge of the left lens.

"Good choice," she said absently. The memory of the sweet

and sour scent of the churchyard flared in her mind and made her hungry. She walked to the window, looking down into the river. The light from the building reflected on the still water, and for a moment, the lines of gleaming white on the dark surface looked like the thing that had scratched her. She studied her glasses as the mark on her face itched and the questions rushed back, burning through her mind more than ever.

"Are you sure you're okay?" Sam asked.

"Sam, have you ever…" She wasn't even sure what the question was, so it withered, formless, in the air.

"Have I ever what?"

"Forget it," Mira said. "Having a weird moment again. So, food."

CHAPTER 4

A long-haired man in a T-shirt marking him out as a community volunteer came to the church's iron gates, unlocked them, then disappeared inside. It was one of the first signs of life Mira had seen this morning. She sipped from her coffee as she tried to lurk nonchalantly on the street corner, which she was fairly sure was a contradiction in terms, but she was going to try. She had risen early, geese be damned, and headed down here, wondering as she did how foolish this course of action was. Still, the unanswered questions in her head weren't going away, and the Red Queen seemed like her only chance of getting to the truth. And if the Red Queen was connected to the church, then she'd watch the church. Like an idiot.

An hour or so later, Mira was on the brink of giving up, or possibly having herself committed, when a familiar figure crossed her eyeline. The Red Queen strode out of the gates and headed off into the city. Mira lowered her gaze and tried to look inconspicuous, then followed at a discreet distance.

The more Mira followed, the more confusing things became. The woman moved with such a sense of purpose from place to place, but never did anything. Every once in a while, she would stop, studying the buildings around her with great intensity before marching off to her next destination. There was an air of frustration that grew with each pause, and Mira suspected that whatever she was looking for, she wasn't finding it.

Mira's pursuit led her to a construction site which she generally went out of her way to avoid, and she felt an involuntary flinch in her shoulders at the sight of it. To her surprise, the Red Queen strolled casually past without drawing a glance or a remark. But as soon as Mira came near, the usual volley of catcalls followed and she tried to blot them out as best she could. Once her irritation had faded, Mira's mind turned to the next strange thing – nobody really noticed that the Red Queen was even there.

Of course, people noticed, but they didn't acknowledge her presence – as if she was merely an occupied space that people manoeuvred around but never interacted with. More than once, the Red Queen passed within inches of someone energetically handing out fliers and was ignored, while seconds later, Mira was obliged to make polite rejections. The one time someone took notice of the Red Queen was when she initiated the exchange herself, pausing to buy a copy of *The Big Issue* and paying, Mira noticed, with a note.

This meandering tour carried on all day and included a full circuit of the city walls. Mira struggled to keep up, especially given the Red Queen's tendency to trust to luck in the face of oncoming traffic.

However, more than once the stranger paused to catch her breath, and often when she did Mira saw her grimace in pain, much as she had done by the fountain yesterday. Mira took some comfort from the fact that if she was following a serial killer, it was one apparently in the grip of period pains. That at least would be something ordinary.

As the afternoon drew on, the Red Queen began looking at her watch after each stop. Around five o'clock, she checked the time once more, swiftly turned on her heel and headed back in the direction she had just come from, forcing Mira to dive into an alleyway. She walked quicker than before, eventually stopping at a small gift shop on the Shambles, an ancient cobbled street of overhanging timber-framed buildings beloved by tourists and Harry Potter cosplayers. Mira peered through the window, and saw her talking to someone, but could not make out anyone else in the room. She retreated to a point where she could see the shop without being seen herself. It was worrying how good she was getting at this.

It was only a few minutes before the Red Queen emerged, with a box of dark red leather slung over her shoulder by a strap. She headed away from Mira, back in the direction of the church. The shops were beginning to close now, and the streets were growing increasingly crowded. Mira darted around the people in her way, but the Red Queen had dropped out of sight. Reaching an open space, Mira caught a glimpse of her quarry walking through the church gates, and ran after her.

The church appeared deserted. Mira paced nervously around the box pews to make sure, but found no one. She stepped cautiously into the box where the Red Queen had disappeared the day before. The trapdoor was now firmly sealed by two chunky padlocks. She tugged uselessly on one of them.

"Can I help you?"

Mira leapt to her feet in surprise and turned to see the smiling but somewhat suspicious face of the long-haired volunteer. She tried not to look like she was up to no good, and, judging from the man's face, failed.

"Hi, yes. I was just wondering about this trapdoor in the floor. I'm not trying to steal anything!"

She flashed her best non-threatening smile, honed to perfection by the retail sector, then realised that was exactly what someone who had been caught trying to steal something would say. The man laughed, awkwardly.

"There's a couple of those, but they're not part of the original structure, they only put them in in the seventies," he said, slipping into the familiarity of tour guide mode. "Archaeologists wanted to get into the foundations, but there's nothing down there. We like to tell kids it's where we keep the gold. Sorry, I need to lock up soon, but we have some leaflets if you're interested…"

Mira left the church, pamphlet of fascinating historical details clenched in one hand, and strode down the street, finally stopping outside a Japanese restaurant, where she leant against the window to rebuke herself. She'd spent the whole day stalking a complete stranger, and for what? What did she think she was going to accomplish? She was going home, and not giving this another thought…

There was a tap on the glass next to her head. She turned and saw the Red Queen waving her in.

Mira's head flicked back away. She was overwhelmed in rapid succession by terror, embarrassment, frustration and the realisation that she'd never had a clue what she intended to do in the first place. She felt a tremendous urge to run away and never look back.

Yes, because that's why you spent all day chasing her around the city, she thought.

"Bollocks," she added out loud, pulled herself up as tall as she could and headed into the restaurant.

The Red Queen was sitting in a booth in front of the window, next to the conveyor belt that snaked around the gleaming white space. Her coat lay across the seat and she wore a tatty waistcoat of scorched burgundy over a rumpled shirt that had clearly not seen the underside of an iron in quite some time. A pile of small, empty plates of various colours were on the table in front of her. As Mira climbed into the seat opposite, the woman reached out and scooped another plate off the conveyor without looking at it. Mira placed her hands folded on the table in front of her and fixed the woman with her most serious expression.

"The police are looking for you," she said as calmly as she could.

"That so?" replied the Red Queen absently as she picked a piece of sushi from her plate, dipped it three times in a small dish of soy sauce, and tossed it into her mouth.

"I told them you were there. I could phone them right now..."

"Let me stop you right there," the Red Queen said with a wave of her chopsticks. "Take a moment to think about me hair."

Mira wasn't sure where to go with that. "It's... curly and, um... reddish? There's... quite a lot of it..."

"Bit conspicuous though, innit? Now, if I cared whether or not the police were looking for me, I'd probably be getting it restyled right about now, wouldn't I? But I'm not, because nobody finds me unless I want them to."

She flashed a triumphant smile, and returned her attention to her meal.

"I did," Mira replied, surprising herself.

"Oh," said the Red Queen. "Yeah, there's you."

"I've been following you for two days," Mira added.

"I got distracted."

"You got distracted for two days?" Mira wanted to laugh.

"No, I got distracted for five minutes," the Red Queen said. "After that I just wanted to see what you'd do."

Mira slumped back in her chair. The feeling that she was starting to do quite well evaporated.

"Frankly," the woman continued, "I'm a bit disappointed. I hoped you wouldn't go for the 'I've called the police' conversation, which is a bit parochial to be honest, so before you never see me again, why don't you tell me what you really came here to say." She punctuated her dismissive challenge by spearing a piece of sushi on a chopstick.

Mira tried not to feel insulted, remembering that this was far more important than her pride. Of all the questions in her head, the biggest floated to the front, desperate for an answer.

"What was it that killed Chris?" Mira asked.

The woman stopped with the sushi halfway between her plate and her open mouth. She lowered her chopstick as the mocking expression on her face melted like snow.

"Were that his name?" she asked.

Mira nodded.

"Was he a friend of yours?"

"Not really," Mira said sadly. "I just..."

"I'm sorry I couldn't save him." The Red Queen reached across the table to take Mira's hand, which she quickly pulled away.

"Save him?" Mira said incredulously. "Why would it be up to you to save him? Who are you?"

"That's a tricky one. Let me ask you summat, and bear in mind it's the only thing between you and a fobbing off. Why did you say *what* killed Chris, not who?"

"What are you saying, that it's some kind of monster?"

"No, *you're* saying it's some kind of monster. I'm saying you're on the right track."

Mira looked hard into the woman's eyes. She felt far too casual about what she was saying, so casual it came all the way round back to serious.

"Where did it come from?" she asked.

The Red Queen waved her hands around the room. "Right here. This city. It were born here, it lived here, it died here, then it came back here, and for some daft reason decided to start killing people."

"It's a ghost," Mira sighed and the woman nodded, a confirmation Mira greeted with a weary roll of her eyes. "There's no such thing as ghosts."

"How long have you lived here?" the woman asked.

"Of course there are ghost *stories*!" Mira replied in exasperation. "But they're not real, they're just... folklore. And then they became tourism. There's no actual ghosts!"

"There aren't?"

"No!" snapped Mira.

"Okay." The woman paused for a moment. "I have definitely wasted me life."

Mira clambered out of the booth, flustered. "I'm leaving. You are clearly mad and I have made a ridiculous mistake, and I'm phoning the police and..."

"I said monster and you went with it," the woman interrupted. "I say ghost and you're off?"

Mira sighed and sat back down. "Fine. I'm listening."

"Let's start at the beginning," the woman said cheerily. "What's your name?"

"Mira, Mira Chaudhri."

"Pleased to meet you, Mira." She extended a hand. "Holly Trinity."

Mira looked through the window in the direction of the church, then turned back with an expression of disbelief. "You have got to be kidding."

"It's as good a name as any," Holly said. "And I'm not likely to forget it. That happens sometimes."

"Tell me," Mira said flatly.

29

Holly looked around, then leaned in conspiratorially.

"Righty-ho," she began. "Those ghost stories you don't really believe in? Well, kind of all true. York is pretty much the most haunted city in Europe. They're all around us every day, but most people never notice."

Mira leaned in closer still and whispered. "Are… are you a ghost?"

"Boo!" Holly shouted suddenly, and lounged back with a loud, throaty cackle that should have turned heads across the restaurant.

"But ghosts don't kill people," said Mira, adjusting to the shifting ground beneath her feet. "Do they?"

"Not as a rule," Holly replied. "If they did, there wouldn't be a whole lot of living people left before long. No, most of them are harmless. In fact, most of them aren't much of owt. Just a memory really. And those who you might think of as still being people, well, they don't cause much trouble. But every once in a while, one gets out of hand. And when it does, muggins here has to clean things up."

"So you're a ghost hunter?" Mira asked.

"Not what I'd call it," Holly said. "I have to work with these people, after all. No, think of me as a sort of guardian. Protector of the city, that kind of thing. I take it they told you Chris weren't the first."

Mira nodded. "Two more."

"Yeah, I started looking into this after the first," Holly explained. "I didn't get to the second in time, but I figured out he were due to appear at the book shop two nights ago – and then you happened."

"Sorry," Mira said. "I got him killed, didn't I?"

"No." Holly smiled reassuringly. "Just between us, I didn't really have much of a plan and, well, it's a bit bigger than I were expecting. I think it would have got someone anyway. I got a good look at it, 'spose that's summat. A 'thank you, Holly, for saving my life' wouldn't go amiss, mind."

"Thank you, Holly, for saving my life." Mira parroted with a smile.

"Just doing me job, Ms Chaudhri." Holly grinned back. "The problem I've got is this thing is a slippery customer. Ghosts normally stick to one location. This one is all over the bloody place. Three deaths in different parts of the city, with nowt in common I can see. It seems to like old school funeral music, but that's not much to go on."

"The singing," said Mira.

"It's called the Lyke-Wake Dirge, and it really is an oldie. Not heard that one in a while." She tapped a chopstick on the table, and began to sing softly. *"This ae nighte, this ae nighte..."*

"Every nighte and alle." Mira spoke the next line immediately on cue, earning a surprised look from Holly.

"I studied history," Mira said by way of a slightly embarrassed explanation. "And I'm also a colossal nerd."

"Anyway, I've got some kit from the shop that should sort this thing, but it's not much use unless I can work out where it'll turn up next."

Mira mentally ordered her list of questions. "What's with the church?"

"Just where I sleep," Holly said dismissively. "So, do you still think I'm mad?"

"More so, actually," Mira replied.

"Right you are, Ms Chaudhri," said Holly, with the air of someone accepting a challenge. "I've got a place to be in a bit, see what I can find out. Come with me, and I'll show you summat cool."

"Why would I want to come with you?" Mira said with a smile.

"'Cause you said what, not who!" Holly replied. "You're well on your way to being in the know. And you saw it in the book shop, I know you did. Right before it gave you that mark."

Mira touched her cheek, and the memory of the thing's scent rushed back.

"I'm not making this up. I can show you things you wouldn't believe," Holly pressed on, before adding rather awkwardly, "Come on, it might be fun."

The crack in the last sentence was tiny, but Mira detected it.

31

"Was that smart arse for 'I live in a church basement, please be my friend'?"

"No, it was gobshite for 'I'm not sure I can pay for this lot'." Holly gestured defensively at the pile of plates.

"Okay, what do I have to do?"

"First things first." Holly clasped Mira's hands in hers, fixing her with an intense gaze. "The things you're about to see, most people don't even know how to deal with them. I need to be sure you're gonna be able to handle it. What I'm about to ask you could save your life, okay?"

Mira nodded.

Holly smiled at her. "What's your favourite Kate Bush song?"

Mira stared open-mouthed. "Kate Bush? Like Wuthering Heights Kate Bush? That's going to save my life?"

Holly nodded.

Mira leaned in closer. "Is it magic?" she whispered.

"Of course it's magic, it's Kate friggin' Bush!" Holly exclaimed. "The Sensual World is the greatest album. I could listen to that one forever. Which is handy. Now are you going to buy me dinner? We've got places to be."

CHAPTER 5

Holly bounded through the city, with Mira trailing in her wake, trying to keep track of the questions she still had unanswered.

"Where are we going?" She decided to start with the here and now, then work backwards.

"Information, Mira," Holly replied without slowing down. "Someone must know where this thing's gonna turn up next. Now, I did have an umbrapersequor…"

"Well, if you will drink cocktails while you're working…" The joke didn't take the edge off Mira's confusion.

"It's a sort of ghost-finding gadget, thank you very much," Holly continued. "But I were in this book shop, see, when some helpful soul startled me and I smashed the bloody thing on a door frame. So now it's back to good old-fashioned knocking on doors."

"Hence today's grand tour," Mira realised.

"Right. Seeing if I could pick up a scent. But I've got nowt, so I need to go and see a man about a dog."

"Like an informant." Mira found this was starting to make a kind of sense.

"You've got it. Only less small-time crook in the back of a pool hall and more…"

"More what?"

"You'll see," said Holly, stopping suddenly. Her eyes were drawn to an ambulance parked on the other side of the street. "Wait here."

Holly walked slowly across the road, unnoticed by the paramedics carefully loading a stretcher into the back of the vehicle. She stood a short way from them, and seemed to be talking to thin air. Mira had no intention of following Holly's instructions and drew closer. As she did, she noticed a pale man with floppy blond hair and large owlish glasses, whom she could have sworn hadn't been there a moment ago.

"How is she?" Holly was asking him. "You know I need to know."

"We're doing what we can for her, as we always do." Mira heard the man speak in a flat, dispassionate voice. "But I'm sorry to say she does seem to be getting worse lately. We thought maybe you could talk to her. It might do some good."

"You know I'm the last person she'd pay any mind. But if I see her, I'll try." A piercing electronic noise interrupted their conversation, and Holly's eyes flicked briefly to its source. "I think they're playing your song."

The man smiled apologetically, and climbed into the back of the ambulance, the paramedics ignoring him as they went about their business. Holly turned away, and jumped as she realised Mira was standing right behind her.

"Good God, you know how to creep up on people!" Holly said with a start. "Is this gonna be a thing with you, because I get enough surprises in me life as it is."

"Who was that?" Mira asked.

"You saw him?" Holly said, clearly surprised. "Wow. You do move quickly. Quickly and creepily. That's interesting. I'll explain him another time. He's… complicated, but nowt you need to worry about."

Mira looked at the back of the ambulance. The last thing she noticed before the door was closed was that the man was barefoot.

"There's no such thing as bhoots," said Mira wistfully.

Holly shot her a bewildered look.

"That's quite funny… if you're Indian and… me," Mira explained awkwardly.

"Come on, let's start you off with summat simple." She strode off again, and Mira followed.

"Okay, this is a good'un."

Holly dived across the road, paying no heed to the passing cars, heading in the direction of a tall man in black wearing a top hat, who stood in the doorway of a pub. An A-board sign was placed on the pavement, which bore a picture of the same man adopting a menacing pose with hands spread dramatically and an intense stare, beneath the words 'Ghost Journey of York' in an elaborate gothic script. The man seemed far more genial than his portrait as he greeted passers-by. Mira waited for a gap in the traffic before following, and saw Holly indicate across to her, a movement she correctly interpreted as 'two tickets, my friend will pay.' Mira gave the performer his money and they joined a growing crowd.

"A ghost walk?" said Mira. "I thought you said we were going to get information?"

"We are," Holly replied. "Best way to find out what's happening."

Gradually the flow of new arrivals petered out, and the guide began his performance, leading his crowd through the winding back streets of the city, and selecting sites to stop where he could launch into outlandish tales of horror and the supernatural that took place *at this very spot*. Holly and Mira slunk to the back during the walk, so they could speak privately.

"What are we doing?" Mira whispered. "Do we just listen to ghost stories in case one of them turns out to be relevant? I don't get it."

"Okay. Why d'you think York has so many ghost tours?" Holly asked.

"Because... there's a lot of ghost stories," Mira ventured. "And a lot of actors."

"Right," Holly beamed. "But where do you suppose the actors get the stories from?"

Mira shook her head. "Word of mouth, libraries, the in... ter... net..." The last word trickled away to nothing at the sight of Holly's sardonically raised eyebrow. "Actual ghosts?"

"Actual ghosts." Holly was warming to her subject. "All the

ghost walkers, at least all the good ones, have a sort of attendant spirit, which feeds them all this information from the other side. Most of them don't really notice it's happening. That's why you get different versions of the same stories. The spirits give them the stories the way they want them told. Anyway, the point is, our friend's route has to pass over the place where his spirit is at its strongest – usually where it died. And when we get there, I can talk to it directly and find out what it knows. You see?" She flashed Mira a delighted grin.

"Are you showing off?" Mira asked.

"Yeah, obviously! Wouldn't you? Hang on, I think this is it."

The ghost walker had stopped on a street corner in a secluded cul-de-sac of terraced houses, and was regaling his audience with a grisly tale of missing orphans. Holly closed her eyes, took in a deep breath, and muttered something that Mira couldn't make out. She took a step forward and walked right up to the guide, unnoticed by the crowd.

"Is this safe?" Mira whispered urgently.

"Of course it is," Holly replied. "These guys are harmless enough. 'Scuse me, have you got time for a little chat…"

The guide continued talking, but the skin on his face appeared to ripple for a moment. Then suddenly there wasn't one face, but two, like images overlaid on top of each other. Mira's eyes hurt to look at it and her stomach lurched. Her mind and body protested against the sheer *wrongness* of what she was seeing, but she was unable to look away. It was as if the man's head and somebody else's inhabited exactly the same space, connected to the same neck. It was impossible, but also all too real. At one moment, they were one head with two faces, the next two separate skulls sat there overlapping, and then the *thing's* features just floated on the surface of the man's skin. The lips were peeled back in an ugly snarl and the eyes blazed, but neither the crowd nor the guide reacted to its presence.

"Hello there, Nicodemus," Holly greeted the face cheerfully. "Long time no see. I was wondering if you could do me a tiny favour."

"Do not expect help from me again!" the creature snapped, its voice so hard and clipped that the vowel sounds barely existed. "I am not your servant, nor do I care for your cause!"

Holly pressed on casually as if she hadn't heard. "There's this thing. Spirit, demon, apparition, God knows what. Popped up about a week ago. Killed three people so far. What do you know about it?"

"Hangman, Hangman, slack your line, slack it just a while," scowled Nicodemus.

"No cryptic," Holly scolded the creature. "We will not be having any cryptic today."

"Begone from this place!" The face lunged out of the guide's head, before snapping back as if his neck contained a length of elastic. The street performer continued addressing his audience, unaware of what was going on around and inside him.

"Come on now, Nicodemus." Holly lowered her voice. "Don't make me force it out of you."

"Use what sorcery you will," sneered the spirit. "I am beyond your foolish tricks."

"Sewer maintenance," Holly said calmly.

Nicodemus' mouth snapped shut. Fear entered his eyes.

"I don't think this street has been dug up in a while." Holly prodded the concrete experimentally with her umbrella. "I think there might be some serious renovations needed down there. A word in the right ear with the council should get things moving."

Nicodemus' eyes narrowed. "You're bluffing."

"I never play games when it comes to the upkeep of public utilities." Holly smiled. "Now, what is this thing, and where will it manifest next?"

Nicodemus sank into the guide's head before speaking. "To brig o' dread, thou com'st at last..."

"What did I say about cryptic?"

The ghost rolled his eyes. "The third crossing. At sunrise. You'll find what you seek. Now leave me be."

"You'll have to be a bit more helpful than that, I'm afraid." Holly pressed on. "I want to know what this thing is, and why it's killing people. And you are going to make yourself useful or you won't be able to move on this street for builders' bums."

Nicodemus' face contorted as he wrestled with the demands, his eyes and puckered lips twisting and moving around impossibly on the guide's face.

"I think I'm going to be sick," gasped Mira.

"Quietly in the gutter if you must," said Holly, her eyes fixed on the ghost. "It's Friday night, you won't be the last. What is it, Nicodemus? I need to know."

The spirit let out a tortured, grating whine.

"The archaeologists will be down there for weeks even before the work begins." Holly grinned wickedly as she tormented the writhing, grimacing creature. "And I know your bones are down there. You could find yourself stuck in the museum for all eternity while someone else takes over your showbiz career, unless you tell me what I need to know."

"Enough!" howled Nicodemus. "I'll give you what you want…"

But before he could continue, a clamour of footsteps echoed from around the corner. A second ghost tour was marching down the cul-de-sac, and came to a halt on the opposite side of the street to the first. The second guide immediately launched into his own rendition of the orphan story, pretending not to notice his rival, who responded by raising his voice to drown out the competition. The new arrival talked louder still. Nicodemus let out a shriek of rage and was gone from the guide's face.

Mira looked up into the sky and thought she saw shapes moving through the air. Wisps of cloud were rising from the top hats of the two ghost walkers like smoke from chimneys, and in the mist, she could see figures forming, with faces snapping at each other like dogs. Curling tendrils of the two clouds formed the shapes of clawed hands that slashed and raked at each other. She blinked and the shapes were gone, leaving only the two guides each trying to boom the other's monologue into submission while striving to pretend they had no idea anyone else was even there.

"Scut and pumpernickel," grumbled Holly. "We'll not be getting owt more from him tonight."

Holly spun on her heel and walked off, twirling her umbrella. Mira staggered after her.

They stopped outside a small church, where Holly dropped down heavily on a bench outside. Mira propped herself against the stone wall and tried very hard not to throw up on holy ground.

"It's alright," said Holly, recovering herself quickly. "It'll pass."

"That... was... a... ghost," Mira said through a series of ragged breaths.

"Yeah," confirmed Holly. "Yeah, it was. Are you starting to believe me now?"

"There are real ghosts?" Mira gazed at Holly in confused wonder, momentarily forgetting the waves of nausea.

"Lots of 'em, all over the place. Ghosts and ghouls and long-leggedy beasties, and more besides. Everything you used to think were hiding under your bed is out there somewhere. Just like I said. D'you want to see some more?"

"Um... yes, yes, obviously, yes," gabbled Mira through an excited burst of laughter, her mind rushing as she floundered in an expanding world.

"Good. Then get yourself home and have a good night's sleep. We've got an early start. The sun should come up about fourish tomorrow, meet me then."

She gave a wave and wandered into the distance.

"Where am I supposed to meet you?" Mira shouted after her.

Holly turned around, with a vaguely disappointed look on her face.

"Skeldergate Bridge," she said. "Were you paying any attention back there?"

CHAPTER 6

The entrance to the west side of Rowntree Wharf was reached by a raised footbridge over a grubby stretch of the River Foss. Mira ran across it, vibrating with energy. Nicodemus' spectral face and grating voice buzzed in her head, and she clung to the memory, not wanting any of it to fade. She took the stairwell to the second floor at a delighted pace, but as she flung open the doors to the corridor, she was stopped in her tracks by a thought that drained all the joy from the moment. There was no way she could tell Sam any of this.

Sam didn't believe in ghosts. To be fair, Mira hadn't either until today, and it had taken actually meeting one to change her stance on this issue. She realised that part of the reason she was so excited was that there was so much more to find out. She wanted to see what would happen next. But the reason there was more to find out was because so much of what she thought she knew had been proved wrong. How do you tell someone they've got the whole world wrong without them thinking you're mad?

Sam's background was in chemistry, his time split between the university's research department and a government-funded laboratory whose dealings she barely understood. She considered herself grateful that their friendship was strong enough to function without "So how was work today?" as a regular prop. But did that make this better or worse? On the one hand, science was all about the incorporation of fresh evidence into one's understanding of a situation, even if that radically altered your current position. On the other hand, she had no evidence for Sam to incorporate. Any explanation she tried to construct in her head started to sound suspiciously like caterwauling 'whooo' noises.

She would need to dial down her excitement, but in truth, the realisation had sucked the wind from her sails almost immediately. This would have to be a secret. Still, secrets were exciting too. But secrets from Sam were different. They'd been through a lot together, and unavoidably had to share so much of themselves. He was always the first person she turned to. She couldn't keep secrets from Sam.

Shut up, that's different. She pre-empted the dissenting voice that was about to pop into her head. *Okay, I guess this is too.*

Mira came to her front door, turned the key, and thought very hard about having a perfectly normal day.

"Hiya Mum!" came a high-pitched shout from the living room. *Oh goody. Abi. That'll do the trick.*

Mira entered the living room to see Sam rising from the armchair with an urgent look on his face, while his sister arranged herself in a cross-legged position on the sofa, an e-cigarette dangling in her hand.

"You okay?" he asked. "We were wondering where you'd got to."

"He was worrying," Abi clarified.

"I'm fine. I just went for a walk," said Mira, then plucked the e-cigarette from Abi's fingers and held it out to her. "But I thought we all agreed not in the flat."

"Soft touch, my bro." Abi shrugged as she took the device back and pocketed it.

"Abi just popped round to borrow a book."

"Oh yeah, right. Yeah, you did that module on regional folk traditions and stuff, didn't you? I need… hang on…" She fiddled busily with her phone for a moment. "*Folk Rituals and Savage Mythology* by Andrew J Denbeigh."

"Yes, yes, I think I've still got that one," Mira mumbled distractedly. "It's in my room."

"Your room," Abi said almost to herself as she hopped to her feet with a knowing smirk. "Cool."

Mira led Abi back through the vestibule to the door of her tiny box room, and crouched in what little empty floor there was to drag a packing box out from under the bed. The corner caught awkwardly on one of the legs and she struggled to navigate it past the other boxes filling the tight space.

"You alright down there?" asked Abi from the doorway.

"Fine," grumbled Mira, as she pulled the box free and lifted it onto the bed. "You know, last time I checked, the university did have a library."

"They get annoyed if you don't bring the books back," Abi said, then gently eased the door closed behind her. "Sam said I shouldn't talk about you seeing a dead bloke so I thought I'd ask when he wasn't here. You doing alright?"

"I'm fine, really," sighed Mira as she picked through the battered contents of the box, inhaling a whiff of musty academia.

"Only, you were gone all day, we thought you might be doing something daft or morbid," Abi continued, the words spilling out at speed. "It's just, my mate Jake, right, he found a dead swan outside his halls on Fresher's Week, and that was a nightmare. And this was a person, so it's gotta be like a thousand times worse…"

"Abi?"

"Yes?"

"Book." Mira handed over a faded hardback with a tattered dust jacket.

"Awesome," said Abi. "I didn't mean to push, you know. It's just I've gotta look after my uni parents."

"It's okay," said Mira, with a smile that she meant in spite of everything. "The chapters on the wheel of the year are important. I might still have some notes somewhere. I'll see if I can dig them out."

"Cheers, Mira," said Abi and shouted as she bounded from the room and straight to the front door. "I'm off now. Tell Mum I'm not dead."

Mira carefully replaced the box as the door slammed, before returning to the living room and slumping on the sofa beside Sam. They glanced sideways at each other and their straight faces evaporated.

"Is it me," said Sam with a vague concern. "Or did it just get older in here?"

"Oh yes, I can feel it in my twentysomething bones," Mira replied. "How's she doing?"

"Good, good, yeah. She's, well, Abi." Sam laid his head back and contemplated the ceiling. "Was that us four years ago?"

"We were never that cool."

"I'm sure I was cool," said Sam, and was rewarded with a slow head shake and a sympathetic smile.

"I was in a band," Sam protested. "I am in a band. That's automatic cool."

"A band with cool in the name no less," Mira added.

"Ironically."

"Which helps," she laughed. "You guys are great, but not so much cool as…"

"Choose your words very carefully," interrupted Sam with a broad smile as he headed for the kitchen. "Or the court may have to accept your playlists as evidence. And tell Abi you said she was cool. Have you eaten?"

Mira suddenly remembered that she hadn't, and the hunger she'd been ignoring made its presence immediately felt. "No, no I haven't. I'll cook, if you want something."

"I think it's my turn."

"Doesn't matter, I'm in a mood to do things." Mira pulled open the fridge dramatically and began picking through the contents. "And you know I meant cool in an annoying way."

"She doesn't do context. You seem like you've had a good day," Sam said.

Mira realised he still hadn't asked where she had been. She could hear the trepidation behind his voice, and guessed why. She was in too good a mood.

"Sam," she said firmly, as she turned from the fridge to face him, rolling a tomato between her thumb and forefinger. "You didn't by any chance spend today looking up warning signs of PTSD on the internet?"

"No, I…" he began before she bored through his defences

with a look. "Well, okay, just a little, but I was concerned. *We* were concerned."

Mira took a moment to enjoy the sense of belonging somewhere. She half-smiled at the tomato, before returning Sam's nervous gaze.

"That's sweet, thank you. But really, there's nothing to worry about. I'm fine."

She decided to swallow the next words on her lips, in case they sounded callous, but for one reason or another, they felt true in that moment.

In fact, I've never felt better.

CHAPTER 7

The third crossing, at sunrise.

A sharp wind blew across the deserted Skeldergate Bridge, the third of the city's road bridges crossing the River Ouse. It was not quite the brig o' dread, but nevertheless a sinister place in the gathering dawn. Ornate three-headed lamp posts of twisted black metal rose from the edges of the bridge like a clearing of dead trees. As the sun crept over the sleeping city, these fixtures cast pools of light and left long, deep shadows on the surrounding area. The city beyond was nothing but solid black shapes, with a smudge of soft grey mist rising off the surface of the river in both directions.

Mira had slept uneasily, too excited about the promise of what this morning might bring. She leaned on the edge of the metal parapet, stared down into the murky waters below and waited.

She suddenly realised she was no longer alone. In the light cast by the next lamp along from Mira, a girl stood watching the dawn. She was clad in a battered khaki jacket that hung enormously on her small frame. She wore a woollen hat of orange and brown stripes, with a fluffy bobble on the crown and two more dangling from plaited cords that hung from the ear flaps. A waist-length mane of ginger hair flowed down her back.

Mira turned back to the river and continued to wait, when she heard a voice at her shoulder.

"I know you."

The girl had moved closer. Her face was round and pale, and oddly blank, and she stood barely five feet tall. She pushed back her coat to reveal a tatty top with a faded silhouette of a dragon on the front in flaking gold. Her eyes were striking – a brilliant golden-green that shone in what little light there was. She looked in her mid-teens, but something made her age hard to place exactly.

"You work in the book shop by the Minster."

"Yes," said Mira. "Yes, that's me."

"Good shop, I like it. Yeah. Some good stuff in the history section." She extended a hand, which clutched a small paper bag. "Liquorice?"

"No, thanks." Mira smiled awkwardly as silence descended. "So... are you a student?"

"You could say that, yeah. I do like to learn things." She chewed on a sweet as she stared at the sunrise. "What brings you out here so early?"

"Oh, I'm... meeting someone."

"Friend?" asked the girl.

"Um... yes, I guess," Mira replied, and wondered how true that was.

"Nice," said the girl. She looked to Mira, swallowed her piece of liquorice and sucked in her bottom lip, as if she meant to say more, but then turned back to the distant orange glow of the horizon.

"What about you?" Mira broke the second wave of uncomfortable silence.

"Oh, bit of an early riser," she said monotonously. "I always like to start the day with the dawn. It's like 'Oh look, we made it to another one'." A sarcastic edge crept into the girl's voice. She waved a hand in the air lazily. "Hooray." A smirk started to spread across the girl's face. "I once knew a bloke who said he would get up at dawn every morning to see if this was the day that would bring his true love back to him."

Mira rolled her eyes at the romanticism. "Bet he lasted less than a week without a lie-in."

"Actually, he only made it through one morning."

They both laughed, and Mira felt the tension in the air dissipate for a second.

"Then I knifed the soppy twat in the kidneys. Can't be doing

46

with that sort of nonsense so early in the day. You sure you don't want some liquorice?"

Mira took a second to process what she had heard, then decided it was way too early in the morning for adolescent attempts at dark humour. Since she couldn't leave, she fumbled for a way to break off the conversation, but the girl was now warming to her morbid theme.

"A bloke died just over there last week," she said, gesturing vaguely into the murky distance. "Only young, he was. Second year of university. Life gets a bit... *overwhelming* for some people, doesn't it? Still, he had someone to talk to at the end. Which is nice, I suppose." She turned back to Mira, with an odd look in her eyes. "Oh look, I've freaked you out, haven't I? Did I freak you out?"

Terror froze Mira as she noticed the small silver knife in the girl's hand and knew very clearly that she had not been joking about kidneys. The girl produced a long, thick cable of bright red liquorice from her bag and began cutting an inch off, slicing against the pad of her thumb. Mira tried to speak, thought about running away, but there was something overpowering about this girl that meant those didn't feel like options anymore. The girl spoke calmly in her flat and even voice as she sawed through the vivid sweet.

"You're going to die, you know," she said. "Well, of course you're going to die. That's obvious. No one's getting out of here alive. But you know how some people die peacefully in bed surrounded by their loved ones? Well, that's not you. When it's your turn, you get to be frightened and alone, without a hope left in the world." She shrugged as she continued to cut the sticky cord. "Now, it could be that this thing you're after will throttle the life out of you. That seems likely. And if it's not this one, there'll be another and another and one of them is bound to do for you sooner or later. And that'll not be very nice."

Mira noticed the girl had cut clean through the liquorice but was continuing to slice back and forth. "Or, it could be she'll just get bored and kill you herself. You don't know her. Not like I do.

I swear to you it's happened before. The herder dies after telling his tale. It's how the story goes."

A drop of blood formed on the girl's thumb, almost black in the half-light. She rolled the piece of liquorice she'd sliced off against the cut and the dark liquid spread across the bright, artificial colour of the sweet. The girl looked up and her sparkling eyes locked with Mira's.

"But, now that I think about it," she mused. "It'll probably be me that kills you. Yeah, I can see that happening. When the time comes, I'll be there for you. But I feel it's only fair to say this now - with you, I will not be kind."

Mira fought back her fear and managed to form a question. "Who are you?"

The girl smiled and popped the liquorice in her mouth. "Ask her."

A sudden crash and an incoherent shout erupted from up the road. Mira snapped her head round in the direction it came from, and when she looked back, the girl was nowhere to be seen. She turned frantically, looking all around her, but there was no sign. Mira gathered her nerves as best she could.

"Fine," she called out to no one, her voice cracked with hollow bravado. "If you're all just going to keep vanishing into thin air, I'm not talking to any of you!" She turned back to the sun and willed her body to stop shaking.

"Mira!" a voice shouted from the same direction as the earlier noise. "Will you give us a hand with this!"

She turned to see Holly walking stiffly towards her, carrying the case she had picked up the previous day. Mira headed towards her, only to be greeted with the box thrust into her hands as Holly continued walking past. Mira buckled slightly under the surprising weight of the small object. She noticed for the first time an image of a portcullis embossed on the leather in gold.

"Here, I've had to carry that bloody thing all the way from the church, and I managed to drop it on me foot. God, it weighs a ton." Holly stopped in the middle of the road, rubbed the small of her back with both hands, then glanced at her watch.

"Righty-ho, we should have a few minutes before he gets here," Holly said positively, before kneeling and placing her hands on the tarmac. She closed her eyes and began muttering almost silently, as if in prayer.

"Before who gets here?" asked Mira, placing the case on the pavement, and looking in both directions for cars as she stepped out into the road. "What's going on? What are you doing?"

"The Hangman, of course," Holly replied. "He's due to manifest on this bridge any minute now."

"It's coming here?" Mira told herself to calm down, and found the instruction worked about as well as it did coming from other people. "What are we going to do? It'll kill us!"

"I've got a plan," said Holly. "Now, will you shut up and let me get on with this?"

She lapsed into silent muttering for a moment, then rose to her feet, ran to look over the edge of the bridge, then headed back to where Mira had left the box.

"What were you doing?" Mira asked as Holly unbuckled the case.

"Talking to the river," Holly replied.

"What?"

"Don't ask me questions unless you want to know the answer."

Holly swung the case open. The inside was lined with plum-coloured velvet and contained two glass boxes with frames of scuffed brass, like ornate lanterns, but empty inside. One was large, roughly a foot high, filling most of the case, the other about half its size. She carefully eased out the larger one and placed it upright on the pavement. Once it was clear of the case, Mira could see there were hinged metal handles at two corners. Holly folded them out, picked it up and handed it to Mira.

"Grip this by both handles, and hold it up pointing towards me," Holly instructed. "Now stand over here."

The empty lantern was remarkably heavy and Mira struggled not to drop it. Holly placed her hands on Mira's shoulders and marched her backwards up the street, then moved a small lever that sat on the top of the device. A loud *thrum* boomed out and Mira felt the object vibrating in her hands. She saw light flickering across her front, as if the glass was reflecting it from some outside source.

"You okay?" Holly asked with a frown. "This may sound odd coming from me, but you look like you've seen a ghost."

"No, um... I'm fine. What am I doing?"

Holly walked back to the case and removed the smaller lantern. When she adjusted its lever, the *thrum* was quieter and higher. Attaching a short length of chain to its top, Holly began to swing the small lantern back and forth.

"Just stand there," Holly called. "Your lantern is a cage. Mine is the door to the cage. He appears, he goes through mine and into yours. No muss, no fuss. Who were you talking to?"

"When?" The sudden shift in the conversation left Mira lost for a moment.

"You were saying summat when I arrived," Holly explained. "Who were you talking to?"

Mira wondered how much she should say about her terrifying encounter, but before she could speak, a breeze whipped up even stronger than before, and this time Mira felt like she could almost *see* the wind. Lines and spirals floated in front of her eyes. But then it wasn't the wind and she could see it coming towards them.

Mira had barely glimpsed the Hangman in the shop, but now she saw it clearly. A shapeless grey mass formed out of the thickening air in front of them, its surface taking on the texture of rough cloth. A bulge grew at the front and rose up, the material flowing around it, until it assumed the shape of a hooded head on hunched shoulders, that bobbed from side to side as if searching for something. The thing's surface glinted as if wet, and when it slipped into the dark patches between the lamp posts, she could make out flashes of electric red and blue moving across its gleaming form. White lines danced beneath the shape, as if she were seeing scratches on a film. But these scratches came to life as they turned into six glistening tendrils that skittered along the ground in two writhing clumps. The Hangman drifted slowly towards them like some enormous jellyfish floating through the air.

Just as with the ghost walker, Mira's eyes hurt at the sight of it. She could hear the singing again, louder and stronger, but the melody was distorted in a way that was unsettling to hear. Holly stood firm and held her lantern out in front of her, to no apparent effect. As the shape lumbered ever closer, Mira heard a scratching sound coming from her own lantern. She could see tiny cracks forming in the glass, and was just about to warn Holly when a loud bang interrupted the creature's song. Holly's own lantern had just shattered into a rain of tiny crystals.

Holly ran to Mira as the Hangman advanced, tentacles slapping wetly against the tarmac.

"Okay, you remember the bit where I said I had a plan?"

"Yes?" Mira asked with mounting dread.

"Well, it just failed. The good news is you can put the lantern down now."

"What do we do? Have you got another plan?" Mira shouted, but Holly wasn't listening. She had dropped to one knee and was once again muttering to the ground. Mira dropped the cracked lantern, grabbed her by the shoulders and shook her, unable to take her eyes off the advancing shape. Six glowing arms lashed through the air as it came closer and the singing grew ever louder and harsher, a clipped *nik-tek* cutting through the watery droning.

"Holly! We've got to get out of here!"

Holly's eyes snapped open and she jumped to her feet.

"Okay, new plan," she said.

Mira didn't get a chance to ask 'what now?' before Holly grabbed her by the wrist, swung her around and against the metal parapet, then pushed her hard across the shoulders. Mira tumbled backwards over the edge and plummeted into the river. Holly waited for the splash, then turned to face the creature looming over her.

"Of course, if I were really clever," she said. "I'd have thought of a way to save both of us."

1604: THE AFTERMATH OF THE CATACLYSM

Alone in the great vaulted space of the Minster, the archbishop knelt and prayed silently for deliverance. For years, he had led this city and its people, provided his protection from the forces of evil. His faith had been their shield, and it had served them well. Until now.

He heard hurried footsteps echoing along the cold stone floor as his servant ran with less than clerical decorum to where he knelt. He turned and looked up into the boy's panting, anxious face.

"They're... they're..." the boy puffed. "They're ready for you, Your Grace."

The archbishop sighed. He realised that it was far more than his misgivings about the present situation that weighed him down – he simply did not want to go outside. Venturing from this place of sanctuary into the site of his great failure frightened him more than he'd expected. Nevertheless, he rose to his feet and headed for the west doorway.

Outside, the smell of smoke and something worse still lingered in the air. It was quiet, and had been so since the dreadful course of events had come to an end. The people huddled in their houses for the most part, terrified to emerge. It was as if the Day of Judgment had fallen on the city. The archbishop assured himself it had not, but that was no comfort – when the end came, he feared how this day's actions would be assessed.

When the archbishop had walked abroad in the days immediately following the chaos, he had seen faces peering at him from doorways, eyes full of grief for what had passed and fear for what might come next. They had implored him for help he knew he could not provide. He had chastised himself for thinking it, but God had not been enough for this city.

As they headed for their destination, they passed a row of freshly dug graves. A man leaning on a spade caught his eye, and nodded with deference and gratitude. And then he said the words the archbishop had dreaded to hear.

"Hail the King in the Mountain."

"Pagan nonsense," the archbishop grumbled under his breath when the man could not hear him.

On the way to the lord mayor's house, they passed more townsfolk, all with that same sense of renewed hope bursting through, and all of whom gave the same greeting. Their vigour was no comfort. By the time they arrived, the archbishop's face was red with mounting fury.

"Are you alright, Your Grace?" asked the servant.

"My boy," grumbled the archbishop. "I fear for this city when our problems require the intervention of alchemy, witchcraft, or the bloody French."

He stepped inside, leaving his servant waiting in the cold.

Thomas Herbert, lord mayor of York, slouched at the head of a long table. The sheriff sat at his elbow, while several of the city's more prosperous noblemen lined either side. The mayor's face was haggard and careworn, and his hands shook gently, the fate that had befallen his city clearly weighing heavily upon him. The archbishop reflected on how York's mayor was second only to London's in power and authority. Those who held the title were strong men, used to the terrible demands of leadership.

And look at him now.

At the far end sat two strangers, garbed in rough travelling clothes of an old-fashioned design. One was a burly man with a deep lined face and a large bushy beard. Next to him was an imperious-looking woman with silver hair. The archbishop greeted the strangers and took his place opposite the sheriff. The man began talking to them in French, which the woman translated.

"My husband and I have observed what has befallen your city," she said. "Please accept our deepest sympathies for your people. If I may ask, how great the loss?"

"The dead are still being counted, but we believe a third part of the city's people are gone," the sheriff replied, after noting that the mayor had not. "You should be aware that as far as the rest of the country is concerned, York has merely suffered an outbreak of plague. We thought it... unwise to reveal what has actually occurred here."

She understood the source of their concern. "You fear your new king."

Thomas looked up, and finally spoke in a faltering voice. "I fear he would seek the source of this disaster among us, and use the most brutal methods to find the witches he has such dread of. I would not have my people endure his attentions after they have seen so much."

"You must realise," said one of the noblemen to the woman in a voice like honey. "That His Majesty would certainly not approve of you. Nor the course of action that you have in mind."

The archbishop snorted irritably. "I do not approve of the course of action she has in mind."

"I can assure you," the woman began. "What we propose to do may save your people from further suffering..."

"What you propose is an affront against God!" the archbishop interjected.

"We have discussed this, Matthew," said Thomas, his voice on the brink of shattering. "It seems in light of our recent losses that... older methods may be necessary. That is no disrespect to the church or to your office, but I will not bury men in their thousands again."

"You have to admit," added the nobleman who had spoken before. "That the spirits of the people have already been raised up by mere rumour of the Ki-"

"Do not say it, Lankin, it is an obscenity," the archbishop declared. "In any case, the crisis is passed. We have survived, we will survive, we do not need this heresy..."

"And what about next time?" Thomas sprang to his feet, furious. "This city shall have a protector, must have a protector."

Lankin leaned across the table to address the visitors. "The subject is a woman. You can understand His Grace's misgivings."

The woman whispered to her husband, who chuckled.

"Lankin." The archbishop turned on the nobleman, with piercing eyes. "What we are proposing to do defies all laws of God and of nature. It is immoral, it is purely and simply a bargain with the Devil. The fact that we will also be granting tremendous power to a woman, a weak vessel who might use it for who knows what despicable ends, merely heaps further damnation on an already abominable act."

"And yet you agreed," the Frenchwoman said. "You came here today. To ask Catholics and foreigners to place their unholy arts at your disposal. Because there is no other way."

The archbishop bridled. She was right. He knew York could not survive further devastation, nor could he countenance a witch-hunt by the crown.

"But you would wish her to have... limitations?" she added, seeing the value of an olive branch.

"Madam, this is what I would wish. If we must have this... this..." A sarcastic edge crept into the archbishop's voice as he said the words. "King in the Mountain among us, I would have it come when it is called. I would have it do our bidding, then be gone. Do you understand?"

The couple conversed in animated whispers for a moment, before the woman returned her gaze to the table.

"It shall be as you say," she said with an impassive smile. "She shall serve the purpose you have in mind for her, and when she does not... she will be as nothing."

The couple rose to their feet as one.

"We will require a place to work, and the assistance of some of your labourers. If I may ask, since a woman is deemed unsuitable, why not a man?"

The noblemen exchanged embarrassed glances, except Lankin, who fixed her with a wry smile.

55

"You specified in your letter that someone would only survive this process if they did so of their own free will. Volunteers were regrettably unforthcoming."

"What were her reasons?" the woman asked, visibly impressed.

"Her own," replied Lankin. "I'm sure a lady of your discretion will understand."

"Quite so, Monsieur Lankin, quite so," she responded. "Now, if you would be so kind as to show us to where you wish us to work. And if it is possible, I should like to meet this remarkable woman."

CHAPTER 8

Mira blinked. A blur of green and brown formed before her eyes. She could feel her body bobbing weightlessly while her face rested against a solid surface. Something gritty stung in her left eye and as she regained consciousness, she became aware that she was freezing. She blinked again, and then raised her head to look around.

She was in the river, but had washed up against one of the banks, lying face down on the muddy surface while her legs floated in the water. It was light now, and a white early morning sky hung overhead. She stood up clumsily in the shallows, and wiped some of the dirt from her face as she tried to get her bearings. The current had carried her a long way. She had passed under the bridge, out of the city centre and into the peaceful green spaces on the outskirts of York. She was lucky not to have drowned...

Ah.

Mira was suddenly aware of a disadvantage of knowing for a fact that ghosts exist. How would you know whether or not you'd become one? She ran a hand through her wet hair and clothes. She felt real. No, this was silly. Of course she wasn't a ghost. She was just a bit shaken from... falling off a bridge. Into a fast-flowing current. Then passing out. While underwater.

She looked back towards the city, but could not see the bridge from here. She must have been in the water for quite some time.

It could be she'll just get bored and kill you herself.

Get a hold of yourself, Mira, she thought. *Just try and find something that proves you're alive.* She considered the matter for a while. *You're cold,* she decided. *That's an actual physical sensation. You must be alive.*

Unless you're cold because you're dead, came the worst-case scenario right back at her.

Fine, in that case I'm soaking wet. I am consciously aware of being soaking wet, therefore I'm alive.

Unless you're soaking wet because you've just drowned.

She looked up and down the bank, hoping someone might walk past and see her. But that was no good either. People saw ghosts all the time. That was how you ended up with ghost stories. Any passer-by might add the tragic tale of the drowned bookseller to York's endless litany of tales to chill the blood.

It could be she'll just get bored and kill you herself.

"Are you gonna stand in that river all day?"

She looked at the top of the bank. Holly was sitting in the middle of a bench, wearing large oval sunglasses, her feet resting on the leather case containing the lanterns, sipping from a tall cardboard cup. A second was perched on one of the armrests. Mira scrambled up the slope and ran towards her.

"Am I..." she shivered and gasped as she tried to form the question. "Am I dead?"

Holly peered over the top of her glasses and took a swig from her cup. "Nah."

Mira laughed as a wave of relief swept over her, before she proceeded to the other pressing issue.

"Okay, so next question," she said in growing agitation. "What the Hell?"

Holly looked confused, and picked up the other cup. "I bought you coffee..."

"You pushed me off a bridge!" shouted Mira. "Off a bridge! Into the river! You! You pushed me!"

"Are you gonna approach that sentence from any other direction?" asked Holly.

"Off a bridge!" Mira shook with fury. "What the Hell, Holly?"

Holly shook her head. "Yes, I pushed you off a bridge, to get you away from a horrible supernatural monster that's killed three people. And I arranged for you to end up in a safe place. And I

58

came and got you. And I bought you coffee. But I am not feeling a whole lot of gratitude right now."

Mira flopped down onto the bench. Holly handed her the cup, then edged down the seat.

"Nothing personal, but you were dripping on me coat," she said. "And, well, you kind of smell bad. You might want to do summat about that if you've got owt important on today."

Mira glared at Holly, and spoke calmly and firmly. "Please, just explain what happened."

"These..." Holly kicked at the box with her heel and gesticulated with her cup. "Are for trapping dangerous beasties, okay? But they need power. Spiritual energy, I guess you'd call it. And the river, well, it's good for that. The spirits of the river are easy to call up and generally helpful, so that's what I were trying to do. Only our boy in't having it. God knows how, but he weren't going in the box. I had to get you out of there, and since I had the spirits on the line, so to speak, I told them to keep you safe and bring you here instead. And then I bought you coffee."

A terrible thought entered Mira's mind. "Oh God... it didn't kill anyone else, did it?"

"No," Holly replied. "No, it's okay."

"How did you get away?" Mira asked, her thoughts returning to the strange ginger-haired girl's warning.

"Didn't have to." Holly shrugged. "It didn't really do much. Just floated about a bit, then vanished. Bit of a disappointment, really. And it's another thing I can't figure out, which he is racking up way too many of for my liking."

"So, it didn't try to kill you and it didn't try to kill anyone else," Mira said. "Basically, you chucked me in the river for no reason."

"Yeeeaaah," said Holly. "Sorry about that." A distracted look passed over her face and she breathed in heavily before grimacing in pain.

"What is it?" Mira reached out, but Holly pushed her aside. She rose to her feet and walked a few wobbly steps before dropping hard to her hands and knees. Her face screwed up tightly, then she started retching. A jet of grimy, brown river water erupted from Holly's mouth and sprayed all over the ground beneath her. The flood eventually slowed to a thin trickle that dribbled down her chin, before finally, after more retching, she threw up a single smooth black pebble. Holly stood up shakily, wiped her chin and smiled to the dumbstruck Mira.

"All better," she said, and then dropped to the ground in a dead faint.

Mira knelt beside her. Whatever had just happened, she was still breathing at least. She plucked her phone from her pocket and uselessly tapped at the dead screen while water trickled out of the casing. Unless she stumbled on some uncooked rice by the riverside, calling for help was off the cards.

She tried to lift Holly under her arms, but the first few steps were enough to prove that this was not going to get them very far. Home was a long way from here. Holly did not stir through being manoeuvred, not even when she was dropped back to the ground, which was impressive or worrying, Mira wasn't sure which. She carefully moved Holly into the recovery position then looked around, hoping that some helpful soul might stumble on them, but there was still no one. But there was a shopping trolley.

It was resting on its side in the river, close to where she had washed up. It wasn't too far out and the water around it was calm. Mira was fairly sure that it hadn't been there earlier, not that she'd been paying much attention. But it was there now, and that was the main thing. She rushed down the bank and waded out to where it lay, the water coming up around her knees and lapping gently at her, but with no strong current. The front wheel turned freely with a shower of droplets when she spun it with a finger. Reaching over, she easily pulled it upright. It seemed perfectly intact – a little rusty, but solid enough to serve its purpose. Satisfied, she gripped the handle and pushed in the direction of the bank.

Nothing happened. The trolley was stuck fast, as if the wheels had sunk into the mud. Gripping the bar tightly, she pushed forward until her wrists started to ache, but the trolley was immovable. As she gave it a further push, she felt the riverbed shift slightly, feeling softer beneath her feet than it had a moment ago. The water moving against her legs became swifter, but was travelling in the wrong direction. The trolley was pulled from her grasp and she stood wavering for a moment, desperately trying to regain equilibrium as the water rushed in circles around her before imbalance took its inevitable toll and she fell backwards into the river with a splash.

Mira emerged coughing and spluttering, stumbling slightly as she got her feet under her. The water was thrown into turmoil by her movements, and as she caught her breath, she thought for a second that the ripples had formed the outline of a face, two small eyes above a vast crooked grin gazing up at her in mockery. Mira hoped to hear a cackle of laughter at her pratfall from the bank, but Holly was still dead to the world. She turned back to look at the offending trolley.

"River spirits," she said. "You're not here by coincidence, are you?"

Mira took a moment to consider the situation, as ridiculous as it seemed. The river had apparently brought her a shopping trolley but wasn't going to let her just take it. Clearly more was expected of her, but what? What do rivers want?

Don't be stupid, Mira, rivers don't want anything. It's just stuck in the mud, that's all.

Nevertheless, she began to wonder if that was true. She remembered her grandmother telling her about people floating diyas down the Ganges to gain the blessing of the river goddess. As a child, she'd taken the existence of Mother Ganga at face value, but now her adult scepticism rolled its eyes at the very idea. Those rituals were about the people performing them and how it made them feel, the river didn't care. Rivers never do.

But what if this one does?

Practicality elbowed its way into the middle of Mira's spiritual crisis and reminded her that she was cold and soaked to the skin. If arcane ritual could provide her with a means of getting Holly home, who was she to argue?

Assuming the river wanted a tribute, Mira was left with the

question of what to give it. She didn't have a diya on her, but this was an English river, so presumably had different expectations. Mira tried to remember what pagans would offer a river god in return for its blessing. She was fairly sure it was either fruit or virgins, neither of which she had immediate access to. But the two coffee cups sat on Holly's bench caught her eye. Starving peasants gave what they were able to, so that was what she would do. She waded slowly and carefully back to the bank, then ran over to seize the two cups and returned to the water's edge.

"O spirits of the river," she began, muffled by a cocoon of embarrassment as she tipped the contents into the water. "I thank you for bringing me... deliverance from my predicament and offer you the gift of... caffeine... so that you may... flow more swiftly..."

Her eyes roamed the bank once more, and this time she was grateful to be alone with her absurdity. From a mystical point of view, she felt fairly sure that this was the weakest sacrificial offering this river had ever received. From a twenty-first century perspective, she was a very wet woman improvising pagan rituals and generally being weird on a riverside in the early hours of the morning. Neither of these things struck Mira as a good look.

Is it worse that I'm doing this badly or that I'm doing it at all?

Nevertheless, when Mira looked up, the trolley had shifted forward slightly. Perhaps it was the thought that counted. She breathed a sigh of relief and lowered a foot in the direction of the water, before pulling back. She crouched down and whispered nervously to the surface.

"I'm coming in to get the trolley now. I hope we understand each other, and I would really appreciate it if you didn't push me over again. Thank you. Right, here we go."

She stepped into the water and headed for the trolley, which drifted slightly towards the bank, as if it were coming to greet her. When she pushed this time, it moved easily. Mira felt as if the current was flowing with her this time, which was as impossible as everything else. She rolled it up the bank, coming to a halt near where Holly lay.

"Okay, now the hard part." Mira sighed, as she looked down at her unconscious companion.

CHAPTER 9

The shopping trolley clattered along the uneven pavements, pushed along by an exhausted Mira. Holly, still dead to the world, was bundled inside, the lantern box alongside her. No amount of bouncing across cobbles and cracks had roused her.

By the time they made it to the city centre, the streets were starting to fill with people. They attracted a healthy share of surprised, amused and disapproving glances and, Mira noted with more than a little annoyance, not one offer of help. There was no way they'd make it up the stairs to Rowntree Wharf, so she took the long way round to the ground level door on the far side. She wasn't about to explain to her neighbours why a shopping trolley was in the building, so ditched it in the car park. That left the final challenge of dragging Holly into the lift and along the corridor to her flat. Her arms were screaming for mercy by the time she reached her door. She had spent the walk home trying to come up with a reasonable explanation for how she fell into the river and acquired an unconscious stranger, and was relieved if slightly disappointed to find none was needed – Sam was out.

Mira dumped the lantern case, which had been so heavy before but now seemed to weigh next to nothing, carried Holly to her room, and laid her out on the bed. She tore off her damp, muddy clothes, set the washing machine to deal with them, and went into the bathroom for a much-craved shower.

Mira was lost in concentration as she scrubbed the filth of the river out of her hair, when she realised that she wasn't alone. Nervously, she peered out and was startled to see Holly seated on the toilet, merrily peeing without a care in the world. She ducked back behind the curtain, trying not to dwell on the noise, which sounded like someone was aiming a firehose into the bowl.

"Sorry if I startled you," Holly said brightly. "Is this your place? It's nice."

"Thanks," said Mira awkwardly. She focused hard on her fuzzy memory of bolting the door.

"Those river spirits," Holly chatted away. "They are helpful, but then you've gotta expel the power they've given you. I thought I'd got it out of me system earlier, but I must've used more than I thought. At least I managed not to wet meself this time. God, that were embarrassing."

Mira tried to imagine Holly being embarrassed by anything, but even given her expanded horizons, it was a tough stretch. She relaxed as she heard a flush and the door close, then gave her hair another going over, grateful for the shower as an oasis of sanity. As she stepped out, she noticed to her bewilderment that the bolt was in the closed position, just as she remembered. On the other side of the door, she could hear Holly talking to herself. She struggled to make out what was being said, save for a surprised, "She was here?"

Mira threw on her dressing gown, opened the door, and prepared for the next round.

Holly was seated on the sofa, picking lazily at Sam's guitar. Two steaming mugs sat on the coffee table in front of her, with a deck of cards in between them. Holly paused and muttered under her breath, before resuming playing. Mira recognised the Hangman's tune as she settled into the armchair facing across from her.

"Thanks for all this." Holly smiled.

"Any time." Mira stared into her tea for a moment as she felt her muscles starting to relax.

"Oh, I met Joe. Friendly sort," Holly said.

"Who's Joe?" Mira asked.

"The ghost, that's who I was talking to," Holly replied, sipping her tea nonchalantly.

"This flat isn't haunted."

"Yeah, it is."

"No, it's not!"

"How would you know, you only started believing in ghosts yesterday?" Holly said. "It's nowt to worry about – I told you, he's a nice bloke. I think he's from the 1920s. I get a bit fuzzy about those years. He used to work here when it were a warehouse until a box fell on his head, but he's surprisingly philosophical about the whole thing."

"Is he in the room now?" Mira asked, clutching at the front of her dressing gown.

"No," Holly said. "He thought we needed some privacy."

"Are you making this up?" Mira replied testily.

"Of course not!" Holly looked offended. "You hang around me a bit longer, you'll start to notice him."

She resumed playing the guitar and sang softly. "If ever thou gavest meat or drink, the fire shall never make thee shrink…"

"Are you sure that's the song?" Mira asked.

"Of course it is, I know me Yorkshire folk." She continued playing, but her fingers began to shake ever so slightly, making the tune discordant.

"I don't know," Mira said. "When it was on the bridge, there was something different about the song. Quicker. I'm not sure it is the Lyke-Wake Dirge, you know. It's something else, but I've definitely heard it before."

"Are you questioning my musical knowledge?" Holly snapped, as she stopped abruptly with a twang of string and put the guitar aside. She sat back and rubbed her eyes.

"Is something wrong?" Mira asked.

"Tired," Holly muttered. "Tired and pissed off."

"You passed out. And when I was following you before, you looked like you were in pain."

"Yeah, I guess you do deserve an explanation," Holly said, and looked out of the window as if wondering where to start. "When we went on the Ghost Walk, you said you felt sick. Did you feel like that today, on the bridge?"

Mira nodded. "Like my body doesn't even want to be around these things."

"That's how it is. When you're dealing with ghosts and whatnot — it's hard work, you know? Draining. That's why most people can't do it, don't do it. It takes a toll." She paused and looked right at Mira. "Now imagine doing it all the time."

"How do you cope?" Mira asked.

Holly scooped up the deck of cards. Her voice grew sad and distant as she idly shuffled them. "Time was it weren't a problem. The things in this city don't get up to mischief that often. But these last few years, it's getting worse and worse. One thing after another to put back in its box, and I am not getting me beauty sleep. I pushed it too hard today. If you hadn't been there, well… I don't know. God, I'm getting old."

New questions began to form in Mira's mind. She wanted to tell Holly about the ginger-haired girl, but wasn't sure she should. Her warnings about Holly still scratched at the back of Mira's thoughts, even though they felt totally at odds with this sudden moment of vulnerability.

Holly drained her mug and stood up. "I should be going. The Hangman'll keep, but he will be back. I should get some kip before he pops up again. Thanks for everything, Mira. Watch yourself out there, okay?"

"Where can I find you? At the church?" Mira asked as she rose to her feet.

Holly paused at the living room door, her shoulders slumped. "Mira, in case you've not been paying attention, this is all a bit dangerous. Might be best if you stay out of it. Let's face it, I've already nearly got you killed once today, and we've not had breakfast yet."

Mira folded her arms and spoke with determination. "Do you need help or not?"

"Yes, obviously." A smile crossed both their faces. "Okay, fine. Meet me at the Assembly Rooms on Blake Street at seven tonight, and bring the boxes. Is that your boyfriend?"

She was pointing at a picture of Sam on the wall, and the sudden change of direction had left Mira flustered. "Er, no. He's a friend, flatmate."

"That's not what Joe says." Holly grinned as she gazed at Mira, who felt like her reaction to the question had been studied and conclusions formed.

"Okay, that one you did make up," Mira replied.

"Maybe," Holly said smugly. "Do either of you smoke?"

"No," said Mira. "Are you trying to make small talk?"

"Actually, that bit might be important." Holly looked around the flat, her eyes finally alighting on a box of matches sitting on a shelf, which she snatched up and gave an exploratory rattle.

"This'll do. See you later."

And with that she was gone. Mira shook her head and chuckled, when something caught her eye. Something red lay alongside the sofa. She reached down and picked up a piece of liquorice. Fear flowed through her, as she looked back to the picture of Sam and wondered why he wasn't there.

CHAPTER 10

Fingers twisted the metal tab, pulling the length of wire taut as its rough surface pressed firmly into Sam's flesh. He rose to his feet, drew back his fingers, and gave the guitar a test strum. Contented with the results, he nodded to Dave, and Pre-Cool Systems commenced rehearsing the opening number of tonight's gig. He made it through all of two bars before the doors of the pub's upstairs room clattered open violently and a frantic-looking Mira burst in, clearly out of breath. Dave relaxed his best rock star pose a fraction of a second too late to not be ridiculous, and Carl and Nathan exchanged grins.

"Oh thank God you're here," panted Mira. "I've been looking everywhere. Are you okay?"

"Yeah, I'm fine," Sam replied. "I said we were rehearsing for tonight, remember?"

"Yes, yes, of course." Mira struggled to gather her thoughts. "No, it's just…"

"You could have just phoned me. You didn't have to go charging all over the city."

"My phone sort of ended up in the river," Mira sighed.

"How did you manage that?" he asked, laughing.

"It's a long story and I had help," Mira replied. "Did someone come to the flat this morning? A girl with red hair?"

"Oh yeah, the student," Sam said. "Yeah, she wanted to know if you had a book you were holding for her. I said you'd call her back. Seemed a bit odd. Do you give all your customers our address?"

"Did she do anything to you?" Mira blurted out the question, not caring how she sounded.

"Bit young for me," Sam replied.

"I'm serious, Sam," Mira said. "If she comes back, just, don't let her in, okay? She's…"

The word dangerous evaporated on her lips as she realised how strange it would sound.

"What?" Sam looked at her quizzically. "What's the problem?"

"Forget it. I'll see you later." Mira hurried to the door, and then turned back. "Oh, yes, sorry, won't be able to be there tonight. Something's come up. Sorry. See you later."

"What was that?" Dave asked once Mira had departed. "She's not going Yoko on us, is she?"

"For God's sake, she found a dead body yesterday!" Sam snapped back defensively.

"Okay, fine, just really don't need another crazy girlfriend in the band," Dave grumbled.

"Not my girlfriend."

"Carl, does that sound less convincing every time he says it?" asked Nathan.

"Now, now, Nathan," replied Carl, testing the weight of a drumstick in his hand. "If Sam says she's not his girlfriend, then she's not. The world is often not the way we'd like it to be."

"Every band should have a drummer with a philosophy degree," Sam sighed.

Mira collapsed into a chair in the bar with her head in her hands as music drifted down the stairs. A flood of panic swept over her. *She was in our home. She said she'd kill me and she was in our home. Oh God, what do I do?* There was no way of explaining this to Sam. Talking to the police was a waste of time. How do you say that some little ginger girl is plotting to murder you in your sleep without sounding paranoid?

"She was here?"

Mira jolted upright. *Oh my God, Holly knows. Holly knows who this girl is. She knows she was at the flat today. That's why it's suddenly too dangerous for me to help her.* Annoyance at having things kept from her drowned her fear.

Right then, Ms Trinity. Time for some answers.

Mira ran all the way to Holy Trinity, and went straight to the trapdoor. To her relief, the padlocks were open. She took a discreet look around for any more helpful volunteers, then lifted the door, dropped down into the hole and was confronted with a small wooden door. It was barely four feet square, with an iron ring on one edge, and Mira was positive it had not been here last time. She gripped the ring and found the door was not locked – in fact, it did not have any kind of catch at all. She pulled it open and shuffled forward, but no sooner had she crossed the boundary than it slammed shut behind her, cutting out all the light and plunging her into blackness.

Mira reached into her pocket for the phone that wasn't there and silently swore. She crouched in the darkness and felt her way along the walls, whispering Holly's name. As she stepped forward, her foot plunged down and landed on a lower level. Steps. There were steps. She gingerly made her way down until the floor levelled out, and stretching up, realised that the ceiling was high enough for her to stand. Feeling her way around this new space, she touched smooth, curved stone walls on either side of her, and flat wood in front, marked with iron nails. This was another door, a full sized one. She felt around the edges for a handle, and found a large knob of cold, rough metal. She rattled it furiously, and the door pushed forward. Light streamed painfully through the opening, and when Mira opened her eyes again, she could see the roughly carved steps she had just clambered down, and the yellow stone walls surrounding her. She turned back and stared at a somewhat startled figure.

A teenage girl stood in the doorway, wearing a black hoodie and jeans. The wires of headphones dangled from beneath her hood and snaked into a pocket. Her blue eyes were wide with shock.

"Nan!" she shouted. "I think she's let someone in!"

A squat figure shuffled out of the shadows to stand beside the girl, and Mira found herself looking at the deeply lined face of a little old lady smiling broadly at her beneath horn-rimmed spectacles and wiry grey curls.

"Oh my word!" she said excitedly. "My mum always said she does this sometimes, but I never thought to see it myself. Hello, dear, do come in. Welcome to the chicken coop."

The old woman grabbed Mira's hand and pulled her through the door, which the girl closed behind them. They were in a square chamber of grey stone, lit by a ramshackle mixture of sources, from a candelabra blazing in an alcove to a string of Christmas lights that hung above the door. While the room felt like part of the church above, it was filled with furniture of various ages and styles, including an antique chaise-longue against one wall, which the girl now sat on, studying her phone intently. There were three further doors inside, all closed. Discarded items of clothing lay scattered all over the place. Taped incongruously to one stone wall was a large poster, with candles in sconces on either side like a shrine. The illustration was of a woman with a pale face, large black eyes and a lopsided smile, her hair composed of blue and pink clouds. Mira leaned closer to look at the text underneath, which in spidery black letters read 'Kate Bush: The Tour of Life 1979'.

"Holly," Mira said with a smile, before turning to the old woman. "Sorry, but who are you?"

"We're the caretakers, dear," the woman replied. "I'm Angie, and that there's my granddaughter Chloe. I'm training her up, aren't I, love?"

The girl shrugged, without looking up.

Mira felt none the wiser. "I'm sorry, I still don't understand. Are you Holly's mother?"

"Mercy, no, dear. I'm not quite that old yet," Angie replied with a warm chuckle. "We just sort of look after things. Make sure she has what she needs. My mother did it all her life, and her mother before her, and her mother before that. My mum taught me to take her place, and now I'm teaching Chloe, aren't I, love?"

Mira couldn't see the girl's face beneath the hood, but could imagine the rolling eyes.

"My knees aren't what they were, and trudging around in that tunnel's no good for me at all these days." Angie began picking up the clothes from the floor and thrusting them into a canvas bag, shaking her head disapprovingly as Mira's spun. "She doesn't half leave this place in a mess sometimes, I don't know."

"But if your mother and grandmother were here before you," Mira said, "that doesn't make sense. Holly's just... I don't know, but she'd have to be..."

"She's quite a bit older than that," Angie replied. "She's been watching over this old town for many a long year. And all that time, we've been looking after her."

"And doing her laundry?" Mira asked.

"My old mum used to say," said Angie, pausing in her task. "She has so much on her plate, that it's up to us to think of the little things. So we clean up after her – see she's got plenty of money, patch her up when she hurts herself, that sort of thing."

"Sounds like you are her mum," said Mira, warming to the genial old lady.

Angie laughed as she extracted a handful of banknotes from her coat pocket and began counting them out into a small pile on top of a chest of drawers that looked Georgian.

"I never thought of it like that, but I suppose it's true. I can see why she likes you... sorry, what was your name?"

"Oh, yes. I'm Mira. Chloe said Holly had let me in. What does that mean?"

"Most of the time, only us caretakers can see this place. Normally, you open the trapdoor and there's just a dark old hole," Angie explained. "But every once in a while, she takes a shine to someone. Decides they're worth trusting. And then they can see the door and the stairs, and find their way in, you know, when she's not sleeping."

Angie grasped Mira's hands in both of hers.

"She thinks you're someone special."

"As long as I don't wake her up," Mira said, and Angie's expression showed that the old woman expected her to know far more than she did.

"Not exactly, dear," Angie replied. "You see, her job is to protect the city, but, well, there's not always anything to protect it from. And when there isn't, she sleeps."

"For how long?" Mira asked.

"Until we need protecting again," Angie said. "And one day, when her work's all done, forever. Did you say she's called Holly?"

Mira nodded, taken aback by the question.

"What a lovely name."

Mira looked into Angie's trusting eyes, and decided to risk the question. "Angie, do you know anything about a girl? She's about Chloe's age, with red hair. I think Holly knows her."

Angie's smile disappeared into a look of deep concern. Her dry fingers closed on Mira's hands and squeezed them tightly.

"Stay away from her," she said forcefully. "You don't want to know what she is, but please, for your own sake, stay away from that girl."

CHAPTER 11

The Assembly Rooms had been a magnificent ballroom in the eighteenth century, while the twenty-first had seen it repurposed as an Italian chain restaurant. It remained a spectacular site nonetheless, the long main hall bordered on either side by towering pillars of swirling golden brown that stretched from the polished wooden floor to the impossibly high ceilings, from which a series of silver chandeliers descended. Classical statues peered down from alcoves along the dining room through which Mira walked. With one hand she held the case containing the broken lanterns. In the other she held a large, plain white carrier bag. She found Holly seated at a small table with a plate of pasta and a glass of what looked like brandy in front of her. Her coat lay draped over her chair while her umbrella rested between her feet. She looked up from her meal, and happily waved at Mira to join her. Mira noted that Holly had made some effort to dress for dinner, wearing a pristine waistcoat of dark grey silk with pearl buttons.

Holly was gazing around the room with delight. "I've not been here in ages. I'd forgotten how beautiful it looks. Oh, try some of this." She pushed her plate to the middle of the table.

Mira helped herself to a forkful.

"Quite a history, this place," Holly continued. "Big, grand balls held here three hundred years ago. And Hubert Scraggles, who were Yorkshire's most debauched and least prolific romantic poet, died of syphilis in a back room. Probably right over there."

She gestured to the far end of the hall, where the open double doors of the kitchen were visible. Mira suddenly didn't feel hungry. She swallowed uncomfortably and handed the plastic bag to Holly.

"I bought you a present."

Holly peered inside and saw two plastic hoops bound together by a fine mesh of blue material. She looked up, puzzled. "What is it?"

"It's a laundry basket. I met Angie at the church. It looked like you could use one."

Holly stared, still puzzled.

"Angie," Mira repeated. "Angie, your caretaker. Looks after things for you? Her and her granddaughter?"

"Oh, right, got you," Holly said. "Is that her name?"

"You don't know her name?" asked Mira.

"I've never met the woman," said Holly, picking at her pasta. "They only come round when I'm out or asleep."

"Have you ever said thank you?" Mira asked.

"I've never met her!"

"You could leave her a note!"

"Why are you making a fuss about this?" Holly said. "She just looks after the place, that's all. I'm sure she's fine just getting on with things. Leave her be."

Mira felt aggrieved on behalf of the woman she had met this afternoon, and riled at hearing her so casually dismissed. There was something unpleasantly entitled about Holly's attitude.

"I'm making a fuss because, firstly, she's old. Secondly, she's lovely, and thirdly, she seems to have spent her entire life picking your knickers up off the floor of some dusty old crypt! On bad knees! And you just take her for granted! You could make a little effort, you know, try and make her life a bit easier."

Holly sat up straight, her face uncharacteristically expressionless. "Look, you might've missed this, but I've got one or two important things to worry about."

"Well, now you can worry about one more," Mira said, and tapped the carrier bag with her foot. "Knickers, basket. Not hard."

"Yes, mother." Holly sat in a rare silence as a knowing smile crept across her face. "All her life?"

"Three hundred years ago?" replied Mira.

"I were gonna build up to that one. I imagine you have questions. You usually seem to."

"I'm not sure where to start," Mira said. "I guess the big one... how old are you?"

"Well, we weren't all that big on keeping track back in my day. But I knocked ageing on the head in the Year of Our Lord 1604. I remember that one, because the archbishop mentioned it in a really dull speech that went on *forever*. I think he wanted everyone to know I were on his team. Or maybe he just wanted me to know what eternity felt like, I don't know. Anyway, as the crow flies, I'm probably somewhere in me mid-four-hundreds, but I've not had what you'd call a normal passage of time."

"I suppose you wouldn't, if you're immortal."

"No," Holly said firmly. "I'm not immortal. I can die. I just haven't yet."

"Tell me," said Mira. "I think I can handle some extra weirdness at this point."

"There are legends." Holly leant in conspiratorially as she spoke. "The King in the Mountain, it's often called. Goes back way before I were born. In these stories, there's some great macho bloke, a man of mickle might as we used to say, who sleeps in a cave somewhere until the world needs him again."

"In eternal sleep until England's greatest need," Mira said in a distant voice.

Holly looked at her bemused.

"It's a quote about King Arthur, from... somewhere. Can't remember who said it."

"There you are, perfect example," said Holly. "I'm like Arthur in... want to say Travelodge?"

"Avalon," corrected Mira.

"That's the badger." Holly flung her hands wide as if she was trying to encompass the city. "When this place needs protecting, I wake up, sort the problem out, then it's back to sleep until next time you lot are in trouble. Get it?"

"No," said Mira. "How does this happen? Where did you come from?"

"York," Holly replied. "I've lived here all me life. Which is saying summat."

"Well, then how did you become this?"

Mira's fascination with these new revelations spurred her on, but she felt a momentary stab of guilt at the look on Holly's face. She became aware that she was straying into sensitive territory.

"It's..." Holly's gaze drifted around the room, as she tried to sort her thoughts. "I'm sorry, Mira. There's a lot of it I don't remember. I think some of it I don't really want to. But, yeah, 1604. Well, that were a bad year. Summat happened. Summat terrible. And... people died. Lots of people. So many."

Holly's jaw tightened around the memory. "The history books all say plague, but it weren't. It were summat worse, summat no one should have to even know can happen, never mind see. I read once that 3,512 people died. We didn't count them at the time. But it felt like half the world were gone."

The pained memory was suddenly washed away in a burst of glibness. "So anyway, dust settles, those of us who are left think, what the scut do we do when this happens again?"

Mira nodded. "A King in the Mountain."

"The idea of a protector were big in these parts way back," Holly explained. "But they knocked it on the head once the Romans got into Christianity. Bit pagan. But things like that don't get forgot. I don't know what happened to the last one. He would've lived more than a thousand years before me. Maybe they killed him. I think they probably just didn't bother to replace him when he died."

An ominous thought occurred to Mira. "Wait a minute, is that why I'm here? Are you looking for someone to take your place? Am I your successor?"

"You bloody well are not, you cheeky mare!" said Holly. "Seriously, is this how you talk to all your mates? Would you mind dying so I can have all your stuff?"

"Okay, sorry I spoke," Mira said. "I don't fancy moving into your place anyway."

"As I were saying," Holly continued. "1604. The grand old

tradition makes a comeback. I volunteer for the job. They make a place for me under the church. A Hen Hole, it's called. I'm guessing you were there today. I go to sleep. Then one day I wake up, I've got some vague sense of a terrible danger that needs sorting out, and off I go to deal with it. But the first thing I find is twenty years have gone by. That were a bit of a shock."

"Why would you volunteer for this?" Mira said.

"It's my city," Holly said bluntly. "I wanted it safe. I wanted it always safe. And I wanted me family to be safe here forever. But by the time I woke up again, they were all gone."

Mira didn't know what to say, she was dumbstruck by the brutality of what had been taken by nothing more than time passing.

"It's been a funny old life," Holly continued. "Because my little naps... some of them are just a couple of weeks, but most of the time it's a long old rest. Years, decades. I think I lost a century somewhere. And I suppose that's good, 'cause it means all's well up here, how I want it. But lately, I am up and about a lot. I get days most of the time. And I'm starting to get the reason for the sleeping. This morning, when I said that dealing with ghosts takes its toll? Well, I don't think I'm getting the downtime I need to keep on going."

She smiled sadly. "I think it's for the best in a weird way. Before, I'd get out of bed, and everything would have changed. The people, the buildings, the streets, it'd be a whole new world. The ghosts'd be the same of course, but on the living side of things, I'd be starting from scratch every time. Sometimes, I just stopped bothering to think about the people, and you can live like that, but then you lose yourself. But now, for the first time in ages, this place feels like home again. I'd forgotten how much I missed that. Because this is a *fantastic* city, Mira. I love this bloody silly place. But my God, it's wearing me out."

The loneliness Mira had sensed yesterday was all over Holly's face.

"Anyroad, your turn," said Holly, wiping the corner of her eye with a cuff. "Bloke in picture. What's the story?"

Before Mira could say anything, the sound of tiny bells rang softly through the restaurant, although nobody else seemed to notice it. Holly rose to her feet and swung on her coat.

"It's time," Holly said. "Look, I got a bit carried away there, and forgot to mention. We're about to do summat unbelievably dangerous, so if you want to go home now, I'll understand."

"I said I'd help, and I'll help."

"You are a woman of mickle might, Mira." Holly grinned. "Grab the case, we're off to the dance."

CHAPTER 12

The ringing gradually faded away, as Holly stood still in the centre of the restaurant with both hands folded over her umbrella. She was muttering quietly, which Mira had already learned was a sign that something otherworldly was imminent. She stopped and flashed a dazzling smile, clearly looking forward to Mira's reaction to whatever was about to happen.

"Go on," Mira said. "You're obviously dying to do some exposition."

"I already have," Holly replied. "I told you Hubert Scraggles the romantic poet died in this place."

"So why are we here?"

"To meet him, of course." Holly pointed her umbrella to the ceiling. "Wait... do you hear it? Oh, you're gonna love this bit."

"I thought you said it was dangerous," Mira said, gripping the case and the carrier bag tightly and trying to make out what Holly was listening to.

"Oh, it is," Holly responded with a shrug. "But the first bit's *really* cool. Forgot to ask, did you pick a song yet?"

Mira was about to point out that she hadn't had much time to broaden her musical knowledge, when she realised that she could hear an orchestra playing. It sounded like they were right in the room with her, and yet somehow far away at the same time. Holly strolled down the central aisle of the dining room, and as Mira followed her, the sounds of the restaurant faded away to nothing. The people continued eating and talking in absolute silence, while the music grew louder and the lights became brighter and warmer. Mira realised they were not alone.

A man in a frock coat and a woman in a ball-gown waltzed

between the tables, the silent diners ignoring their presence. Out of the corner of her eye, Mira caught sight of another pair, then another, until the room was filled with dancers, all weaving their way in and out of the oblivious, muted patrons. The music was booming now, the source so close, and Mira detected a buzzy, electronic quality to it, at odds with the period outfits of the growing throng.

The air felt thick, heavy and perfumed, and Mira's head throbbed. But this was different from her earlier encounters with the spirit world. This felt pleasurable, but too much so – her mind was over-stimulated by waves of sensation. Her vision blurred and a sickly-sweet taste filled her mouth. She looked over to Holly, whose long coat, bushy hair and high boots created a similar silhouette to the Regency gents among the crowd. She glided around the room with ease, strutting with her umbrella wielded like a cane and greeting the dancers one by one, sometimes curtseying, sometimes kissing hands or presenting her own to be kissed. Other times she was more formal, offering a courteous handshake. For someone so lacking in niceties in the modern world, Holly was the ultimate social chameleon in this one.

A couple circled near to Mira, and for the first time she looked closely at the face of a dancer. Her unnaturally smooth white skin was crisscrossed with fine grey lines, like tiny cracks in porcelain. Her scarlet lips were pursed and frozen in place, while her eyes were deep and dark. Mira swayed drunkenly as she stared into those eyes, which were no more than two empty, round black holes in the woman's face, seemingly bottomless. She backed away, trying to spot Holly, who she saw deep in conversation with a couple, one hand resting on the woman's corseted waist while the other stroked the vivid green material of the man's waistcoat. She saw Holly discreetly slip something into the woman's bodice as she stumbled closer, but then collided with a tall Edwardian gentleman. She stared up into the same empty eyes and blank expression. Her bags slipped from her fingers and clattered to the ground. He extended a hand, which made a grinding sound as it unfolded, then clasped hold of hers.

Suddenly she was dancing, or at least whirling chaotically. The lights of the room smeared across her vision as her feet skittered, and she realised she could no longer feel the ground beneath them. The music wasn't music anymore, just an undulating pulse that filled her head and made it pound. The face of her partner remained blank, and Mira thought she could see tiny flakes of plaster drifting from his skin to burn away in the glare of the lights. For a moment, another face flashed across her vision, long and distorted with yellow eyes full of hunger. But in a second, it was gone, and in another, a hand had grabbed her wrist.

"I believe this is my dance."

Holly was standing beside her, and she shook the man's hand firmly, holding the grip for a moment before he bowed and backed away. Mira breathed heavily, trying to calm her racing heart. She could feel the rush of the dance fading, subsiding back into the general air of warm, sugary excess.

"Are you alright?" Holly asked, gripping Mira's arms and gently shaking her. "I am so sorry, I didn't see us get separated. You still with me? It can get a bit weird, this place."

She dashed back to their table and returned with her brandy. "Have some of this, it... well, I don't suppose it can hurt."

Mira sipped the brandy and tried to give her thoughts voice. "What... what is this place?"

"This is Scraggles' place," Holly said. "And this lot get to haunt it with him. Anyone who died in and around the Assembly Rooms, they belong to him. Forever. We've crossed over into his plane, not a safe place to be. I haven't seen him yet. I can take you back if it's too much."

Mira tried to shake off her disorientation. She focused on the taste of the brandy, which was vile, but at least real. "No, no, I'm okay."

"Oh good, because his nibs has just turned up. Grab the case, we might need it."

"Why?" Mira asked. "They're broken, aren't they?"

"Yeah, but he don't know that. Come on."

Holly moved to the edge of the hall, where a man stood apart from the rest of the ghosts. While the dancers were clad in finery, he wore a stained, threadbare dressing gown of faded green and gold over an equally grubby off-white nightshirt that trailed to the floor. His gaunt face looked grey and pockmarked, but as they drew closer, Mira could see the flesh was rotten and covered in weeping sores that cracked open as he smirked at them. Lank, pale blond hair hung to his shoulders, and a brocaded cap sat atop his head with an oddly festive dangling tassel. Holly strode up to him, and he bowed a little too obsequiously as she approached.

"*La Belle Dame Sans Merci*," he said in a hissing voice. "I am honoured."

"*La poete mort sans publishing deal*," Holly replied. "Long time."

"Do you like the ball?" he asked. "I really feel it is approaching perfection."

"I'd have thought you'd have more people by now," Holly replied, her tone flat.

"Regrettably, this hall has become a less popular departure point for the great beyond. Sad, really."

"Is that why you're branching out?" Holly asked.

"You heard about that?" Scraggles replied with a smile that stretched his rotten flesh to breaking point. "Yes, an interesting experiment. Take that gentleman over there."

He pointed a bony finger at a bewhiskered Victorian in a tweed suit and derby, dancing with a woman wearing a floral minidress who could only have come from the 1970s.

"He didn't die here. Merely had a hand chopped off in the street outside over a gambling debt. But parts of a whole remain one thing in my home. I was able to take the hand, and eventually the rest of him followed. He died many years later, in Brough I believe, which is unfortunate. But his spirit belongs to me nonetheless."

Mira could see Holly trying to cover her disgust. "I don't know how you came by this place, Scraggles, but..."

"Yes, you do." Scraggles cut Holly off and regarded her with a defiant air, daring her to challenge him.

"Yes, I do."

Mira caught a flash of sadness entering Holly's voice, before she resumed the confrontational small talk.

"How's the poem going?"

"Which one?"

"*The* poem."

"Developing nicely. I feel I may finish within a century. Of course, there's no hurry. My muse will never die."

"That's new." Holly pointed to the far wall as she changed the subject. Looking where Holly indicated, Mira saw the reason for the strange quality of the music. A mixing desk dominated the space, and a DJ worked to pump out the sounds of harpsichords and harps through an arrangement of towering speakers. His hands danced slowly and elegantly across his controls while his head lolled as if asleep.

"Oh, my most recent arrival," said Scraggles proudly. "He died a few years ago. Overdosed in the gents. Dreadfully lucky to get him."

"What happened to your usual band?" Holly asked.

"They dance now."

"That's nice."

"Forever."

"Less so." Holly stared at the DJ as he sleepily worked his controls. "Hang about, I know that fella!"

She bounded over to the desk, and gave the DJ an enthusiastic high five, which he returned with a lazy, dreamlike motion before resuming his work, his face remaining entirely blank throughout the greeting. Mira was alone with Scraggles, who fixed her with a predatory grin.

"How very thoughtful," he whispered. "Did she bring you for me? I do hope so. Some fresh blood may be just what I need, so to speak, to bring my ball to full and beautiful life. I've been working on it for so long, like a painting, and it is magnificent, but... in my mind, I see it as it should be. And you are there. Will you dance for me? I think you will."

He reached out to touch her, the flesh of his hand pulled tight across old bones. Mira raised the lantern case to her chest, the portcullis symbol facing the poet, who pulled his arm back.

"You know what this is." Mira tried to sound calm. "Well, unless you fancy spending eternity in a little glass box, you'll keep your hands to yourself."

Scraggles regarded her defiance with wry amusement.

"Are you up to no good again, Scraggles?" Holly asked as she returned.

"Am I so dangerous," Scraggles asked, with a sarcastic air of feigned innocence, "that you feel the need to bring a tendicula with you? And what other tricks and traps do you have upon you? Tell me."

He indicated the carrier bag Mira had dropped at her feet.

"It's a laundry basket," said Holly, who flinched in embarrassment as Scraggles smirked.

"How domestic," he drawled. "I assume this is a business call?"

"I wouldn't come here just to chat," Holly replied.

"Very well, come with me." Scraggles drifted away from the dance. "Your dabbawalla can join us, if you wish."

"Sorry about that," grumbled Holly, then downed the remains of her brandy. "I keep such pleasant company."

"If we are going to be associating with people from the glory days of Empire," Mira said. "It might be best if you carry your own bags."

CHAPTER 13

Scraggles glided imperiously through the kitchens of the restaurant, followed by Holly, who had stopped on the way to discreetly refill her glass at the bar. Mira nervously brought up the rear, still clutching the case and the bag, both of which felt reassuring for very different reasons. The silence that had descended over the dining room had taken effect here as well, and the staff worked swiftly and methodically with barely a sound. A harassed-looking young cook dropped a metal bowl, which fell to the ground with a delicate ping. Mira worried they would be seen, but everyone remained oblivious to the three intruders in their midst.

As a furious-looking chef mouthed reprimands at his clumsy subordinate, Scraggles stopped in the middle of the room. He sat cross-legged on the floor, and with a languid gesture, invited them to do the same. As soon as Mira sat, she felt like the ground had dropped out beneath her and she had fallen into a deep hole in the Earth. She snapped to a juddering halt in an instant and the kitchen was gone. They were in a small, shadowy room, surrounded on all sides by heavy curtains of rich velvet in an assortment of dark colours. She was sitting on a hard-backed antique chair of pale wood. Holly and Scraggles were seated with her at a round table made of scratched mahogany, with a cluster of short, thick red candles burning in the centre. The smells and sensations of the ballroom were stronger and more overpowering here. Mira got the impression that if this place, whatever it was, had windows, they hadn't been opened in a very long time. Scraggles puffed casually on a hookah that sat beside his chair, and Mira was impressed to note that Holly still had her brandy, which she swilled in its tumbler but did not drink. Mira heard far off noises, and looked up. Through a round opening in what she had to call the ceiling for want of a better term, she could see the distorted shapes of the kitchen, as if glimpsed through a fish eye lens set into the floor. Cold, pale light filtered through the opening, and motes of dust swirled in the air.

"So, then," Scraggles said with a long exhale of acrid smoke, "to business."

"You must have guessed why we're here," Holly said.

"Oh, of course. The new boy."

"So he's new. That's a start," Holly said. "I thought maybe he'd been around a while..."

"The dirge is confusing, isn't it? Music often is. Some things of great antiquity can seem as fresh as they ever were, while the work of a past year can feel ancient." Scraggles idly tapped the surface of the table with a dirty nail. "But you still haven't explained why exactly you expect me to help you."

"Well, I was thinking I might threaten you, see how we go from there."

"The tendicula," Scraggles said with a weary sarcasm.

"You're not my problem, Scraggles. You're only a threat to the dead, and that's someone else's territory. But if you stop me from catching this thing, you become my problem."

"Succinctly put." Scraggles cracked a sour grin. "Of course, you didn't seriously think I wouldn't notice that your little weapon is broken."

"Ah."

"That I couldn't sense its power as soon as you walked in was my first clue, but the ease with which your colleague waves it about rather gave the game away."

"So is this the part where I ask nicely, and you decide to be helpful out of the goodness of your heart?" Holly asked.

"I suspect not."

"Rather not go for feminine wiles, if you don't mind. I'm not saying I couldn't flirt for Yorkshire on a good day, but I'm not sure me eyelashes could manage a bat right now."

"We could game for it, I suppose, that might be amusing."

"I did wonder if it would come to that again." Holly smiled. "Primero?"

"Why not?" Scraggles produced a deck of cards from the depths of his robe, and begin shuffling. "It's been a while since I played, but it is one of life's great pleasures, isn't it? Or indeed death's. I always liked the story of two gentlemen in London who sent a man onto a ship in the Thames, then scuttled it so they could bet on whether or not he would drown."

"Okay, I've been in the river once today. Can we not do that one?" Mira piped up.

Scraggles flashed her a crooked smile. "Oh, I think Primero will more than suffice. This time. Your stakes?"

"The Hangman. I want to know when and where it'll turn up next. Oh, and I'll have that back an' all." Holly gestured to his left hand, and Mira noticed for the first time a tarnished silver ring.

Scraggles extended the finger to study it.

"I'm sorry, that's a little high for my liking," he said, making it clear that he wasn't sorry at all. "What say we play for the information, then if you win, we can always have a second hand for this old thing."

"Seems fair. What do you want?" Holly asked.

Scraggles casually stroked his chin, making an unconvincing show of being deep in thought.

"Your dusky friend can put up her tendicula, I'm sure I'll find some use for what's left of it," he finally declared, not even looking in Mira's direction, but clearly enjoying her seething. "And as for you, my dear, you can stake your friend."

"Done," said Holly, as casually as if she'd been asked to play for buttons. "But I get to deal."

"What?" Mira jumped to her feet. "No, not done! Undone!"

"Mira, it's fine. I'm good at this game, honestly…"

"I don't care how good you are, you're not using me as a bloody poker chip!"

"Mira, please…"

"No, I am through with this." She looked around the room for a way out. The opening in the ceiling was small and inaccessible. She reached for the nearest curtain, tore it back and stepped forward into nothing. A great black void stretched out as far as she could see in all directions. Wisps of cloud circled the small cocoon of the curtained room, which as they drew closer assumed the shapes of the dancers from the restaurant. A strong, cold wind roared around them, pushing Mira back towards the table. There was nowhere to run.

"The deal is made," Scraggles said severely. "Shall we?"

Mira returned to the table and sat, trembling with rage.

"If you don't mind." Holly reached across the table and took the deck from Scraggles. "Mira, I know you're upset, but I promise, nothing bad is going to happen. I really am very good at this game."

She began shuffling, but the cards sprang from her hand and scattered across the table.

"I hate you," Mira said coldly as Holly gathered up the deck.

She dealt four cards to Scraggles, four to herself, which she studied intently, then four to Mira. It suddenly occurred to Mira that she had never heard of Primero, and that her life was riding on a game she had no chance of following, let alone playing. She picked up her cards and breathed out slowly at the sight of the satisfied-looking faces of the king and queen of hearts, along with a seven of the same suit, and a three of clubs. She still had no idea what she was doing but decided that this hand was probably a good start.

"Shall we say Numerus 40 to begin?" said Scraggles, and Mira was once again totally lost. Holly nodded, and Scraggles tapped the table. She dealt him two more cards, and after a moment's thought, he discarded two from his hand and laid them face down in front of him.

"Hangman, Hangman, slack your line, slack it just a while," whispered Scraggles ominously, but Holly did not rise to his desire to appear important. They both turned to look expectantly at Mira, who tapped the table a little harder than she had meant to. Holly passed her two cards, which turned out to be a welcome ace of hearts and a six of spades. Still confused, she tossed the two black cards from her hand. Holly gave what appeared to be a reassuring wink, before dealing herself two cards and discarding two.

"Well, if we're all still in, shall we take it up to 50?" Scraggles asked. Holly gave a carefree shrug, while Mira just looked baffled.

"Lowest score needed to win the hand," Holly explained.

"Okay, fine. I'm sure that's... fine." Mira had three good cards, it didn't seem unreasonable that she had 50.

"A degree of desperation is always fascinating," said Scraggles, running a finger across his cards. "Only three dead, and you're willing to trade an innocent for the slenderest chance to stop this creature. And yet I'd wager you don't even have the first clue what it is yet. Two more, please."

Holly obliged him, he placed two cards back on the table, and then it was Mira's turn again. She gave the surface a delicate tap with one finger and Holly once again gave her two cards, a four of diamonds and, to her delight, a Jack of Hearts. She kept her court cards and her ace and tried very hard to maintain her poker face.

"I won't say you're wrong," said Holly, taking two cards and discarding two. "But then again, it doesn't really matter what it is. It just has to stop. And yes, I will make whatever sacrifices I need to."

Her eyes flicked to Mira's clearly anxious face. "Only not in this case, because nothing bad is going to happen, because I'm really very good at this game."

She flashed Mira a smile, and looked hurt when it was not returned. In truth, Mira had very much wanted to reciprocate, but knew not to. The unlikely appearance of exactly the card she was hoping for had tipped her off to what was really happening. Holly was cheating. It was obvious now that she thought about it, that's why she'd been so keen to deal. But she wasn't cheating for herself, of course, Scraggles would notice – he was watching her like a hawk. But he was hardly paying any attention to the stupid little dabbawalla who had no idea what she was doing, and Holly was using that to set her trap. Let the rookie win.

"Then *vada*. Show me everything."

Scraggles tapped the table and grinned as he laid out his cards – an ace of diamonds, a six of spades, and the sevens of hearts and clubs. Mira let out a burst of nervous laughter at the sight, then triumphantly slapped her own cards down on the table.

"Sorry, Hubert, but I think I might have you beaten there. Now shall we have a little chat about the Hangman?"

It took Mira a moment to realise that Scraggles was looking very pleased and that Holly was shifting uncomfortably in her seat, and for the first time since they had met, looked scared.

"That's not really worth anything," said Holly.

"Not even the minimum bid," added Scraggles, revelling in their discomfort.

"But it's a royal flush! A flush has got to be worth something, surely..."

Holly took her hand and explained in a soft, somewhat pained voice. "You needed at least 50. Court cards are only worth 10. But sixes and sevens are worth triple. I'm sorry."

"I had sixes and sevens! Why didn't you tell me about the sixes and sevens!" shouted Mira, yanking her hand away and sending cards flying across the table. "I thought you were cheating, I thought you were deliberately giving me good cards..."

"I do not cheat at cards," Holly replied, but clearly knew this was no time to be hurt by a slight to her honour. "I were just gonna win the game meself, that was the plan. It didn't matter what you did."

That was *the plan*. Mira noted the past tense and did not like it. Holly looked increasingly ill-at-ease, and Mira had a nasty feeling that things had not worked out as intended.

"Then what were all the knowing smiles and winking in aid of?" she asked.

"I just wanted to make sure you weren't freaking out..."

"Well I bloody well am now!"

"If you're quite finished," Scraggles said witheringly. His visible pleasure at their discord faded as he became impatient to claim his victory. "May I see the hand that was going to win you this game?"

"Yes, well... I've got... these..." Holly awkwardly put her cards on the table, a random jumble of suits and numbers. Mira didn't need to know any more of the rules, the look on Holly's face said it all. A wordless cry escaped her lips as panic consumed her.

"Holly, what have you done?" she said, tears beginning to form in her eyes as the terrible weight of the situation took hold.

Holly picked her cards up with trembling fingers. She looked confused and helpless, all her confident swagger drained away. A sickening prospect dawned on Mira.

"Oh my God," she gasped. "You don't know what you're doing..."

Holly looked up from her cards, a bewildered emptiness to her expression.

"She said I'd die, she said I would die with you, and now I will because you don't know what you're doing!" Mira cried. "I trusted you and... you're all talk! You never had a plan, you told me you never had a plan and I trusted you anyway and this is what happens! This is how they all died!"

"I'm... I don't know what happened, I'm good at this..."

"Apparently not." Scraggles rose to his feet, and with a grinding, cracking noise, his body seemed to elongate. His chest became almost snakelike as he stretched across the table and his jaw distended into a wide, predatory maw. The ends of his fingers shrank away into needle-sharp talons as he reached across the table. Mira leapt from her chair and ran to the edge of the tiny space, while Holly brandished her umbrella in front of her like a rapier.

"Now come on, Hubert," she said. "You don't have to do this."

"You made your wager." A wiry, black tongue flicked between Scraggles' thin lips. "The house always wins."

"Righty-ho then." Holly's thumb moved over a catch on the handle of her umbrella, and a length of chalk emerged from the tip. Swiftly, she moved around Mira, drawing a circle on the floor surrounding her. Scraggles lunged forward, but his hands stopped sharp as if against a wall. Mira saw the skin of his palms turning white as he pressed them against whatever was holding him back.

"Now, she can stay safe and sound in that magic circle, until you and I come to an arrangement. What do you say?"

The boldness had returned to Holly's voice, and Mira saw that every sign of weakness had been for the dead poet's benefit. The twisted creature that had been Scraggles glared avariciously at her with malice in his yellow eyes. He paused for a moment, turned back to face Mira, and without looking, lashed out with one impossibly long arm. The blow sent Holly flying through the curtains and she was gone, her umbrella clattering uselessly to the floor. Scraggles lumbered around the chalk circle. While his upper body had stretched, his legs had shrunk, and he moved with an ape-like rolling gait. His jaw twitched as he spoke, and crooked brown teeth snapped inches from Mira's terrified face.

"Oh, don't you worry, this enchantment will fade soon enough. I said you'd be mine, didn't I? I'm always right about these things, you know." His voice had a strange sing-song quality as it rasped through his misshapen mouth. He dragged a claw across the barrier, and sparks formed in the air around it. "I'll soon have you out of there, and then we must get on with killing you. Can't have things from your world down here. Not the way, not the way."

"Not even when they help you win at cards?"

Scraggles and Mira turned to see Holly clutching a fraying curtain, which she used to haul herself back into the card room, landing heavily on the dusty floor. She rose up, shaking out her wild hair with both hands.

"Chuffin' hell, is it blustery out there," she said. "Anyway, as I were saying, you want to take another look at your winning hand before you go on playing the charming host. Y'alright in there, Mira?"

"Still hate you," Mira replied, but she found her faith in Holly rushing back, no matter how much she told it not to. It did not seem justified – it certainly wasn't deserved. But right now, she had to admit it was all she had left.

Scraggles looked at the cards on the table. There was something about that ace of diamonds, something out of place, something shiny and... *new*.

"You're right, you know. It is confusing." said Holly, picking up her brandy and taking a sip. "Some things of great antiquity can seem as fresh as they ever were, while the work of a past year can feel ancient."

Scraggles flipped the cards over, revealing three identical copies of a boar's head emblem. But the fourth card showed the face of a man in a cocked hat with an elaborately waxed moustache, his portrait framed with the words Jack Daniels.

"I slipped that one in when you weren't looking. I suppose I did cheat a bit, actually," Holly said, replacing her glass on the table and turning to Mira. "I've got to ask, was it too much when I dropped the cards all over the table? I were a bit worried there, I thought I were really hamming it up, but neither of you were paying much attention, so I suppose I got away with it..."

Scraggles flourished the card in front of her between two talons and cackled. "And this, somehow, will save you? The great King in the Mountain, and all you have are a mountebank's tricks?"

Holly strolled around the table, and Mira noticed a match clutched between her thumb and forefinger.

"Funny thing, a deck of cards. It's lots of separate things that are all one thing." She gasped theatrically, and placed a finger to her open mouth in a broad imitation of inspiration. "A bit like your man with the hand."

"Indeed." Wariness crept into Scraggles' voice. "I look forward to discussing this further at the ball, after your death. This will not help you."

He crumpled the card in his hand and dropped it to the floor.

"No, I suppose it won't. Not on its own." Holly's smile was all mock apology. "But then again, I did give the rest of the deck to all your mates up there on the dance floor..."

Scraggles froze. A look of what might have been fear crossed his distorted face. Holly raised her arm and snapped her fingers. The queen of spades was suddenly in her hand as if by magic.

"And I kept this one for meself."

Before Scraggles could react, Holly thrust her match into one of the candles, then dropped it into her brandy, which burst into flames. She leapt back to stand beside Mira, holding the glass by its base in one hand, with the card suspended above it.

"Playing the hand with that ace in it should be enough to make the rest of the deck part of your world. Now, what do you suppose will happen if I set fire to this?"

"My dancers…" Scraggles gasped.

"Freed from a living death," Holly said. "Like I said, you're not my problem unless you choose to be."

Scraggles' elongated body shrank back into its more natural human form. "Take her and go. You will not be harmed, I promise."

"More than that. I want what I came for." Holly stood firm.

Scraggles wrenched the ring from his finger and held it out.

"Mira, reach out and take the ring, but keep your feet inside the circle." Holly's voice had a commanding authority that compelled Mira to do as she was told. "Now put it somewhere safe. He won't hurt you. Will you, Scraggles?"

Scraggles grimaced as Mira pulled the ring from between his leathery fingers and stuffed it into the pocket of her jeans.

"Now go," hissed the poet.

"Ah-ah, not done yet. Where and when, Scraggles? Because one way or another, this ends. The Hangman does not kill again, not here, not in my city. You can either help me stop this, or watch everything you have burn."

"Coppergate. Go to Coppergate. To your tawdry Norse village. Now please, put that card down…"

"When, Scraggles? I asked you when."

Holly let the queen slip closer to the flames. But this did not worry Scraggles; in fact, the fear on his face had been replaced with his familiarly unpleasant air of smug assuredness.

"I'm sorry, I don't understand the question," Scraggles replied.

"Don't play games with me, Scraggles. When will it manifest?"

"It won't. It doesn't need to. It's already there. And as to whether or not it will kill again in *your city*, only one thing will decide that." Scraggles grinned, his face once again monstrous. "How fast can you run?"

"Cheers, Scraggles," said Holly. "You're a diamond."

She dropped the queen into the flames. The crumpled card at Scraggles' feet exploded.

CHAPTER 14

Greg snorted and slammed the paper down on the table. Caroline peered over, and saw the faces of the three victims staring back at her, beneath a headline declaring 'Strangler Kills Third'.

"Well, that's that," growled Greg. "We're a bloody airport novel now."

The two detectives sat in the front window of a small pub, all low wooden beams and uneven floor beneath dusty carpets. Greg scowled out of the window over his bitter, while Caroline scanned the paper, her fingers moving up and down over the stem of her glass of red wine.

"You know how this works," she sighed. "People know, they report stuff, they lock their doors at night…"

"They'll be giving him a name next," Greg grumbled.

"Very likely," Caroline replied.

"I hate it when they give them names," Greg said. "I'm not sodding Batman, I don't need my wrong'uns to have stupid bloody nicknames."

"Says the only man on the force who uses the word 'wrong'uns'."

Caroline continued to read. As if he hadn't heard her comment, Greg pressed on with his extended grouch against the twin evils of serial killers and journalists.

"I bet he'll love it when they do," he said. "I know the sort. Sitting in his mam's basement feeling all big just because some smart-arse journo gives him a stupid bloody name. Makes him feel like something more than a person."

Caroline lowered the paper and fixed Greg with a look he had seen on her face many times before.

"Not this, Caz. I can't be doing with this tonight…"

"I'm just saying..." she began before he cut her short.

"You know, when other coppers go for drinks with colleagues after work, it leads to sordid affairs, which leads to ugly divorces, which leads to gallstones. What do I get? I end up in the bloody X-Files."

"You already did the affair and the divorce," Caroline pointed out. "The other one too."

"Well, I'd rather do them again than go looking for little green men!" he complained.

Caroline sat back and resolved not to let go of the thread she was unravelling.

"Has the coroner been able to identify what they were strangled with?"

"No," Greg replied wearily.

"Did we see anything on any of the CCTV footage?"

"You know we didn't. It was all static," Greg snapped back. He looked around the bar, aware he was about to say something it would not do to have overheard. "You know half the cameras in this city are falling to bits anyway."

Caroline smiled and leaned further in. A glint in her eyes pierced through her usual studied cynicism.

"No," she whispered. "The cameras outside the book shop were replaced three months ago. Brand new. Perfect working order. The ones outside the park are less than a year old. But the footage has the same problems we always have. Like somebody's wiped it. Why does the CCTV in this city never work?"

"I don't know, why?"

"I don't think there's anything wrong with the cameras," Caroline said, her eyes blazing with excitement. "I think it's something else that causes it. Maybe there's something about this city. Maybe there's something that can't be recorded, so the cameras never work."

"Or maybe they replaced them with cheap cameras they bought in a car boot."

"I'm serious, Greg."

"Yes, I know you are. You always are when you get on to one

of these daft ideas. That's the problem." He drained his glass before continuing. "Look, Caz, the cameras don't work because they're crap cameras. That's all there is to it. Which is why it's a good thing we're so bloody brilliant at what we do. And I am far too old and cantankerous for you to get me believing in ghost stories."

"Run for it, Mira!"

Fire was everywhere, blue fire with tongues of blinding magnesium white. Holly and Mira charged out of the kitchen as the blaze engulfed the room. Mira shielded her eyes against the brilliant light of the inferno that surrounded them, but felt no heat coming from it. She could see the cooks, seemingly untouched and unaware that their workplace was filled from floor to ceiling with flames. Mira could hear Scraggles roaring in pain and rage, a guttural bellow that sounded nothing like a human voice. The noise spurred her on to keep pace with Holly.

As they ran out into the dining room, they found the swirling flames had spread and filled the vast room all the way to its vaulted ceiling. The diners, like the cooks, acted as if nothing were out of the ordinary, but the ghosts were another story. Their bodies were swept into the air, spinning and twirling as their clothes and skin blackened and flaked away to nothing. As each one disappeared in turn, there was an ear-shattering crack and a ball of incandescent light shot into the ceiling. Mira could barely see or hear as she stumbled after Holly, just visible through the glare. And then suddenly it was all gone. The flames vanished, as if all the oxygen had been sucked from them. The two women stood in the middle of the dining room as if nothing was out of the ordinary. Mira looked down and noticed to her surprise that without thinking she had remembered to bring the laundry basket with her. She let both the bag and the tendicula case fall to the floor as she tried to gather herself.

"Right, we…" was as far as Holly got before Mira slapped her hard across the face. The dining hall was plunged into silence, followed by outbursts of muttering. Everyone either turned to watch the ensuing scene, or tried half-heartedly to ignore it, as Holly's apparent invisibility was shattered by the blow.

"Ow! What were that for?"

Mira pointed back in the direction of the kitchen. "That was cruel. You know how cruel that was."

"Can we talk about this later, we've got to go…"

"I thought I was going to die!" Mira shouted. "And you let me think that!"

"Well, okay, yes, bad," Holly protested. "But look at it this way – I pretended to leave you to die, but then really saved your life. For the third time. So I think I've earned a little bit of leeway."

"Don't," Mira said. "You don't get to make jokes about this. You made me think you would just… throw my life away to get what you want. You just use people, like we're your… stupid, useless gadgets!"

She picked up the case and hurled it at Holly, who stumbled back a step as she caught it.

"What would Scraggles have done to me if you hadn't been lying?" Mira asked, trying to reign in her fury.

"Well, yes, he'd have killed you, but I wasn't…" Holly explained.

"And what then?" Mira said, her tone hard and cold. "What then?"

A flippant remark formed for a second on Holly's lips, but she thought better of it.

"Nothing good," she said softly.

"Nothing good. And you made me believe that was coming."

"Mira, I just…" Holly said. "Look, the Hangman is gonna kill someone else if I don't stop him right now. Also, I think we're about to get chucked out of this restaurant. We need to go. Please."

Mira picked up the carrier bag, and reluctantly nodded her assent. She followed Holly as she ran for the door.

"Look, Greg, I know what I've been saying sounds crazy," said Caroline as they stood in the doorway of the pub.

"It doesn't *sound* crazy," Greg replied. "It actually *is* completely bonkers. There are no fairies at the bottom of the garden, Caz. There's a man, and you and me are going to find him."

"Fair enough." Caroline smiled as she turned to leave. "Tomorrow, then."

Greg walked off, taking a short cut back to his car through a small square lined with shops and galleries. It was dominated by the brightly lit windows of the city's Viking museum, and towering images of Norsemen in gleaming helmets and tangled beards glowered down at him, watching his progress like a gallery of ancient gods. His eye was drawn to a hardback book on a plinth in the window of the gift shop, the cover embossed by an image of a shield engraved with a serpent chasing its tail, and the title *Choosers of the Slain* in big gold letters. The name provoked a wordless reproach from Greg. The place was deserted, as it usually was at night, but this time Greg had the feeling he wasn't alone. He could hear singing. The Vikings watched him as he left.

Holly sprinted across the centre of the city, with Mira trailing a few steps behind. It was Saturday night. How had Mira forgotten it was Saturday? The streets were crowded and they ducked and weaved between the oblivious people, the din of a busy night in the city enveloping them. Mira was tired and her body complained bitterly at what she was asking from it, still asking after such a long and demanding day. But there was no stopping, she knew that, not if what Scraggles had said was true. So she ran. Her anger at Holly popped up every few steps when she remembered it was there. She congratulated herself on thinking of the big picture for the times it didn't, but then reminded herself not to stop being angry.

Finally, they reached the square they had been sent to. And there Mira saw it.

The Hangman floated in the middle of the deserted courtyard, singing its eerie, glugging tune. A man's body dangled lifelessly, cradled in its glowing tendrils. It seemed to become aware of them and twisted the neck of its victim, turning the man's head to face backwards. Mira gasped as she stared into the empty lifeless eyes of the detective who had interviewed her just two days previously. Holly set down her case and tossed her umbrella into the air, caught it and flung it overarm like a javelin. It passed into the Hangman's body with a faint ripple and was gone.

"I don't think that helped," Mira said, with mounting dread.

"I got his attention," Holly retorted. "If he comes after us, he's not hurting anyone else."

The detective's jaw flopped open and one of the Hangman's tentacles emerged from his mouth like some great reptilian tongue, lashing back and forth in front of his dead face.

"And what do we do when it comes after us?" Mira asked.

"I'll get to that part in a bit."

The Hangman tossed the corpse aside and advanced towards them, all six tentacles moving in frenzied arcs through the night air.

"Have we got anything else we could use?"

"Yeah, we've got a laundry basket."

Nik-tek.

"Run!" shouted Holly, grabbing the case with one hand and Mira's wrist with the other. They fled through the city, moving away from the crowds and charging through the backstreets where they had followed the ghost walk just yesterday. Holly seemed to know where she was going, so Mira followed. She didn't look behind her, but she knew it was there, chasing her every step. The singing rang in her head, and she wasn't sure what she was hearing and what was imagined. For a moment she wondered if anyone else was seeing their pursuer. All she knew was that it was not going to stop, so she didn't either.

She realised where they were heading as the Minster towered over them, growing closer and closer, until they came to the piazza of pale yellow stone on the building's south side, a place Mira walked through every day on her way to work. The life-size, bronze statue of the enthroned Roman Emperor Constantine gazed down on them, leaning on his sword atop a head-high stone plinth. She could see the sign of the book shop in its small side street, but Holly made straight for the main south door of the cathedral.

"What are you doing? You can't get into the Minster!" Mira shouted.

"You just watch me!"

"But it's locked!" Mira said and fumbled in her pockets for her work keys. "Maybe we could hide in the book shop…"

"I am the protector of this city. No one can lock me out!" Holly yelled triumphantly, and pulled the smaller door set into the great arched double doors open, only to be interrupted by a scream. The Hangman was right behind them. One of its tendrils had looped around Mira's ankle and was hauling her towards it. Holly seized both of Mira's hands and pulled hard. The two of them tumbled through the doorway and slid across the cool marble floor. Holly leapt to her feet and yanked the door shut behind them. She leant with her back against the wood and slid slowly to sit on the floor.

"How…" Mira gasped. "How did we get in here?"

"I told you. I'm the protector of the city," Holly gasped, crawling across the floor towards her. "What's the good of a place I can't get in to protect? Locks never keep me out."

She tried to stand, then flopped down on to the stone. Mira hauled her over and pulled her up into a sitting position propped up against an information desk.

"Are we safe here?" Mira asked.

"I think so. This place should be off-limits to the likes of him." Something heavy crashed against the door. "I hope."

They sat side by side in the dark, two tiny figures in the vast, vaulted space of the cathedral. Light filtered through the enormous stained-glass windows and cast its patterns across the grey expanse of the floor. Mira was badly out of breath, her head spun and her legs ached. Holly didn't look much better than she felt. Once again, the door shook as something slammed against it.

Holly spoke quietly, but her voice still echoed in the emptiness. "Mira, please believe me. I would never have let Scraggles hurt you. I promise. I just needed to play the game to make it all work. But I'm sorry I scared you. I didn't think."

"It's okay," Mira said softly. DS Unwin's tormented face filled her mind and drowned her anger. She began to be aware of the terrible weight of Holly's responsibilities.

"I've not been in here in ages." Holly's voice was acquiring a sleepy, slurred quality, and her head drooped against Mira's shoulder. "Did you see the scaffolding outside? There's always scaffolding. You know why?"

Mira placed an arm around Holly's shoulder and pulled her closer. "Tell me."

"Long ago," Holly said dreamily, "there were a magic war, right here in York. And at the end, a demon laid claim to this city. Said it were his to do with as he pleased. And no one could stop it, not the lords or the church, not even me. But there were this monk. Brilliant man he was, so clever, so beautiful. And he says to the demon 'Look here!'"

She raised an arm in an uncoordinated gesture, then let it flop to her side.

"He says, 'You can't have the city yet, we're not done building the Minster. Let us finish, then it's all yours.' It were having work done even then. And the demon, he don't know owt about architecture, but you can't have a city without a Minster. And he thinks, this is a good deal, the humans can do all the hard work for me. And ever since then, some part of the Minster is always under construction, in case he comes back, so's we can say, 'Still not done yet'."

She gave a dry and dusty laugh. In that moment, Mira fancied that Holly looked every day of her five centuries' age.

"What happened to him?" she asked. "The monk."

"A wanton woman led him astray." She smiled wistfully. "She thought his talents were of more use outside the church. She were right an' all. But then she left and he waited for her to... come... back..."

Holly's eyes closed, and her breathing grew ever slower and shallower. The door shook once again.

"Oh Erin," Holly whispered. "Erin, I'm sorry, I'm so sorry..."

Her head flopped forward and her body lay still. The door shook with another impact. Mira had never felt more alone.

1604: HAIL THE KING IN THE MOUNTAIN

The city was celebrating, as well it might. It was, by any standards, an important day. A great bonfire blazed in the centre of town as evening drew in. Music played, people danced and feasted, and everyone knew they had nothing to fear. All of them were happy. Except one.

On the grassy bank of the city walls, a girl was crying. Uncontrollably, unendingly. She had watched the celebrations beginning from this remote distance, and the tears had come no matter how hard she fought. Hours later, there were still so many more to be shed.

A man walked along the wall and saw the girl. He wore robes lined in fur that spoke of wealth, power, privilege and other qualities indisposed to pay any heed to a sobbing peasant child. But nevertheless, he hopped over the edge of the wall, and sat on the grass beside her.

"Don't be sad." His voice brought authority and wisdom even to an instruction that could not be obeyed. "This is a fine day. A day to remember. Yes, all will be well. An eternal protector to watch over us while we sleep. As God does, I suppose."

The girl continued to cry silently. The nobleman noted for the first time the small knife lying in the grass, the spots of blood staining the sleeves of her dress and the dark scratches on the arms beneath. He reached into his robe and produced a leather drawstring pouch, which he slowly began to open.

"I should introduce myself. My name is Lankin. I know who you are, of course, and I know it must be hard for you to see things clearly. But I can promise you, in all things, someone has a plan. Not God, obviously, but someone. And people have their parts to play in this plan. Most are insignificant, but still of use every now and again. And then there are those with grander roles. Since there are dragons and Turkish knights in this mystery, so there must also be the saints and the learned doctors. People of consequence. Today has certainly brought us one of those."

The girl ran a grubby hand across her dripping nose and commenced an outburst of wailing. Lankin ran his fingers through his iron-flecked beard thoughtfully and pressed on.

"Which is not to say there aren't other, equally important roles a clever girl could turn her talents to, if she were of a mind. If you were open to the possibility, I know where you might be of use one day. I think there's a bright future in store for you, my child, regardless of the grief you feel for…"

"I hate her." The girl cut him short with a ragged shout, full of malice. Lankin reached down and turned her face towards his, looking deep into her red-rimmed eyes. He smiled kindly, gently stroking her cheek with his thumb.

"No," he said. "No, I don't think you do. Not really."

He withdrew his hand and they sat in silence as musicians struck up another song for the joyous crowd.

"Of course," Lankin mused, holding out the leather bag to the girl. "I've always felt the most important thing in this life is to show willing. Would you like a blackberry?"

CHAPTER 15

Hubert Scraggles sat slumped on the floor in the burning remains of his empty world.

Ash, soot and fragments of burned cloth covered every surface and drifted slowly through the air. The people of the living world that surrounded him talked and ate and laughed with not a sound to be heard, oblivious to the layers of white powder that built up on them, dissolving into their drinks and coating the food that they ate.

"Hullo, Hubert."

Scraggles looked up and saw the girl in the bobble hat framed in the great arched doorway at the far end of the restaurant. He scrambled to his feet and unconsciously scurried back a few steps. The girl danced through the hall, her clumpy boots kicking up clouds of ash as she pirouetted, gazing in glee at the ceiling, for all the world like a child seeing snow for the first time.

"Can you feel it, Hubert?" she asked as she reached him. "My colleagues are doing their bit. Spiriting away all the people you've kept here, giving them the peaceful rest they were supposed to have. She does like to stir up trouble – and you're not even what she's here to sort out. Did you talk, Hubert?"

She circled the anxious figure of the poet. "You know, not many people die in this place anymore, or even leave convenient bits of themselves. I bet it's going to take you ages and ages to build it up to what it was. Did you talk, Hubert? Of course, that's if I let you. I could just take away what I gave you and leave you all alone forever. Did you talk, Hubert?"

The girl stopped to stand directly in front of Scraggles and flashed him a beaming smile. Her left arm snapped upwards to point at one of the tables, while her eyes remained locked on him.

"She's going to die. Quite soon, actually."

They turned to face the table, where a woman laughed silently as the handsome man in front of her filled her glass.

"Something's about to happen. Something not very nice. Did you talk, Hubert?" The girl moved closer to the table, and her smile faded to a cold, impassive mask. "This is Michelle. Any minute now, this bloke's going to slip something into Michelle's drink. But chemicals are funny things. They don't always behave. Did you talk, Hubert?"

She drifted closer, her hand running unnoticed through the smiling woman's blonde curls.

"So Michelle's body won't do the things he wants it to. But then it won't do the things she wants it to either. And then it won't do anything, not ever again. And he'll always think of her death as a cruel thing, as if he were ever meaning to be kind."

She returned to where the poet stood, and registered the barely contained excitement on his rotten face.

"Do you want her?" the girl asked. "You can have her when it's done. Michelle can stay here with you forever. The first of your new collection."

She fixed the squirming Scraggles with a piercing stare. "*Did* you talk, Hubert?"

"She knows where your creature is. She will try and destroy it, no doubt."

"She'll give it a good go. And?"

"She has the ring," Scraggles added.

"And?"

"She does not know the creature is yours, just that it is new. But she knows you gave me all this."

"*And?*"

"She suspects, but nothing more," Scraggles said. "Don't think me so foolish as to cross L-"

"Shh." The girl placed a finger on her lips, and looked to the

109

ceiling as if checking if she had been observed. "See that you don't. I have appearances to keep up. Ta-ra for a bit."

As she turned to leave, her arm stretched out over the man's shoulder and her hand stroked his chest. When she was halfway to the exit, a flash of terror passed over his face for an instant. His eyes roamed the room and his hands dipped inside his jacket, looking for something he realised with mounting horror that he no longer had. Michelle looked concerned as she noticed his anxiety, with no clue as to its dreadful cause.

"But you promised!" shouted Scraggles to the retreating girl.

"Go back to your hole, poet man," she replied as she faded out of the empty world.

CHAPTER 16

Sam weaved his way through the crowded bar to the table where his friends sat, his fingers growing colder as they stretched around the cluster of glasses in his hands. The owners had reserved a snug for the band, and as he drew closer, he heard bursts of laughter. Abi's was easily identifiable, louder and shriller than the others, and the voice that had lurked in the back of his head since she was born made a mental note to count the glasses in front of her.

As he arrived at the table, Nathan and Abi greeted him with raucous shouts. Carl nodded sagely while sipping from a pint of tap water and Dave didn't look up, his gaze fixed on the text he was furiously composing.

"Here he is, it's Doctor Love!" said Abi as Sam pulled up a seat at the end of the table. "Sit yourself down! We were just talking about you, weren't we, boys?"

"About you and your Missus," explained Nathan, taking up Abi's lead.

"Theoretical Missus," Carl clarified, calling a point of order with a raised hand.

Abi snapped a finger in Carl's direction. "We have a little bet on as to why you're not acting on your very obvious carnal desires. Now, come on, tell us everything."

Sam sipped his beer wearily and put on his best big brother face. "Abi, we're mates, you're pissed, drop it."

"You see, I thought you might be scared, which is ridiculous, because it's Mira, for God's sake. Now, Dave." The singer's head snapped upright as he heard his name mentioned. "Dave, in his usual charming manner, says you haven't got the balls, but to be fair I think he has trouble with the concept of people fancying anyone who isn't him. Nathan reckons you're too deeply wounded by Bitchface…"

"Emma."

"Call her Bitchface, it feels good," Abi commanded, her face briefly hard before she burst out in drunken glee, continuing to expound the fruits of her research. "Oh, and Socrates over there… he said something about a cave and a fire."

"The fundamental difficulty of perceiving reality in any form but its current state," Carl deadpanned.

"Yeah, I zoned out a bit when you were talking."

"Wow, you guys are just living the dream with your celebrity gossip." Sam shook his head. "Sorry to disappoint, Abi, but Mira and me are still, and forever more, just mates. Carl, say something deep. We need to move this conversation on."

"I've got nothing," Carl replied drily. "I can't just turn it on like that."

Dave's phone buzzed in his hand. He scanned it excitedly as he jumped to his feet and left the table. Carl sat back, his face a thoughtful mask, glanced across to Nathan, then reached into his pocket for an e-cigarette, which he wiggled between his fingers while turning his gaze to Abi. She nodded enthusiastically, and the two of them departed.

"Right," said Nathan. "Now that Baby Bear's out of the picture, you want to talk about what's really going on?"

"Don't you start," groaned Sam.

"Come on, mate, we can all see it. Even Dave can see it." Nathan leaned across the table. "Look, I can understand you not wanting to have this conversation with Abi. God knows, I wouldn't share the details of my private life with her even if she was my sister. But me you can talk to, so get on with it."

"Stop being sensitive, you're a bass player."

"You're doing the one-liner thing, that's cool, I can wait," Nathan replied with a sly smirk, then rose to his feet, slapping a hand down on Sam's shoulder as he did. "Come on, step into my office."

Sam shook his head, and followed Nathan to the bar. By the

time he arrived, the barman had poured out two shot glasses, one of which Nathan handed to him.

"Right then, honesty shots," Nathan said with a wide grin, clinking his glass to Sam's.

"Don't call them that, we're not fourteen," sighed Sam. "Why is everyone so obsessed with us getting together? Can't I just have a friend? A female friend?"

"Of course you can, you should, it's healthy," said Nathan, before slugging his back in one swift move. "But that's not what this is, and I expect better of you. Can I get two more of the same please?"

Sam downed his shot and shook his head. "You're a dick."

"I'm a dick who's going to keep buying shots until he gets an honest answer," Nathan clarified, as he scooped up the second pair of glasses and handed one over. "Which means we're either going to get very drunk, or I'm going to need to borrow money off you for the rest of the month. If pressed, I am prepared to drop this in return for getting to pick the set list for the next gig."

"Oh God, no, I value our audience."

"Well, then."

They downed their drinks and Sam finally cracked under the pressure. He gathered the arguments that had washed around his head for the past year.

"It's not just up to me, is it?" he said. "Like I keep saying, we are just mates. That's what we are. It's what she wants, so that's how it is. And you know what? I really like it. I don't want to lose that. If she felt the same, maybe it would work, but what if it didn't? We'd just end up ruining our friendship. So there you go — that's my confession. You happy now?"

"I knew it!" The shout made them both jump. Abi was right behind them.

"How long have you been standing there?" demanded Sam.

"Long enough," said Abi with a victorious smirk. "Nathan, you want to line me up one of those, because I. Just. Won."

She raised her hand for a high five, which Sam did not return.

"Congratulations," Sam said with a disapproving grimace. "I

don't suppose you're planning on giving up being a pain in the arse? It's been nearly twenty years now, I thought you might get tired."

"Why quit now when I'm getting so good at it?" Abi clapped her hands and then gratefully received her drink from Nathan. "I knew it."

"It still doesn't matter, does it?" snapped Sam a little too loudly, suddenly feeling very exposed. "None of this matters, because it's all my bullshit! Mira just wants a mate!"

Abi and Nathan shared an amused glance, then tapped their shots together.

"Are you going to tell him or shall I?" Nathan asked.

"Tell me what?"

"Oh my poor sweet brother," Abi sighed. "You really are a bloody idiot sometimes."

NINETEEN YEARS AGO: SWEET DREAMS

"Once upon a time," the old woman said with a warm smile to the little girl tucked up in bed in front of her, "there was a man walking alone in the forest. He had come a long way already and he still had a very long way to go before he was home. And he was very lonely in the forest, as he had not seen another soul in such a long time."

She shook her head sadly at the traveller's plight, while the child gazed at her in adoration.

"But as he walked through the forest, he met a woman, all dressed in white, resting in the shade of a tree. And she was the most beautiful woman he had ever seen. He asked her where she was going, and do you know, she was going to his village as well. But you see, while her face was the most beautiful thing he had ever seen, her voice was *horrible*. She spoke with this high whiiiineeey wheeeeeezy sound."

The little girl giggled at the impression of the strange woman, and the old lady couldn't help but smile broadly and lovingly at the child's amusement, the lines on her face lengthening and deepening as she did.

"But he was very lonely and she was very beautiful, so he asked if she would like to travel with him through the forest." The old lady leaned in closer, her voice dropping to a whisper. "But as they walked, he began to notice something very strange about her. They passed into a clearing in the forest and the light of the full moon cast down upon them. And do you know what he saw?"

The little girl shook her head, her eyes widening as she waited for an answer.

"She didn't have a shadow!" said the old woman. "There was his shadow stretching on the ground in front of him, but where she stood... nothing!"

The child pulled the bedclothes closer around her. She knew from experience that this was getting to the good bit.

"And as he looked for her shadow, he noticed something funny about her feet. He could just see them underneath her sari as she walked, and he suddenly realised..." The old woman looked around the room, as if to make sure no one else was listening. "...they were backwards! Backwards! With the heel at the front and the toes sticking out the back! Imagine that! But that wasn't the strangest thing. Do you want to know what the strangest thing was?"

The little girl nodded excitedly.

"When she walked," the old woman said, "her feet never touched the ground. He looked behind them, and he saw his footprints and only his footprints. Now the man had heard terrible things about this forest. Some people said there were ghosts that lived in the trees called bhoots, and that unwary travellers who met a bhoot were never heard from again."

The little girl's fingers clutched the blanket firmly.

"And he became very, very, very afraid. Because he knew she wasn't a woman after all. She was something else. And though he didn't want to see, he turned to look at her face again. And he saw..."

"Mum, what are you doing?"

"I'm telling her a bedtime story, Manisha. Don't interrupt," scowled the old woman at her daughter, who stood in the doorway with hands on hips and an eyebrow arched in disapproval.

"No, Mum, you're telling her a ghost story," Manisha sighed.

"She likes ghost stories, don't you, dear?"

"I know she does," said Manisha, coming into the room. She sat on the edge of the bed and stroked the girl's hair. "But you don't like the nightmares you have once Granny's gone home, do you? And Mummy doesn't like being woken up in the middle of the night because there's a ghost under the bed."

"Pardon me for bringing a little magic into the world." The old woman chuckled.

"Oh, I think I've got all the magic I can handle right here," Manisha smiled at her mother, then leaned in to kiss her daughter. "Go to sleep, Mira. And remember, it's just a story. There's no such thing as ghosts."

CHAPTER 17

Nik-tek.

Mira's eyes snapped open with a start. She hadn't noticed herself drifting off, and had no idea how long she had slept. She reached for her phone to check the time, only to remember once again that it was lying soaked and useless at home. The Minster had grown cold and dark, its impossibly high ceiling barely visible in the shadows. If Holly's church had made Mira feel small with its cluttered interior, the Minster made her feel utterly insignificant with its vast emptiness.

Holly hadn't moved.

Mira stumbled to her feet, stiff from lying on the chilly stone floor. She leant over Holly and gently touched her shoulder. Nothing. Mira placed a hand on her cheek and found it was icy to the touch. She pulled up her sleeve and felt for a pulse, but wasn't sure if she could detect one or not. If Holly was breathing, Mira couldn't tell.

Holly's death was a possibility that had never occurred to her. Her own had been a more pressing concern. But now it seemed to have actually happened, she struggled to manage her reactions. She wanted to feel sad at the loss, or angry at the pointlessness of such a lonely, empty end. But the selfish, pragmatic side of her mind barrelled those feelings out of the way with waves of panic and one overriding, terrible thought – it was all up to her now. She remembered how lifeless Holly had appeared by the riverside this morning, and tried to reassure herself that this was no different. It was just the shadowy, gothic surroundings that made it feel like she was gone. But then she looked again at Holly's pale face and still body, and her fears came flooding back.

Mira looked up at one of the stained-glass windows on the south wall, afraid that she might see some sign of the Hangman through it. There was none. Maybe it had gone, maybe it was still out there. Mira's hand brushed her pocket and she felt the unfamiliar shape lying there. She pulled the ring out and looked at it. It was a simple silver band, old and tarnished and engraved with a design of writhing ivy. She slipped it on to her finger, which felt vaguely symbolic, but not empowering in any way. She wasn't sure what she had expected to happen. If she were likely to turn invisible or gain some magical power from wearing it, Holly would surely have used it earlier, and Mira felt foolish for imagining the possibility. Still, it did leave her feeling oddly in control, as if she bore some measure of Holly's authority. It didn't make her immediate course of action any less terrifying – she knew she had to go outside and check if the Hangman was still there. She walked unsteadily towards the door, pushed hard against it with shaking hands and stepped into the night.

Outside, Mira saw no signs of life. The Piazza was a pool of cold, pale light cast from the ornate lamp posts standing at either end, while in all directions the city was nothing but darkness. The Minster loomed through the shadows behind her, an ominous presence where previously it had been a sanctuary. Constantine sat on his throne, regarding her with cold judgment. The tendicula box and the bag with the laundry basket lay where they had fallen. Distant sounds could be heard from the city, but this secluded square was deserted.

Mira hugged her arms against the cold and wondered again how long she had slept. Perhaps it had been twenty years, like Holly. *Oh God, Holly, what do I do?* She tried to shake off her burst of grief, which wasn't helping, and thought about her options. Home wasn't far. Holly's church was nearby as well. She could go and... do what? She wanted to be doing something, but couldn't think of what might be useful. She wanted to talk to Sam. Sam would... not have the first clue what to do when you're being chased by a giant supernatural jellyfish and the only person who can stop it is dead and you don't know what to do, but she wanted him to be here and be comfortingly amusing at her, then make a cup of tea using the excellent tea and coffee making facilities in this fifteenth century cathedral and *for God's sake, Mira, you're panicking, historically accurate panicking, but panicking nonetheless that doesn't change the fact that Holly's dead and you don't know what to do!*

Mira turned on her heel to go back inside. The Hangman was right in front of her.

The spectre hovered in the air, its tendrils waving gently in the light breeze, as if underwater. It looked bigger than ever. Its surface glistened in the light, while its empty cowl loomed over her, the darkness beneath like a vast mouth poised to envelop her. She stared deep into that black space and breathed in the overpowering watery stench of the creature. The singing was louder than ever, but somehow clearer, the notes sharper and more discernible, the odd gurgling quality falling away as she stood closer to it than she had ever dared before.

Mira knew she should be terrified. The twisted, dead faces of Chris and DS Unwin should have been the only thing she could think of as the thing that killed them floated in front of her. But instead, she felt an odd kind of clarity. She thought of Sam, imagined him playing his guitar, and as the tentacles drifted forward to encircle her, their stark, white light illuminating the space in which she stood, she opened her mouth and began to sing.

"This ae nighte, this ae nighte, every nighte and alle…"

The great noise of the Hangman chimed along with her, its body billowing as if it were taking deep breaths. The tempo of the Hangman's singing was faster than she was used to hearing the song, and she adjusted to keep up.

"Fire and fleet and candle-lighte…" she continued falteringly. Mira had never considered herself a good singer, but it seemed to be doing the trick now. The creature's six arms pulled outwards away from her, still surrounding her with a web of light.

"And Christ receive thy saule…" she sang, and the Hangman chimed in with a clipped *nik-tek,* that threw her off track for a moment. The retreating tentacles writhed and once more swayed towards her as the Hangman reared up almost disapprovingly. Mira felt a stab of panic that was instantly swept away as a memory swam into her mind. She imagined herself sitting in a pub with Sam and his friends, pedantically lecturing Nathan on why something made absolutely no sense whatsoever, and growing irritable at his protestations that it didn't matter so long as it sounded good.

I hope you're right, Nathan. She resumed the chorus as he had preferred it.

"This ae nighte, this ae nighte, every nighte and alle," she croaked her way through the song. The Hangman's arms resumed slowly withdrawing into its body, apparently satisfied with her efforts.

"Fire and fleet and candle lighte," Mira pressed on, before swallowing her intellectual pride to belt out the revised final line of the chorus. "And Old Nick take your soul."

She had no idea what came next, but it didn't matter. The tendrils retracted into the Hangman's body completely, and the left shoulder of the creature collapsed, as if the air had been let out of it. Bit by bit, the Hangman shrank away, its body folding in on itself until it vanished.

Mira stood alone in the cold and empty courtyard.

"I sang a song," she said. "And it went away."

The thought was so absurd, even by the standards of this week, that she burst out laughing until she was unable to stop. Tears welled in her eyes and her legs struggled to keep her upright. She collapsed and landed on one of the stone steps, then leaned back to lie across them, still laughing. She stopped abruptly when she saw Holly.

She was standing in the doorway of the Minster, leaning heavily against the frame, her unruly mop covering her face. Mira leapt to her feet and ran over.

"Holly, it was here!" she gabbled. "It was right here, but I sang a song and it went away. I know what the song is, and if you sing its song with it, that makes it go away, and…"

She drifted into silence. Holly looked awful. Her face was pale, clammy and soaked in sweat, and her eyes were half-closed.

"Styoo," she murmured between forced breaths.

Mira looked frantically around the Piazza, trying to see what Holly was talking about. The bronze emperor loomed obviously over them.

"Did you say statue?" Mira asked.

Holly nodded weakly, and draped an arm over Mira's shoulder. Together, they stumbled in the direction of the seated figure, and Holly slumped hard against the plinth. Her shaking hands grasped for the emperor's shin and the sword he was leaning on, and with some help from Mira, she slowly heaved herself up and collapsed in his lap. She lay back, her head and legs dangling over the edge of the statue, one arm dropping forward while the other rested on the emperor's shoulder. There was an odd serenity to the sight, and her ragged breathing calmed to a more even pace. Her eyes closed and a peaceful smile formed on her face.

After a moment's rest, she sat up, and stretched an arm around the statue's neck, then carefully brought her legs down to stand in front of it. She rested her left hand on its shoulder while the fingers of her right stroked the face. As Mira looked on bemused, Holly leaned forward and pressed her mouth to Constantine's metal lips, twice. She then gripped the statue's head with both hands and proceeded to give the immobile sculpture a long lingering kiss, her shoulders and hips writhing around as she did.

Mira's mouth opened briefly, but then she shook her head. *No, she thought to herself, I can't even pretend to be surprised at this point.* Instead, she looked in all directions, hoping fervently not to see anyone. She might have been getting acclimatised to Holly, but she didn't like the idea of other people seeing this display, or associating her with it.

After what felt like a particularly uncomfortable age, Holly leapt down from the plinth and half-ran, half-staggered in Mira's direction with a broad grin on her face, her vitality apparently restored. In fact, she looked more than a little drunk.

"Mira!" she shouted. "Thank you, I... haven't done that in a while. Definitely needed it though. Yeah, that's the stuff." She registered Mira's expectant expression. "It's... um... a thing. Energy, pick-me-up sort of deal."

Mira shook her head. "You just snogged a statue. You might have to explain that one a little more specifically."

"They put a... thing... outside the Minster, just in case I wear meself out. Not s'posed to use it unless it's an emergency, which this was. Bit of a headrush though. And there's always been a..." She flapped a hand in the statue's direction. "Thing-thing so I can get at it, and these days it's big Caesar bloke."

"You cop off with the statue and it makes you feel better?"

"Yeah, basically. It used to be a tree stump, but this is more fun." Holly beamed and swayed. "I were about to say summat and you did the face. You were excited! There was a... thing. Different thing, and you were all happy about it and I were too knackered to listen. What did I miss?"

"The Hangman was here," Mira said. "And I was right, it's not singing the 'Lyke Wake Dirge'! Well, it is, sort of. It's a cover version, from the nineties, but they changed some of the lyrics! They were a sort of punk folk band, all try-hard darkness. I knew I recognised it, one of the guys in Sam's band wanted them to do it. Anyway, I just sang back to it and it disappeared!"

"You sang a song and it went away?" Holly looked at her with a puzzled expression.

"Yes!"

"You must be a bloody awful singer."

"No!" Mira waved her hands as she spoke, the energy of her earlier victory returning. "No, you don't understand, it... stopped. It stopped when it heard the song and it was like it was... sated or something."

Holly began pacing back and forth, her face knotted with concentration.

"Hang on, I know this, I knew this, this is familiar, it's, it's... Yes!" She jumped a little in the air as she spun back to face Mira. "Red Rosemary!"

"Red Rosemary?"

"Red Rosemary!" Holly cried with glee. "It's a story me father used to tell us. There's this sort of… bad fairy, gets up to all sorts of mischief, and he's always whistling this tune. And he goes to this house belonging to a… shepherd? Want to say shepherd. Maybe a woodcutter. Anyway, your general fairy-tale rustic type. But see, the shepherd, he recognises the song the fairy is whistling and sings it back to him, and instead of the fairy doing owt awful, they just sing a song together, then he goes away."

"So I've made it go away?" Mira felt proud for a moment, before the absurd injustice made her furious. "It killed four people, and all we had to do to stop it was sing a song?"

"Well, in the story, the shepherd doesn't teach his wife the song. And the fairy comes back while he's out, but she can't sing to him, and then, well…"

"What?" Mira wondered if she would regret asking.

"He rips her heart out and fries it in hog fat and rosemary. Then he feeds it to her kids."

The image lingered in the air for a moment.

"Was your dad a bit weird?" asked Mira.

"He had his moments," chuckled Holly. "Wow, I haven't thought about that story in, ooh, forever. It terrified me when I were a kid. I went through this phase where every time I heard a new song I had to learn all the words just in case the fairy came to get me."

"Where does that leave us?"

"Folklore's not an exact science," Holly said thoughtfully. "But there's loads of tales like that. From what you said, and if the stories are owt to go on – you've probably bought us a day."

"Right, so we've got time to come up with a plan…" Mira said, already trying to organise what she knew.

"No, I've already got a plan. I were about to say we've got time for cocktails."

"Cocktails?"

"Mira, I am completely awake, more so than usual even thanks to old Snoggyus Maximus, and there's nothing for me to fight! I'm free!" Holly said delightedly. "No evil, no monsters, nowt! Do you know how often this happens to me? The night is young and I am not, so let there be cocktails! Your treat!"

"Oh, I forgot," Mira reached into a jacket pocket and produced a handful of banknotes. "Angie left this for you at the church."

"Fine, my treat. But cocktails!"

CHAPTER 18

Holy Trinity church stood silent as the night drew in. Light filtered weakly through the main window, and the tree outside blew in the wind, the leaves flickering like a distant fire. Inside, just one tiny light cast itself valiantly against the looming shadows. It came from inside the pulpit, where the girl in the bobble hat sat cross-legged on the small patch of wooden floor. She had lit a candle, which she did not need, and stared in quiet fixation at the guttering flame while she waited in silent solitude. The fire reflected in her gleaming eyes and she pondered the night's events, some of which suited her purposes and some of which did not. Her next step remained to be chosen. But for now, she would wait. Wait for company.

"So here's what I'm thinking," Mira began as Holly placed two drinks on the table, then hopped onto her tall stool. "That band was a one-hit wonder at best. They can't have lasted long, and I doubt anyone but Nathan remembers them. That gives us a year, right? Maybe the Hangman died whenever their version of 'Lyke-Wake' came out."

"Nope, night off." Holly silenced Mira with a flourish of her hands. "No monsters, that's the deal. Time to drink hard liquor in red lipstick. Talk about summat else." She raised her glass and tapped it lightly against Mira's. "Mickle might," she said by way of a toast.

"Like what?" said Mira, trying to think of any common ground they might share that did not involve the pursuit of the Hangman, but coming up dry.

"I want to know about you and your bloke. Come on, what's the story?"

"There's not a story."

"See, now I *know* there's a story," Holly said, sucking on her straw. "If there really weren't a story, you'd have told me what you thought the story was and it wouldn't be a story, so it'd probably be a bit boring, and I'd pretend to listen and say that's nice, then change the subject, but when someone says there isn't a story it's because there is a story, and it's probably a story worth hearing."

Mira looked at Holly's glass. "How much of that did you just drink?"

"There may have been rum at the bar," Holly admitted. "But me point stands. Not together, kind of want to be, but not doing owt about it. Thereby hangs a tale."

"I see. You think you've got me all figured out, do you?" Mira retorted.

"I just see what I see," Holly said. "Come on, don't Bechdel me, girl, I want to get drunk and talk about boys. I've not done it in a good long while, I'm sure it used to be fun."

"How do you even know what the Bechdel test is?" Mira laughed.

"I pick up stuff and try and remember it," Holly said. "You never know what might come in handy. And you are consistently changing the subject, which lends credence to my theory that there's a fantastically juicy story you're not sharing. Come on, I need to get vicarious over here, I've not got much going on for meself, as you can probably gather."

"Really?" said Mira with a smirk. "Not even with clever and beautiful monks who save the city from demons?"

Holly's mouth dropped open in shock. "Holy mother of flip, did I actually tell you about that?"

"You went a bit third person, but I could tell. I think being in the Minster made you nostalgic."

"I'm not surprised. Wow. I haven't thought about him in an age. Good times, definitely good times. So long ago." Sadness passed across Holly's face for a moment, before she snapped back to the present. "But that were then, and if I've told you that, you're even more guilty of holding out on me. So come on.

I want to know how long you have been madly, and passionately, and frustratingly unrequitedly, in love with the bloke with the guitar, and how many cocktails it will take to get the whole story out of you?"

She leaned across the table with wide eyes and the broadest, cheekiest, Cheshire cat smile.

Mira lowered her gaze in embarrassment.

"Um... three?" she replied.

"Now you're talking."

Elsewhere in the city, two men stood alone in the empty square, the point where their respective routes home diverged and decisions would have to be made. They kissed, something neither would have been bold enough to do in a public place on most nights. But this night had been good, and no one would disturb them here. As their arms wrapped around each other, one took a step backwards, pulling the other closer to him, when he felt his foot touch something. He broke off and looked down at the paving stones. The lifeless eyes of Greg Unwin stared up at him.

"I was with Dominic and Sam was with Emma," Mira explained. "And we're all mates, but Sam and Emma are living together, like proper couple living, in this really cool flat, and that's where we'd all hang out. I'd moved into this shared house with people I kind of knew, and oh God, that was a mistake, because they never cleaned and they all hated each other and one of them played the drums, and... Oh God, that bathroom. I just remembered that horrible bathroom... hang on, did I say something funny?"

"No, not at all, go on," said Holly, swallowing her amusement at the stream of consciousness.

"So, I'm with Dominic," Mira continued. "But Dominic's really work-oriented. When he switched off, he was great, but when he was in full-on study mode, he just didn't want to be disturbed. So when I can't stand my place anymore, but don't want to bother him, they had a spare room, and it sort of became mine. I was there a lot. Emma wasn't always around, she had a job with odd shifts, so it'd just be the two of us, and we'd spend a lot of time alone together, but we're both coupled up, so it's not a thing."

"When did you find out about Dominic and Emma?" Holly asked.

"I didn't get to that part yet!" Mira exclaimed. "How did you know that's what I was going to say?"

"Bit obvious though, innit?" Holly said. "He's not working as hard as you think, and her job's less bother than he thinks, but they've both got a good excuse to have at it while you two are platonicking."

"As soon as Dom and I graduated, they were off," Mira sighed. "Together. Should I have seen it coming?"

"Well, don't be too hard on yourself but… yeah."

"Anyway," Mira said, "there was no way Sam could afford that place on his own, and I practically lived there, so it just made sense for me to move in. And we really both needed a friend around. Not a lot of people I knew stayed in the city after graduation. I guess neither of us really knew what we wanted, so we just sort of stuck around. And I got a job in a book shop."

"Big Bad Dom was out of the picture," said Holly. "So why not…?"

Mira shook her head. "I don't think either of us wanted anyone else at first. Like I said, we both just wanted a friend, and that's what we got. And it helped so much to have that, it really did, but then…"

"It became normal," Holly said.

"Yeah." Mira nodded. "We just got used to how things were."

"You know, for someone mad enough to give my life a try," said Holly. "You're not half rubbish at your own."

"It's been noted," Mira agreed. "Mostly by my mother."

"Lucky you, mine would never have said that. 'Know your place, girl' was more her speed. Now, if you ask me what you should do…"

"What should I do, Holly?" Mira teased in a sing-song voice.

"Well, this may sound simple, but then I'm a simple soul at heart. You could just go for it," Holly said. "Tempus fugit, carpe diem and sundry other Latins – life is short, so make hay before it chucks it down."

"Your life isn't short," Mira said.

"It's a lot of short bits though," Holly replied. "My life is pieces, with huge bloody great gaps. I try and enjoy the bits, but they always end. And that's what you need to do, Mira. Enjoy the bits, so to speak. Because only one of us is gonna live forever."

"Thank you. I feel so much better now I've been confronted with the spectre of mortality," Mira said sarcastically.

"I've steered us down a bit of a dark alley here, haven't I? Sorry."

"It's okay, you can get us out again." Mira smiled. "Tell me more about seducing your monk. I need to get vicarious too. What century was that?"

"Seventeenth," Holly said. "During the Civil War."

Mira grinned and clapped her hands together. "Ooh, nice! Are there cavaliers in big hats in this story?"

"I'm gonna go out on a limb and say it's been a while," Holly sighed.

Caroline stood in the square, looking down into the face of the man she had worked with for so long and shutting out the noise as she had done all those times before. Not to think this time, not to gather clues, just to remember. Soon someone was going to come and tell her to go home, that she shouldn't have to work on this case anymore, that it was too close, too personal, too involved. But until they did, it would be her and Greg and another crime scene. *There's a man,* she thought, *and you and me are going to find him.*

"Five years," Holly slurred sadly. "Five long, lovely years of him. Most I've ever had of someone since all this started and I loved the bollocks off him."

"I think we need to go home now," Mira said, squeezing her hand. "Serious, this time. I have to go and not go to work tomorrow because I'm traumatised. And also it might be Sunday."

"See, this is how it is, I connect, I think I'll have someone, and then it takes them away," Holly said. "I got settled, I got complacent 'cause he were always there and I was too. And we were together and happy, and I went to bed and she took him. I mean, he were gone, like everyone else. Look at you, you're gonna be me best mate. You are."

"Thank you," Mira said. "I will try my best."

"No, you will, but then you'll die," Holly said. "You're gonna die or move to Selby, and it'll be just me again, 'cause it always comes back to that until I get maudlin and I want somebody and the whole thing starts up again. I'm a bit busy these days so I can have a mate if I want and that's you, but one day I might not be. We'll both be like 'she just vanished' but you'll have time to get over it and I won't."

"Isn't there anyone like you?" Mira asked. "People who live forever?"

Holly's eyes darkened and she slumped across the table. Mira paused and decided it was time. She wasn't too drunk to notice the slip Holly had made.

"You said she took him," Mira said. "You mean the girl in the bobble hat, don't you?"

Holly snapped upright and seemed to sober up in a heartbeat. The look on her face made Mira feel like she'd just punched her.

"It's me night off," Holly said imploringly. "I don't get nights off."

"I know," Mira said. "And I'm sorry, I truly am. But I need to know. She said she'd kill me, and she knows where I live. She came to the flat this morning. She spoke to Sam. He has no idea what's going on, please Holly…"

"She said that?" whispered Holly, a look of desperate sadness on her face. "Oh God, no."

"Holly, you love to talk," Mira said. "You love to show me things, and explain this mad world you live in. I get that part of the reason I'm here is that you want an audience. You love having that and I'm enjoying being that for you. But it means that when there's something you don't want to talk about, then that frightens me."

"She's..." Holly tried to compose herself. "Honestly, Mira, she's normally harmless. Just another cog in the machine, like I am. But sometimes, she likes to make trouble, especially for me. I hoped she wouldn't find you, at least not for a while, until I could figure summat out, but she must have known from when we met..."

"Does she mean what she says?" Mira asked. "Has she killed people? Did she kill him?"

"Yes," Holly said coldly. "She'll kill anything I love."

"Why?"

"She just doesn't like me very much," Holly replied.

"So what, she's like your arch enemy?" Mira tried to lighten the mood, and instantly regretted it. "How dangerous can she be, she looks about twelve."

"She's fifteen. And she always will be."

"She's like you, then?" Mira asked. "She doesn't age?"

"She is what she is." A sliver of pain crept between Holly's casual words. "Mira, I will understand if you want to walk away from this. God knows, you've done more than anyone should, and I shouldn't ask you to put yourself, or Sam, in danger. You're right. I do like having an audience, reminds me how cool I am. But I don't just want that. I'm not being pissed and sentimental when I say you're me mate. I want a friend again, just like you did, and I know I shouldn't dare, but I *really* want one. I won't ask you to stay, but if you do, I promise I will find a way to keep the two of you safe from her."

A long silence descended before Mira spoke. "Will it help if I sing to her as well?"

"We can only hope." They both laughed.

"This isn't going to be my last drink, is it?" said Mira.

"Yeah, definitely good to have a friend again." Holly clinked her glass against Mira's. "Mickle Might."

CHAPTER 19

"I'm just saying, you two are just fantastic and stuff," said Abi as she swayed back and forth across the pavement. Sam tried his best to guide her in the right direction. "And she's into you, I know she is. I can feel it, you know it's just right and everything…"

They were on the home stretch now, and the end of the walk couldn't come soon enough for Sam. Drunk Abi was one thing, drunk victorious Abi another, but tonight he had drunk, victorious, meddling Abi. He was not looking forward to sleeping on the sofa, but letting her walk back to her halls was clearly not an option.

He'd zoned out much of her babbling, which had grown increasingly circular, and come back to the cold, hard truths he'd always clung to. Mira was his friend, and that was what she needed, especially in light of her recent experiences. To push that aside for his own feelings felt selfish, cruel even, and he'd need a far more convincing character witness than his sister's drunken ramblings to know he wasn't making a terrible mistake.

He'd thought these things so many times, and was impressed that he could still almost believe them. The faces of the last woman he'd loved and the man who'd been his friend were not going away. In his mind, they were always calm, quietly delivering their devastating fait accompli and watching his pain like a wildlife video. At the time, he hadn't got angry. They'd made him feel like that would be unfair. He'd just watched them go and then quietly imploded afterwards.

His friends thought he was scared. His sister thought he was scared. And deep down, beneath his carefully constructed moral arguments and sense of what was right and fair, he knew that actually he was just terrified. Terrified of getting hurt again, terrified of losing something precious, one way or another. He'd trusted Mira with nearly everything, but the more he did, the heavier the things he kept back became. He felt dishonest and weak, but knew the alternative was worse. He hated it when he couldn't switch it all off and enjoy what he had. He really couldn't be doing with desire when contentment was right there.

He was distracted from his grim thoughts by a blaze of lights. A number of emergency vehicles were clustered ahead of them. As they drew closer, he noticed a streak of yellow tape cutting off the square around the Viking museum, and took hold of Abi's hand. She immediately pulled away and ran to look.

"Oh, wow, it's a crime scene!" shouted Abi. "Sam, come on! Let's have a look! Maybe there's a body and stuff, and like, you could have a deeper understanding of Mira, because you've been through the same terrible experience…"

As she spoke, she stumbled backwards and barged into someone leaving the area. Sam recognised the detective with the scar on her face he had spoken to earlier that week. Her eyes looked sad and watery, and he felt suddenly uncomfortable, even more uncertain how to be around her than he had been before. Abi was clearer, and pulled herself up straight in a crude imitation of sobriety as she sensed the presence of an authority figure.

"Sorry, Miss," she said. "Just so you know, I'm nineteen and I definitely won't be doing any driving tonight."

"Mr Nesbitt, isn't it?" Caroline said in a quiet and distant voice after a moment of scanning and recognising his face.

"Yes, yes it is," Sam said, and gave in to his concern. "Are you alright?"

"You should see she gets home safely," the detective said half-heartedly.

Sam watched the solitary figure disappearing into the distance.

"Yes, I'll go straight to bed like a good girl!" shouted Abi, blissfully unaware of the tension in the atmosphere.

Sam scowled at her, then led her in the direction of home.

134

"So, am I going to tell Mum how much you had to drink?" he asked.

"Depends," she replied. "Am I going to tell Dave when you lost your virginity?"

"I hate you sometimes."

Abi reached over and squeezed his cheeks. "Of course you do, I'm your baby sister. It's what we're for."

Holy Trinity remained as empty and silent as it had all night. And the girl still waited. She hadn't moved from her position in the pulpit and her candle was all but burned out. She could feel the time had come at last, and quickly extinguished what was left of the flame. There was movement in the church, as something emerged from the darkness, casting ominous shadows across the walls. She heard the singing as it reverberated off the old stone, the sound filling the space and shattering the calm stillness of the night.

Mira exploded into a burst of giggles as she and Holly belted out the chorus of 'Total Eclipse of the Heart', with varying degrees of tunefulness and lyrical fidelity. The girl peered over the edge of the pulpit as they danced through the church, filling the space with joyous noise. Holly leapt to stand on the tomb and thrust her arms out for an inaccurate declaration on the precise beginning of forever, before wobbling on unsure feet and pitching forward, landing in Mira's arms, laughing hysterically. She made a half-hearted bid to snap back into a more serious mood.

"Righty-ho, here's the plan. I need to sleep until..." She glanced at her watch. "All day. While I'm doing that, I want you to surf the net..."

"Surf the net?" Mira burst into more laughter at the anachronism.

"Sod off, I'm old!" Holly said with a grin as she made her way to the trapdoor. "If you're right, the song gives us a year, and we've got five places – where the murders happened and the bridge. There's gotta be a connection, summat that happened in those places around that year, when the Hangman were still alive probably. If we can figure out who he is... was... we might be able to get ahead of him, work out where he'll show up next. Come here tomorrow night with what you've found, and we'll have a think. Oh, and try and make some progress with Sam, you know you want to. Don't worry about getting out of here, the doors'll all lock behind you when you go."

"Okay, I will do the research. If I'm not so hungover I can barely move." Mira suddenly remembered she was still wearing Holly's hard-won ring and pulled it from her finger. "Here. Your precious. I don't know why it's so important."

"Oh yeah, that." Holly smiled as she looked at it. "Yeah, this'll come in handy."

"And so will this." Mira handed Holly the laundry basket. "I expect you to have made use of it when I come round tomorrow. Goodnight, Holly."

Holly half-climbed, half-fell through the trapdoor. As Mira walked away, a shout of "Mickle Might!" emerged from the shadows, followed by the sound of a slamming door. Mira left the church, laughing to herself. Once she was outside, she tried the handle of the door she had closed behind her. Firmly locked, as promised. The gate was the same. Home was near.

The girl opened the door of the pulpit with a creek and crept through the gloom. She walked to the trapdoor and lay down beside it, curling her arms and legs into herself. Finally, she reached into a coat pocket, and produced a small, red sweet, which she placed on top of the hatch.

"Nighty-night, Hol," she said with a smile.

THE DAY HE DIED

Suddenly, he was falling. The water below rose up to meet him, but it seemed to be moving so terribly slowly. He felt the wind on his face, rushing past with such speed, as everything else dragged impossibly out for what felt like eternity. His arms whirled helplessly through the air, as the music played. The CD player in his coat pocket continued to pump tunes to the headphones that rested on his head as if everything was normal, and he wasn't falling.

From Brig o' dread when thou may'st pass, to Purgatory fire thou com'st at last.

He struck the surface of the water face-on, and the impact was hard, as if he had landed on cement. But then it wasn't hard, and the light and sound of the world went away, leaving only cold, a piercing overwhelming cold that consumed him. The water rushed in to claim him, filling his nose and mouth and his whole body as he was dragged down into the darkness.

If ever thou gavest meal or drink, the fire shall never make thee shrink.

He could still just make out the muffled sounds of the music slowing down as the water seeped into the mechanism of the player, draining its life away. The headphones drifted from him, carrying the last death rattle of the song with them.

If meat or drink thou ne'er gav'st nane, the fire will burn thee to the bare bane.

He became aware that he wasn't alone. He forced his eyes to remain open, the dark, dirty waters stinging them as he watched the figure approach. Not swimming, but walking – strolling along the river bed, as casually as if this were a park, a city street, anywhere but the inky depths of the river.

This ae nighte, this ae nighte, every nighte and alle;

As the figure drew closer, he saw it was a girl, her long hair streaming out around her. Even in the lightless murk, he could make out the pale red colour. She extended a hand to him and he forced his arm to push against the weight of the water and the deathly chill that suffused him to reach out to her.

Fire and fleet, and candle lighte;

He felt her hand take his, felt the coarse wool of her fingerless gloves and the strangely warm fingers that grasped, tightly squeezing his hand with impossible strength. He looked into eyes which shone even in the darkness, and the triumphant smile beneath them.

And Old Nick take your saule.

CHAPTER 20

Mira let her reading glasses clatter to the table, causing the tape and glue holding the arm together to finally give way, and rubbed the bridge of her nose in frustration. She sat at the table in her living room, wearing pyjamas far later in the day than she normally would. In front of her sat a notebook covered in scribbled thoughts, many of them crossed out, and a laptop, the light from which was hurting her eyes and making the rest of her head join in. She told herself once again that this was not the laptop's fault.

She looked up in the direction of Sam's bedroom door, to remind herself that others were feeling worse this morning. She'd come home to find Sam asleep on the sofa, and guessed that his bed had been donated to Abi. She had yet to show her face, but the occasional groan and worrying wretch had been audible. Mira had brought her a cup of tea earlier to find her blissfully snoring, and had left her to it. She was grateful for the privacy considering the task at hand.

Surf the net, Holly had said, as if it were that simple. Mira wasn't sure how much of a grasp Holly's seventeenth century brain had of the internet. Maybe she thought it was some kind of oracle she could just ask for answers. In all fairness, it had delivered the song in question by Chilled Monkey Brains, who had proven as cringe-inducing now as they had been when Nathan had introduced her to them. But googling deaths in York was a less exact science than augury, which was not even a science to begin with, never mind exact. She'd do as well trying to read the unsavoury contents of the washing up bowl Sam had placed by Abi's bedside in the event of an emergency.

So far, Mira had discovered that eighty-six people had died

in York the year the song was released. One of them might have been the Hangman, but all she had was a list of names and an address for ordering copies of their death certificates. She wondered how suspicious it would look if she requested all of them. Her search history already looked like it was wearing black nail polish and answering to Ravenna, and she had precious little to show for it. She flopped down on to the table and willed her head to shut up and leave her alone.

Faced with a distinct lack of progress, Mira felt her mind beginning to wander down other avenues. She took another check for signs of life, then furtively tapped at the keys until the words King in the Mountain sprang on to the screen. She followed where the phrase led her, and leant in, fascinated by the story that spilled forth.

A King in the Mountain, or sleeping hero, is a prominent motif in folklore and mythology. The tales tend to involve a legendary or historical hero sleeping in a remote cave or supernatural world, often accompanied by armed retainers, and awaiting a time when they will be summoned to defend the nation, or oppose some looming threat. The stories almost always mention the king having grown a long beard, indicative of the many years he has slept.

Mira smiled to herself at the image of Holly sporting acres of facial hair before she continued.

In the most common version of the story, popularised by the Brothers Grimm, a herdsman is searching the mountain for a lost animal and strays into the king's cave. The king awakens and asks if birds still fly on the mountaintop. When the herder replies that they do, the king orders him to leave, as it is not yet time for him to return. The herder goes back to his village, adversely affected by the experience – often he ages rapidly or his hair is turned white. In most versions of the story, the herder dies after telling his tale.

Mira leapt back from the screen, as if she might put as much distance between herself and the familiar words, and all that they implied. She felt a sudden urge to look in the mirror and hunt for white hairs. She reminded herself that this was foolish, that Holly would never have dragged her into this if her death was inevitable. She was prepared to believe in a lot, but premonitions of certain doom were a step too far.

It could be she'll just get bored and kill you herself.

A loud buzz distracted her from her fears and made her jump. Her first task of the day had been to dig out a battered old phone from a shoebox under the bed and transfer her mercifully intact sim card. She'd been rewarded with three voicemails from her mother that she had no intention of dealing with today. This call was from Grace, so putting it off was not an option.

"Hello?" she said weakly.

"Hello, Mira," said the cheerful voice on the other end. "How are you feeling? Better, I hope."

"Um, yes, a bit, thank you." Mira silently mouthed an obscenity as she realised where this conversation was about to go.

"Oh, that's good, good," said Grace. "It's just, well, we were wondering when you might feel ready to come back to work? Don't feel there's any pressure, I know it was a terrible thing you went through, and obviously you shouldn't have to be around the shop until you feel ready. We'll cope just fine, don't you worry. It's just Tony's Laurel, well, she's being induced at the end of the week, so we could maybe use some extra help after that, but only if you feel up to it…"

"Yes, um, right." Mira prepared to lie as convincingly as she could. "I'm sorry, I… I'm not sure I'm ready yet. I've not been sleeping well. I keep having bad dreams about that night. I just… maybe I need a few more days?"

"Take your time, we'll manage," said Grace, the words 'but it won't be easy' hanging unspoken in the air.

Mira winced at her own betrayal, as her eyes flicked to the York Press website in front of her, today's tasks pulling her back from the conversation. The screen nagged at her, and suddenly she realised why. Her heart leapt at the deductive leap, then sank when she realised she was going to have to ask some very strange questions.

"Grace," she began, as casually as she could. "I was just wondering. What was that whole thing about not talking to journalists? We haven't, I mean, there haven't been any getting in touch at all. I just wondered why you thought we might need to worry about that."

"Oh, it was probably nothing. I just got a bit carried away, that's all. Don't worry." Grace spoke with a forced cheeriness that betrayed itself. "Although, they might ask about Chris. If they ask about Chris, don't say anything."

"Okay, but why were you worried about that in the first place? Has something else happened?" Mira found a manic edge creeping into her voice as she leapt to a conclusion. "Has someone else died?"

There was silence at the other end. Mira wondered whether to start looking for another job before or after hanging up.

I found a dead body and I'm very, very upset. I can ask creepy questions if I want to.

"Are you sure you're feeling alright?"

"Yes," said Mira, then realised that was the wrong answer. "Well, no. It's just... I keep going over that night in my head, and... you know how this city is, all the stories. I thought maybe I saw something, that's all."

"Well, we're not haunted, I can tell you that much," Grace said fondly. "Look, you know that poster, the chap who's gone missing? Well, it turns out his dad used to work for me. Never made the connection until some student rang asking about him. Digging up what happened, which was nothing to do with me. But I didn't want anyone else sniffing round."

"Why? Who is he?" Mira leapt on the hint that had been dropped. "Did something happen to him?"

"He drowned," she said. "It's an awful thing to say, but I was a bit glad to be rid of him. Nasty temper on him, that one. It's just, you know how this town gets, all the stories and the morbid tourists. I couldn't be doing with all that."

Mira smiled. Grace was possibly the only small business owner in the city who didn't want to be connected to a ghost story.

"What was his name?" she asked.

"Fennell. Derek Fennell. Yes, that was it."

Mira could sense Grace wondering whether it was wise to encourage this newfound morbidity in her clearly troubled employee.

"Look, Mira, I don't mean to interfere, but you really don't sound like yourself. Do you think maybe you should talk to someone? Bad experiences like this, they can mess you up if you're not careful."

"Yes, no, I'm sorry," Mira said. "I've just been thinking about it all too much."

"Well, if it would take your mind off things to be busy, we're always here," Grace said. "But there's no pressure. You should do something fun today, get your head out of all this gloominess."

"Yes, I will. Thanks for calling, Grace, I'll see you soon." She switched off the phone and lowered her head into her hands.

So, today we're lying to Grace, pretending to have PTSD to get time off work, not actually having PTSD despite people you know dying horribly in front of you, and screening your mother. Congratulations, Mira, you're officially a sociopath. It'll serve you right if you get sacked.

The phone call brought Mira crashing unexpectedly back to Earth. It was like she'd spent the last few days living in another world – which, in a way, was exactly what she had done. Now she had a day clear of Holly, real life was starting to intrude with a vengeance, and it carried its own demands. She reminded herself that the Hangman had yet to put in an appearance during office hours, and ghosts only come out at night, don't they? She could go back to work and help Holly in her spare time.

Help Holly. Protect the city from the forces of darkness. In her spare time. It sounded less convincing when she broke it down. Still, today was Sunday and now she at least had something to go on. If selling books had taught her anything, it was that it was always easier to start with a name. Derek Fennell. She set to work, and was soon making progress, which helped her to avoid thinking about other aspects of real life that she was going to have to contend with today.

"Where were you last night?" asked Sam, right on cue.

"Oh, you wouldn't believe it," Mira replied. "But I met this woman, and it turns out she's a ghost hunter. And we went to a ball. A ball for ghosts."

"Wow," he said, clearly impressed. "What was that like?"

"Really weird, which I guess is to be expected. There was this creepy romantic poet, who was actually a monster, and he won me in a game of cards. But my friend, the ghost hunter, she saved me."

"That was good of her," Sam smiled.

"Yeah, and then, we ran into the man who killed Chris, and he was killing a policeman," Mira explained, excitedly. "Only he's not a man, he's this sort of giant octopus thing. It chased us halfway across the city, until we hid in the Minster. Then I sang it one of Nathan's terrible punk songs and it went away. So then, my friend, the ghost hunter, who's over four hundred, snogged the statue of Constantine, and then we went out and got steaming drunk, and she got me to admit that I love you. I really do, I suppose I always have, even back before Dom and Emma and everything, and I knew I had to say something as soon as possible. Oh, and there also might have been karaoke."

"Okay, that's amazing. You definitely win last night," said Sam. "Our gig went alright."

"Oh, that's good, I'm glad. Shame this is an imaginary conversation."

"Might be for the best," said imaginary Sam. "I'd probably have freaked out if you'd really said any of those things. Especially the last one."

"You've got a point." She sighed at the truth of what he was saying. "I suppose I'd best keep it to myself."

"Yeah, I think so," Sam agreed. "Although, if we ever do have this conversation for real, it might be a bit less awkward if we weren't both naked."

Mira glanced down at her body, then over at Sam, and swallowed.

"Gosh, would you look at that."

Mira heard the door, and her hands reflexively leapt to cover herself before she remembered that she was dressed in real life. Still in her pyjamas at two in the afternoon admittedly, but that counted. Sam came into the living room laden down with shopping bags, which he dropped on the kitchen counter before gently opening his bedroom door.

"Afternoon," he whispered. "How's my little pisshead?"

"Dead to the world, but she seems fine," Mira replied as Sam slowly pulled the door closed. "Although she may have made use of the bowl."

"You see, this is why you should be glad to be an only child," he sighed. "Didn't see you last night. When did you get in?"

"Not entirely sure," Mira said. "Late? Definitely late. How did the gig go?"

"Not bad, not our best," Sam said. "So what did you get up to?"

"Oh, just out with… someone." Mira regretted the choice of that last word even as she said it. *Someone? Way to go, Mira, you know what that's going to sound like.*

"Were you on a date?" Sam turned from the shopping he had started to unload, looking like this was the most important question in the world, although Mira couldn't quite judge if he was pleased or not.

"No!" she said more quickly and forcefully than she would have liked. Sam had clearly picked up on the presence of a secret lurking behind her reaction. Mira could see him arranging his thoughts into the most appropriate shape, like a child discovering Lego for the first time.

"I mean, obviously, you could, if you wanted to, and, you know, you don't have to keep it a secret."

"I know," she said, matching his awkwardness word for word. "I don't need you to tell me I can go on a date if I want to, which maybe I do. But I didn't. But I would. But wouldn't have to tell you, but I might tell you. But I didn't. Go on a date, that is, not tell you about a date that I… didn't go on. And I'm telling you that."

The ground stubbornly refused to swallow either of them up, which after the last few days, Mira had cause to hope might be a thing that could actually happen.

"Oh-kay," said Sam slowly. "Glad we've got that cleared up?"

Mira decided to try being halfway honest, although it didn't take long to realise that even halfway might be a little too far in this case.

"I met this woman at work, she's… a writer. I've been helping her with her research, and we went for a drink. Then some other drinks. She's… funny."

"Funny ha-ha or funny peculiar?" Sam asked.

"A little from column A, a little from column B," Mira laughed. This was starting to feel like their normal routine again, at least as long as she didn't think about it. Which she just had.

"Is the library still open?" she asked in a flash of inspiration. In truth, she did have some leads she needed to chase up in their records, which made her feel a bit better about wanting to flee.

"I think so," Sam replied, clearly thrown by the non-sequitur.

"Okay, I need to go to the library, so I should go now before it shuts. I'll catch you later." Mira said brightly, picking up her shoes from where they sat in the corner.

"You're going to the library in your pyjamas?" Sam asked.

Mira stopped halfway through pulling the first shoe on and tried to think of the funniest, cleverest explanation for her sudden descent into half-wittedness. None came.

Elsewhere in the city, the flickering lights from a bank of screens flashed across a dark room as Jermaine worked the controls. He was tired and impatient and looking forward to the end of his long shift, but he could somehow tell he wasn't done just yet. He waited for the words he knew he was about to hear.

"Run it again," said Caroline from the shadows at the back of the room.

"Alright, but I don't know what you're hoping to find," said Jermaine. "Look, here's DS Unwin going into the square and then the cameras start acting up for the next twenty minutes. I'm sorry, but there's just nothing here."

"Run it again," Caroline repeated.

Jermaine sighed, and played the sequence again. Once again, the figure of Greg Unwin turned a corner into the square, before the screens burst into a mess of static. Jermaine sped through to the next visible footage, which showed the space empty apart from the body.

"The IT guys think it's electrical interference," said Jermaine, rubbing his temples. "Happens all the time. The amount of useful footage we get out of this place, we may as well not be here..."

"Run it again," Caroline interrupted his complaint.

Jermaine wound back the recording to the point where Greg became visible and played it again.

"Look, is this going to take much longer? I was supposed to have finished work hours ago..." he began.

"Stop," said Caroline, rushing forward to stand beside Jermaine's chair, glaring intently at the static-filled screens. "Go back a bit. Slowly."

Jermaine shrugged and rewound the interference, then ran it again. At Caroline's prompting, he paused it, then meticulously went frame by frame through the snowy blur. Slowly, on the edge of the screen, the static seemed to retreat as two figures entered the picture. The first only appeared on screen for a fraction of a second, the static instantly enveloping them. But the second remained visible for a few short frames. When they were paused, Caroline could just make out a face, a face that she recognised.

"Well, Ms Chaudhri," she whispered. "What on Earth are you up to?"

CHAPTER 21

Holly's crypt reverberated to the sound of Kate Bush. The music came from an antique gramophone with an ornate curving horn, sitting on the floor with a vinyl LP spinning on the turntable. Holly lay stretched out flat on the chaise-longue, wearing a simple and fairly shabby blue dress. Her bare feet rested on the arm and danced back and forth in time with the music. She was studying a leather-bound book of some antiquity, the cover embossed with the same portcullis symbol as the tendicula case. A number of other volumes sat stacked in a tottering heap on the floor beside her. Holly snapped the book shut and returned it to the pile as Mira entered the room.

"We're not happy today, are we?" she asked, studying Mira's vexed expression.

"No, we are not," Mira said. "It's all your fault."

"What have I done now? I've tidied up, look."

Holly sat upright and stretched, revealing tufts of ginger hair beneath her arms, then gestured to the laundry basket in the corner as she got up to turn off the music. Mira slouched against a mahogany sideboard, setting down a bundle of papers, and knocking aside a strange device, which she picked up and ran through her hands absently. It was a sturdy tube, with a length of copper wire coiled around it, connected to a car battery by a long rubber lead. A gleaming metal sphere sat at one end, with a small, flat soft pad sticking out from the round surface.

"Yesterday, Sam was my best friend," she said. "We were always there for each other, we could talk about anything. But now you've put all this stuff in my head..."

"I didn't put anything in your head, I just spotted what were clearly there already," Holly interrupted as she returned to the chaise.

"And now I can't even form a sentence around him!" Mira said, waving the gadget around. "And he can't either! You've made my home into the most awkward place on Earth!"

"He's weird around you too?" Holly said, leaning forward in fascination. "Well, that just proves I'm right. He obviously feels the same, no problem. Just get yourself vinegared up, like I told you to."

"Well, in the first place: 'vinegared up?' And secondly, you've never met him, how can you possibly know what he feels?" The aggravation in Mira's tone was mirrored by a buzzing noise coming from the object in her hand.

"I know you, I've seen the flat, got the lie of the land. I talked to Joe..."

"Don't bring Joe into this, it's weird enough back there without... Holly, what on Earth am I holding? Is this some kind of ghostbusting thing?" The device was getting warmer in her hand and throbbed gently against her palm. "Please tell me this isn't going to blow up."

"No," said Holly. "That's not what it's for."

Baffled, Mira looked into Holly's eyes, looked at the device, then back at Holly's pointed expression. The penny dropped, and she immediately put it down, at which point it began vibrating its way across the chipped and scratched surface.

"Okay," said Mira, disconnecting the battery and taking a step back. "Just so you know, there have been significant advances in this technology since the industrial revolution."

"Really? Do tell."

"No!" said Mira, trying not to smile. "You said you needed to sleep."

"I have other needs."

"Not having this conversation." Mira grabbed the papers and flung them to Holly. "Come on, we're here to talk about monsters."

Holly caught the pages and flicked through them, as Mira came to sit beside her.

"Fine, what am I looking at?"

"This is Derek Fennell," Mira explained. "He used to work in the book shop, until he died."

"Did he stop after that?" Holly said with a grin.

"He drowned, in the river." Mira ploughed on over the wisecrack, excited at her discovery. "A few years after the song came out. From where the current took the body, the police thought he must have…"

Holly completed the sentence. "Fallen off Skeldergate Bridge."

"Nobody knows if it was an accident or if he jumped, or was pushed." Mira took the papers from Holly and shuffled through them to find what she was looking for. "Sandra Fisher, the second victim, killed at home alone in her flat in Holgate. Did some digging on past owners and guess whose mother used to live there? That's three of our locations. And Grace, my boss, she remembers him, she said he had a temper. Maybe this guy was violent when he was alive, and still is now, only much, much worse. The Hangman even *smells* like the river, I noticed it before but couldn't place it."

"I don't know." Holly looked thoughtfully at the documents in front of her. "It's a bit odd so much time has passed since he died, but it could be…"

"I thought about that, look, there's more," said Mira, throwing sheets aside to find what she was looking for, and thrusting it into Holly's hand. "Read that."

Holly examined a photocopy of an old newspaper, with a note at the bottom ringed in red.

"The York Press," she read, "would like to issue a formal apology regarding the article dated the third of October relating to the death of Derek Fennell, in which parties who are entitled to remain anonymous were named. We are sorry for any distress this may have caused."

"They had a hard copy of the paper at the library, and I found the original article." Mira pulled out another sheet from the pile. She had underlined one sentence near the bottom.

"Mr Fennell is survived by one son, Peter MacMillan,

aged twelve," Holly read aloud. "Someone didn't want the kid mentioned and kicked up a fuss."

Mira handed over one more piece of paper. It was the poster from the shop notice board, showing the image of an unshaven, untidy looking man with straggly black hair and a distant expression, above an appeal for information.

"Peter MacMillan went missing three months ago. Nobody's seen him since," she said. "When I was a student, you'd hear these stories around campus, where somebody had been walking home drunk one night and hadn't turned up the next day. When people go missing in this city, they usually find them…"

"At the bottom of the river." Holly nodded. "So you're thinking Peter's drowned too and maybe that's woken up daddy?"

"I'm not the expert here," Mira replied. "But, yeah, could that happen? Or, I don't know, maybe Peter is the Hangman and he's looking for his dad. Going back to all these old places to find him and getting angry that he's not there."

"Watch you don't catch yourself writing a ghost story, we don't know everything," Holly warned. "Mind you, Scraggles were talking about people drowning, and it'd be just like him to laugh at what we don't know. These two guys… I think you might be right, there's summat here. What's your next move?"

"Peter's mother printed the posters. She set up a website looking for information," Mira said. "I'm guessing it was her that didn't want Peter being connected to Derek. I thought you might go and talk to her. Maybe she knows something, something that might help you get ahead of the Hangman, or find out what he wants so you can make him stop."

"Go where?" Holly asked warily.

"She lives out in the East Riding somewhere, but it's not that far…" said Mira, as she shuffled through the papers in search of the address.

"That might be a problem," Holly said. "I can't leave the city."

"I'm sure everything will be fine without you for one day. Oh, here we are…"

"No, Mira, I literally cannot leave the city," said Holly. "Not ever. That's the deal. They didn't make me live forever so I can go gallivanting off around the country. They did it so I could stay here and look after the place. I can't go anywhere else."

"What happens if you do?" Mira asked.

"I don't know – I never tried. It was impressed upon me very strongly not to," Holly said. "I mean, obviously the city's bigger now than it used to be, and that's been taken into account as far as I can see, 'cause I'd be a bit of a rubbish guardian if I could only protect the bits that were here four hundred years ago. But the city limits, no matter how far they creep out to, that's the line and I do not cross it."

"All this time, just in this city," Mira sighed. "And I thought I was stuck in a rut."

"A few years back, I had to go and deal with a possession at the university. It were the furthest I'd ever been from home," Holly said. "I remember all the way out there on the bus, I were absolutely terrified. Not because of the demon, he were easy, but because I honestly didn't know if I were *allowed* to go that far. And I'm sitting on this bus with no one to talk to, thinking any moment, I might just drop dead, or maybe all the ageing I haven't been doing will catch up wi'me and there'll just be this four-hundred-year-old mummy sitting on the number 44. Or maybe it's like a big invisible wall that I can't cross, except I'm on a friggin' bus, and the bus ain't gonna stop. It were alright in the end, but God, was I knackered that day. I think I were having to expend all this energy to be that far from the centre. I really wanted to fall asleep on the bus home, but I thought they might not notice I were there and I'd die from being accidentally driven to the depot."

Mira took a deep breath, and committed. "I'll go."

"Well, I was gonna ask," Holly said. "And it won't be dangerous. You'll just be talking to a person. I'll see if I can scare owt up down here, I might have more luck now we've got summat to go on. You know what, you should take Sam with you. It'll be like a date, but not a date, so it won't be weird."

"Maybe I will." Somehow her newly complex relationship with

Sam appeared simpler when viewed through Holly's eyes, which was comforting, but also worried her. She wasn't sure how much Holly really understood about everyday life.

"Holly," she said. "You know I'm going to have to go back to work soon, don't you?"

"I suppose. I hadn't really thought about it," Holly replied.

"Well, I will. I mean I'll go and see this woman. I can do that, no problem," Mira added hastily. "It's just... we spent all day yesterday together and it was great. Apart from the bits that were terrifying, obviously. And getting chucked in the river wasn't fun, and my legs are still killing me from all that running, but what I'm trying to say is... I won't be able to do that every day. Do you understand?"

"Yeah, yeah, of course," said Holly, and Mira caught a flash of disappointment in her eyes.

"I mean, I'll help." Mira tried to console her. "I said I'd help. I'll help whenever I can. I just need to pay my half of the rent, and maybe do normal things from time to time?"

"I get it, it's fine," Holly said, but did not convince. "And seriously, take Sam with you. Spend some time alone, experience the bright lights of..."

She flicked through the papers to find the address.

"Howden?"

"I'll do that." Mira smiled. "Listen, I should be getting back. See if we can actually still talk to each other."

"You'll be fine," Holly said. "Come back tomorrow, and we'll compare notes. Oh, and write your number down, I might need to call you."

"You have a phone?" said Mira, as she scribbled down her mobile number.

"Of course I've got a phone. Doesn't everyone have a phone these days?" She looked around the room distractedly. "At least I think I've still got one. I'm sure it's here somewhere, I've not used it in a while. Is twelve years a long time to a phone?"

"No, no, I'm sure that will be... well, maybe a little. Anyway, I'll see you tomorrow." Mira turned to leave, but felt a pang of guilt that she'd be leaving Holly by herself.

"Mira, wait..." she heard Holly call after her.

"It's fine," said Mira. "I'm not trying to wriggle out of this, honestly. I get it, I do. You don't have to do the big lonely hero speech again. It's scary, but I really do want to be here, so I'll be here, whenever you need me, I promise. I'm not trying to get rid of you, don't worry."

"That's nice," Holly said. "But actually, I were just gonna tell you you've got your skirt stuck in the back of your tights."

Mira closed her eyes and breathed out slowly.

"Of course I have," she sighed. "It's been that kind of a day."

Mira slipped into the flat and leaned back against the inside of the front door, composing her thoughts. Preparing to talk to Sam was a new experience for her – it'd always come so easily in the past. Now she felt like she was about to fail her driving test again. She hoped that Abi would be up and about, to distract her from it all. She poked a head into the living room to see Sam lying on the sofa, skimming casually through his phone which he shut off quickly as she walked in.

"Hi," she said timidly. "How's Abi doing?"

"She's fine, she's gone home," he replied, pulling himself up to a sitting position. "Did you find what you were looking for?"

Mira tried to mask her fear of being alone with her best friend as she sat down in the armchair across from him.

"Yes, thanks. Sorry, I was being a bit weird, earlier, wasn't I? And yesterday as well, now that I think of it. I hope I didn't freak you out, it's just... look, I've got a lot on my mind at the moment and there was something I meant to say, and I thought..."

"Mira, it's fine," he said. "I know what's going on and I understand."

"You do?" Mira said with a rush of hope.

"What happened with that guy," he said, his words sounding carefully chosen. "Finding him like that, it must have been horrible. I get it. And if you need to talk to someone about it, I'm always here. But if you don't, that's fine, and be as weird as you need to be if that helps."

Mira screamed inwardly at the genuine sympathy in Sam's voice and expression. All he wanted to do in this moment was be her friend and she wished she could remember how to be grateful for that.

"Thanks," she forced herself to say. "But it's not… Listen, are you doing anything tomorrow…?"

A knock at the door saved Mira from completing her awkward question.

"Abi," Sam said.

"I'll just park that thought there for a minute," Mira said, and rose to her feet. Once clear of the living room, she let out a groan of irritation.

"Find one dead body and everyone thinks you're a basket case," she whispered to herself under her breath. "Oh God, what are you doing?"

She pulled the door open forcefully and was about to ask Abi what she had forgotten, but was instead confronted with the girl in the bobble hat.

"Hullo," she said, with a childlike wave and a mocking smile. "I thought it was about time you and me had a little talk."

Mira suddenly felt one of the remaining pieces of the puzzle slotting into place.

"Hello, Erin," she said.

1604: A CLEVER GIRL TURNS HER TALENTS

The woman screamed, a ragged shriek that reverberated off the cold stone walls. Her red-rimmed eyes bulged out of her gaunt face as she frantically scanned the room that reeked of her own filth. If the men noticed the smell, they did not betray it, continuing to calmly ask the same questions without a hint of feeling. In the far corner of the room, the man and the girl watched, equally detached from the distressed figure that was the centre of everybody's attention.

"They're not doing anything to her," said Erin. "I don't understand."

Lankin smiled. He observed the scene before him like an astronomer at his telescope, mentally noting the details with detached curiosity, as if these events were a million miles away rather than taking place before his eyes.

"There are many forms of torment the human race has devised. It's not all branding irons and bridles," he explained, taking pleasure in the lesson. "They call this Waking the Witch. It is hoped that by simply depriving the subject of sleep, they will become too exhausted to maintain their façade and their true, demonic nature will become clearly visible. Marvellous. Such a grasp of the world."

Erin looked up at him, her brows knotted in confusion. "But they don't have a clue what they're doing. She's not a demon, she's just a woman. Isn't she?"

Lankin nodded as a man leaned in closer to the woman's sobbing face, pulling her head upright by her hair. Behind him another began reading from a monstrous slab of a bible.

"Oh yes, they're quite wrong. Blundering in the dark, really. And yet they have grasped a fundamental principle of existence on some small level. They just don't know what to do with it."

"Which is?" Erin asked.

Lankin regarded his pupil's curiosity with affectionate admiration.

"Wakefulness," he said. "To be awake, and to know one's purpose and goals is a vital thing. Those who are not cannot be said to be truly alive. These men grasp that on some level, but are misunderstanding that knowledge. They believe they are forcing this woman to awaken so they can deal with her as she really is. However, what they think is her true nature is merely a story they have constructed. Her true nature is something they are destroying and the dream they have concocted is something she will conform to. They think they are waking her up when they are putting her to sleep in what I suspect will be a fairly permanent way."

Erin contemplated the idea for a moment, before forming her conclusion. "They're stupid."

"Yes," Lankin said with casual dismissiveness as another scream pierced the air. "People are funny like that. They're very good at embarking on a course of action that accomplishes the exact opposite of their stated goals, then calling the results a success."

"Because they're not awake." Erin began to grasp the lesson.

"Or they know that others are not, and hope to deceive them. To be the king of the sleepers," Lankin clarified. "But I'm sorry to say that these gentlemen are nothing more than slumbering giants."

The corner of Erin's mouth curled upwards. "Maybe she should wake her own witch."

"Well, possibly." Lankin was momentarily thrown by the response. She was learning quickly. He held out a bag of blackberries, and Erin took one and popped it into her mouth. Lankin relaxed, and resumed his lecture. "It's not always for the best, I find. Now, what do you see?"

"Naffheads," Erin sneered. "Bullying naffheads."

"Look closer," Lankin whispered in her ear.

Erin fixed her gaze on the scene before her and saw another figure in the group. He was dressed like a farmer, and clutched a rake. The men moved around him, oblivious to his presence.

"They can't see him," Erin said. "Is he like you?"

"No. But he is what I wanted you to see," Lankin explained. "He is a tier-up of loose ends. He's here for her. He will wait until her strength fails and then…"

"What? What happens?"

"You'll see."

Erin bit her lip in frustration and returned her attention to the lesson. "If a person isn't awake, it doesn't matter what happens to them. If nobody is awake, nobody else will mind what happens to the first person. You want me to kill for you, and you want me to know why that's not wrong. I don't see how he figures into all this, mind."

"Because I'm going to give you to him," Lankin explained coldly. "His kind has certain attributes that are of use to me. So you will go to him, he will give those abilities to you, and you will use them for me. And all of us will know why we do what we do."

"And them?" Erin indicated the priests, whose questioning was drawing to a close.

"You really are a very bright girl," said Lankin proudly. "I've arranged for their prisoner to be joined to a particularly malevolent spirit. When she dies, it will break free and slaughter them. So, in a way, their story will come true. I'm going to let these men die screaming in the pain and fear they sought to inflict, and you can watch if you like."

"Good."

"Do you miss her?"

"No."

"You are angry and unhappy," Lankin whispered. "I know. And you know how to lie. It's what you reach for, even with me sometimes. That's good. Hold on to that, you need to hold onto that, because the people I will give you to are as cold and honest as the process they deal with. I need you to be as you are, and they will want you to be like them. But they will lie to themselves, if you lie to them."

He placed a hand on the girl's shoulder as the prisoner slumped in her seat and the farmer gently rested a hand on her head.

"She may sleep, but you, my child, have always been so awake…"

CHAPTER 22

Erin bobbed from foot to foot happily. "So, are you gonna invite me in?"

"What do you want?" asked Mira, her hand grasping the door handle tightly.

"I told you. I just want a chat," Erin replied. "And maybe a cuppa. A cuppa'd be nice, but only if you're having one, don't go to any trouble."

"Get out of here," Mira snapped, the frustration of the day feeding her anger.

"That's a bit rude." Erin feigned a hurt expression. "Are you feeling alright? Are you having a bad day? You didn't look too happy when I saw you in town earlier. Bit distracted. Did you know you went to the library with…"

Mira slammed the door, but a battered black boot snuck into the gap. Erin's tiny, white fingers gripped the edge of the door like a vice, and she pushed it back open with surprising strength.

"I really would like that chat, if you don't mind," she said. "I understand if you don't want to do it here. Your man's in, isn't he? I don't need him to die just yet. But he will. Now, repeat after me: 'Sam, I'm just popping out for a minute, I won't be long'."

Mira felt her anger subsiding and her fear of this strange girl rising up to swallow her. She did as she was told, stepped out of the flat, and walked with her down the corridor in silence. Erin produced a tatty paper bag of sweets from a coat pocket, selected one for herself and held the bag out to Mira, who ignored it. When they reached the two lifts at the end of the passage, Erin called one to go up and waited.

"I take it she's told you about me?" Erin asked.

Mira nodded.

"Everything?"

"Enough," Mira replied.

"Interesting." Erin smiled knowingly to herself as the lift doors slid open. They walked in and stood side by side in the tiny space, not looking at each other.

"Just to get my bearings, has she got to the bit where she promises to keep you safe?" Erin asked. "She likes that bit. Makes her feel all big. She won't follow through, of course. It's just words with her. Always has been."

"If you hurt Sam..." Mira began, unsure how she would finish that sentence.

"Who said anything about hurting Sam?" Erin responded. "I never said anything about hurting Sam."

"You just threatened to kill him!"

"No, I didn't. I said he'd die. There's a difference," Erin said with an air of patronising patience, as if she were talking to a particularly stupid child. "I mean, everyone dies. Well, not me, I don't, but everyone else. You, Sam, even her, sooner or later."

The doors opened on the third floor and Erin walked out, gesturing for Mira to follow her. The corridor was identical to Mira's own, the same hideous green wallpaper, the same round light fittings lining the walls like portholes, the same zigzagged carpets and large, bright red circular columns running down the centre. Erin tapped each with her hand as she passed.

"You've never been up here before, have you?" she asked.

Mira shook her head.

"No, that's the modern condition in a nutshell," Erin chattered away happily. "All in your own little... nutshells. Not noticing each other, or what's going on around you half the time. The city gets bigger and bigger and you lot shrink away to nothing, huddled around fire and fleet..."

"And candle lighte." Mira completed the lyric wearily. As much as she was frightened of Erin, she was also finding her irritating. "We figured out the Hangman's song a while back, so you can drop the subtle hints."

"Of course you did, bit of a design flaw that," Erin said. "You're a clever little puppy, though, aren't you? The last one were clever too. Did she tell you what happened to her? You should ask. Thereby hangs a tale, as she likes to say. I didn't kill her, I swear. But if you like, I can show you where I put what's left of her. Oh, here we are."

Erin stopped at flat 34, opened the door and stepped inside. She gestured to Mira to join her.

"Come in," she said. "It's alright, no one'll notice, not if you're with me."

Mira stepped over the threshold with some trepidation. She felt certain something terrible waited for her inside, but fear of the strange girl stopped her fleeing and curiosity drove her on.

Erin led her through the flat to a bedroom, where an old man lay sleeping, drawing in shallow breaths with a ragged snore. A younger woman sat in a small chair by his bedside, looking on him fondly with a sad smile.

"This is Harry," Erin monotoned. "Harry's going to die."

Mira grabbed Erin's arm. "You are not going to kill this man! I won't let you..."

"Oh for God's sake! Did I say you were clever? Well, you're not, now stop being so bloody slow!" Erin shouted, pulling her arm free. The people in the room remained oblivious to the raised voice. "Look around you and have a think about what's going on here. He's old. It's time."

Erin calmed herself and sat down on the bed beside Harry. The woman stroked the back of the old man's gnarled left hand as he shook gently in his sleep, while Erin took his right in hers.

"Harry's had a good long life," Erin said gently. "But now it's ending, like everybody else's does. This is Mary, by the way. Mary's his daughter. Mary's got three kids, and Harry watched them all grow up from tiny babbies to have their own happy little lives, isn't that nice? Harry's going to die, but he's going to die at home in bed, with the person he loves more than anything in the world holding his hand. Would that we were all so lucky. Who's going to hold your hand when it's your time? Besides me."

Mira began to understand what she was seeing. Her mind buzzed with thoughts of cowled skeletons clutching scythes, games of chess in old movies and a story her grandmother told her about a princess who outwitted a god. It was all so far removed from the strange girl in the colourful hat.

"Are you...?" She forced out words too bizarre to even contemplate. "Are you Death?"

"Not exactly," Erin replied. "Think about it. There's so many ghosts in this city. But in the grand scheme of things, there's a lot more people, especially when you take into consideration how long York's been here. Why do you think everyone doesn't end up haunting this place when they pop off? Who gets to make that call?"

"You."

"There's a whole bunch of us, actually," Erin continued, gently patting Harry's hand. "She calls us death collectors. That's her little joke. This place needs managing, you see. It's just a bit too supernatural for its own good. So we come in at the end, and between us we decide where you go afterwards. Now for Harry here, we thought a nice, peaceful sleep seemed right and proper, with all his cares and worries washed away. So that's what I'm here to give him."

Harry's chest rose and fell once more then stopped, and for a moment, Mira thought she could actually see the final breath, like a wisp of smoke curling away towards the ceiling, before Erin's hand snapped shut around it. She opened her fist and breathed gently on her palm, then sat back contentedly. Her eyes moved across the room and Mira tried to follow her gaze, to make out whatever it was she was seeing. Her work done, Erin stood and walked away just as Mary finally allowed herself to cry after too long.

"You see, I'm not a monster," Erin explained as she passed Mira on the way out. "I just like to make them on my days off."

She strolled out of the flat with a carefree demeanour, and Mira followed, closing the door behind her and finding, unsurprisingly, that it had been locked all along.

"Why did you show me this?" Mira asked. "What do you want, what's this all about?"

"I wanted you to understand. To understand that you don't understand. Not really," Erin said, looking down the corridor. The voice that had been so calm and flat now began to rise in pitch, as she turned to glare at Mira. "Do you think you can just become her plucky assistant, like this is some daft story? We are bigger than you. You don't belong here, don't you see that? Why don't you just go back…"

"Where I came from?" Mira said, the familiar words strengthening her resolve as she stood her ground.

Erin stuck her tongue out in response.

"If you think being a smug Guardian reader's going to get you not dead, you really are stupid. I'm giving you one last chance. You walk away from this, you walk away now."

"No," said Mira firmly.

"You'll die," Erin snapped, her body trembling with nervous energy as the edge in her tone grew sharper and more aggressive. "And not like this, not quietly in bed. You asked me if I'm Death? Well, the Hangman is Death. He's my Death, and he kills people the way *I want them to die*. No peaceful sleep for them. No bloody nice Nurse Erin to hold their stupid mortal hands. The worst things wait for them, wait for you, forever. When I'm done, this won't be a city you want to live or die in, and if you stick around, that's what you'll get."

"You're wrong," said Mira gathering her courage about her. "I do understand. You turned that poor man's last moments into a sick sideshow just to make me feel insignificant. You want me to be afraid of you. And you know what? I was, I have been so afraid. But now I'm here with you, I'm not anymore. You've said you're going to kill me. But you haven't, so I don't believe you. I think you're trying to scare me because that's all you have. No wonder you hang out on bridges, you're actually a troll. And if being killed by the Hangman is as bad as you say, then I'd better help Holly stop it happening to anyone else. Now I think we're done for today, don't you?"

Mira felt a flush of pride at her defiance, right up until the moment Erin punched her in the face.

CHAPTER 23

The blow sent Mira flying and spinning across the corridor, and she had no chance to be startled by the power in Erin's tiny frame. She crashed into one of the pillars and landed in a crumpled heap on the floor in front of it. Looking up through blurry vision, she saw Erin advancing on her, producing her knife from inside her coat.

"Sorry, you were being annoying," Erin said. "I could see you thinking 'This kid's all talk.' Well, just so we're clear on this: I'm not a kid and I am not all talk."

She kneeled down and pressed the knife to Mira's throat. Mira closed her eyes and held her breath as terror consumed her. She found herself wishing she had phoned her mother this morning. Erin was ranting again, her mouth close to Mira's face. The sickly smell of the sweets was on her breath.

"You are going to die. Here, today. And it will be me that comes for you when you do. And you will just stop. For you, there's no bright light, no peace, no ghost story, I'm not even going to waste eternal torment on you. You will just *end*. Now, in case that wasn't your final answer, can I ask again: are you afraid of me now?"

"Leave her alone, Erin," shouted a voice.

Mira opened her eyes to see Holly standing at the far end of the corridor.

"Shan't," replied the girl with a satisfied smile.

"Oh yes, you bloody well shall. I am not having this." Holly marched down the corridor towards them, a fury in her voice and bearing that Mira had never seen before.

"Really?" said Erin, jumping to her feet. "You're going to come down hard on me over this? I mean, I could understand it with some of the others – they were clever, they came in handy, but what possible use is *that* to you? You've had to save her life every day since you met her, is it not just getting a bit boring?"

"I wouldn't expect you to understand," Holly said coldly.

"Aaaawww," Erin replied in a childlike voice. "Is she your friend, is that it? Has Holly got a little fwiend now? Bless. You know, they should have just given you an immortal cat or something, it'd have saved us both so much hassle…"

Before she had finished speaking, Holly grabbed Erin by the lapels of her coat and slammed her hard against the wall, hauling the girl off the ground. The only reaction it provoked was a burst of high-pitched laughter.

"Oh yes, the bit where you get pointlessly rough with me!" Erin giggled. "I love it when I get you to do that! Not seen you like this in a while. It's not love, is it? Sorry, can't really keep track of which side of the rainbow you fly on, although I think she might be spoken for…"

Holly flung Erin to the floor, but she bounded instantly to her feet. Mira's eyes settled on a fire extinguisher attached to the wall, and she began crawling painfully towards it. Erin stifled her giggles, not in the least bit intimidated as Holly towered over her with a face like thunder.

"Oh Holly," she said, her face beaming like Christmas morning. "You're getting interesting again. I think the three of us are gonna have a lot of fun together. I mean, obviously one day I'll get bored and kill her but until then…"

Mira approached her from behind and swung the fire extinguisher until it crunched into the base of Erin's skull. The smile instantly snapped off her face and she stared blankly at Holly for a second before cartoonishly flopping face down on the floor. Mira dropped her makeshift weapon and collapsed, sitting curled and shaking in a stranger's doorway. She looked at the dark stain spreading across the back of Erin's hat, then up at Holly, who wore an oddly embarrassed expression.

"Well," said a voice muffled by the carpet. "I was not expecting that."

Erin clambered uneasily to her feet, streams of blood running through her long hair and dying the ginger locks a dark purple. She stuffed a hand under the back of her hat and gave an exploratory rub, pulling it out with sticky gore coating her fingers. She turned to glare down at Mira, who could only gape back in shock.

"So, I'm curious," asked Erin. "When you say she told you 'enough', what exactly did that cover? I mean seriously, Hol, you didn't even get to 'indestructible'? What, did you just go as far as 'evil' and leave it at that?"

"You're not…" shouted Holly, then let out a sigh of frustration. "Erin, will you please just leave?"

"Okay, since you asked nicely, I'll be off. Gotta look for a new hat." Erin began to saunter away, then suddenly turned, raising a finger in an unconvincing pretence of remembering something. "Sorry, nearly forgot. Isn't there something you meant to say before I go?"

"Don't push it," snarled Holly.

"No, that's not it. Come on, you know what I want to hear," she cajoled. "Say it. Sayitsayitsayitsayitsayit…"

"Love to Dad," Holly snapped furiously.

Mira looked at them both aghast.

"That wasn't so hard was it?" Erin said in triumph. "He misses you, you know. Well, you would, wouldn't you, after all this time? Family is very important, Holly, remember that. Ta-ra for a bit."

Holly, her face a mask of humiliation and rage, stood frozen as Erin strolled past. It was only when she heard the door slam at the end of the corridor that it fell away and she rushed to where Mira lay.

"Mira, I'm so sorry. Are you alright?" Holly said as she inspected the blossoming bruise on Mira's face.

"She's your sister," Mira replied.

"Yeah," said Holly after a pause. "Yeah, she is."

"When were you going to tell me this?" Mira said.

"I was build…"

"Building up to it! For God's sake, Holly!" Mira shouted. "The things you said she'd done, what I told you she's been doing, and she's your sister, and you didn't say!"

"Would you?" asked Holly and slumped to the floor beside her.

Mira felt the shock subsiding as they sat in silence, the frenzied pounding of her heart returning to normal. Holly's head hung low and she looked utterly defeated.

"You said your family were all dead."

"I said they were gone," Holly corrected her. "I never said where they went."

"The Hangman," said Mira. "She made it. Or controls it, or something. Did you know that?"

"No," said Holly. "But... she has done things like this before, and the Hangman never felt natural. Her turning up... I thought it might be down to her. I just sort of hoped it weren't."

"She's going to try and kill me again, isn't she?" asked Mira, then added, "I really just asked that, didn't I? This is my life now, oh God..."

"Mira, look, I caught the last bit there, where you stood up to her, which, by the way, was absolutely fantastic. You were awesome." Holly took Mira's hand, but then noticed the look that told her she wasn't helping. "But you don't need to hear that now so I'll move on to the point, which is that I think you're right. I think she is all talk on this one."

"How can you say that?" Mira said. "You said she killed your friends..."

"But she hasn't killed you, and she's had plenty of chances, especially tonight," said Holly in what she hoped was a reassuring voice. "And maybe she just wants to make me suffer, wondering when she's going to get you, or maybe there's summat else. Maybe, I don't know..."

"Maybe what?" said Mira. "Tell me everything, I've more than earned that."

"I think," Holly whispered, as if imparting a great secret, "I think she works for someone. Not the death collectors, someone else. Someone who gets her to do all these things. She's always denied it, of course. She'd have me think it's all just spite, but I

168

know someone is pulling her strings, and if she's not gonna kill you, maybe it's because she's been told not to."

"Who?" Mira asked. "Is it... is it your dad?"

Holly shook her head. "No. No, it's not... look, me dad's a ghost, if you must know. That's not what this is about. I don't know who it is. I just know there's someone, I can feel it. And they've got a plan, and Erin and all her monsters and the things she's done – it's part of the plan. I mean, think about it, she's the perfect assassin. Death Collectors are indestructible, they have to be, people will die in dangerous places. But more than that, they can kill you in this life and the next!"

Mira took little comfort in Holly's words. The vagueness of the threat she described and the uneasy tone that had crept into her voice felt unbalanced, paranoid even.

"Holly, are you sure this isn't just you... wanting her to not be like this?"

"I have no illusions about Erin," said Holly. "Inside that callous, vindictive little bitch beats the heart of a callous, vindictive little bitch. Whatever her reasons for doing this, she enjoys it, and it just kills me every time I see what she's become. I'm just saying there's summat bigger going on behind her. Hurting me is just what she gets out of it."

"Why?" asked Mira. "Why does she want to hurt you?"

"There speaks an only child," said Holly, as she stood, extending a hand to help Mira to her feet. "We'd better get you home. You good to walk?"

"I think so," Mira replied, rising shakily. "Is there anything else I need to know?"

"Well, I don't actually fancy you, in case you were worried about that."

"Thanks. That wasn't actually the scary part, but good to know." Mira placed a hand to the tender parts of her face and grimaced as she touched the large bruise forming on her forehead. "How do I look?"

"Like you walked into one of these pillars," said Holly. "What are you going to tell Sam?"

"I'll tell him I walked into one of these pillars," Mira replied.

"Oh good, this relationship's getting off to a cracking start." They shared a hollow, uneasy laugh. "Mira, I said I'd protect you from her and I will, but you know how I were saying you should take Sam with you to see that missing bloke's mother? Well, maybe you really should. And do it tomorrow."

"All talk?" asked Mira.

"One thing me and my sister have in common," said Holly. "We talk a lot."

THE CATACLYSM OF 1604

The door of the barn banged open and shook on its rickety hinges. It was dark both inside and out, but three figures moved easily through the shadows, a woman and a girl supporting a man, who hung limp between them. It had been dark for three days now, and their eyes had grown used to it.

The woman laid the man down in the hay, and the girl collapsed beside him, shuddering gently and making a low keening sound. The woman made sure the man was still breathing, then moved purposefully around the barn, checking for ways in. An axe lay discarded on the floor and she stopped to pick it up. Satisfied with her surroundings, she returned to the others, and helped her other companion upright. The girl was sobbing and her fingers clawed frantically at her clothes. The woman held her close and whispered in a soothing voice.

"Hey, come on now, Littl'un. We're safe now," she said. "And Father's going to be alright, you'll see."

She could feel the shaking of the girl's body subsiding and her breathing growing steadier. She relaxed her hold to look into her eyes. Even in the dark she could make out the tears running down her face and gently wiped them away.

"Come on now, what did I say to you?" she said with a smile. "Whatever happens, I'll keep you safe. I promised you, we'll make it through this, and we will. Just be brave for me, and everything will be alright."

The girl nodded, and slipped back into the woman's embrace, when something smashed hard against the outside of the barn with a dull crash. The wood creaked under the impact, and heavy footfalls could be heard outside as whatever it was made its way around the building. A wet snuffling noise and unintelligible speech were audible through the cracks in the panels and they could just make out shapes moving in the darkness. The woman rose to her feet and reached for the axe, but the girl held on to her even tighter, clutching at the sleeves of her dress, until her fingers were gently prised away.

"I'm not going to leave you, I promise," she whispered. "Stay with Father."

The woman walked slowly towards the door, the axe raised. She leaned in close to the wall and peered through a crack. The something was peering back. She leapt back with a start as the door was forced from its hinges. A fierce and swift blow struck her to the ground.

The girl looked up at the maddening shape in the doorway and her mind reeled. Horror consumed her as it lurched forward into the barn, drawing closer and closer. But she did not cry out, and was able to look away. Gazing to her left, she saw the woman rising to her feet, the axe gripped tightly in her fist.

"Stay away from my family," she growled and swung the axe.

The girl watched in wide-eyed wonder. Her sister was here. Everything would be alright. Nothing would hurt her. Her sister was here.

CHAPTER 24

Mira studied her reflection in the mirror as Sam drove through the Yorkshire countryside, tugging at her fringe to best cover her bruises. The familiar sights of the city had given way to open green spaces, but her thoughts remained troubled. She had slept badly, the implications of the previous day's confrontation unsettling her mind far more than any of her recent experiences had done. Just as her trust in Holly had been reassembled, she found it shaken by this talk of some vague, controlling power behind the threats they faced. She had followed Holly faithfully through so much, but Erin was a blind spot, no matter how much Holly tried to deny it. Mira's instincts told her that Holly's belief in some kind of supernatural nemesis was just a way of avoiding the unpleasant truth of her sister's nature.

"You still haven't told me what this is all about," said Sam. He'd been all too eager to accompany her, motivated by his desire to support her through a traumatic experience. It certainly wasn't for any other reason, she thought, and ticked herself off for being selfish.

"My friend wants me to go and interview someone, research for her book," Mira said, telling half a lie. She had phoned Susan MacMillan, Peter's mother, the night before and arranged to come and talk to her about her son's disappearance for the mythical book. She took some comfort from the fact that she had at least told them both the same untruth, but decided to redirect the conversation around anything that required further deception. "I've never been to Howden before, sounds nice."

"We had a gig here last year. You should probably prepare yourself for disappointment," he said. "What's the book about?"

It occurred to Mira that a true crime book about the late Derek Fennell's mysterious demise would be the most convenient explanation in the short term. On a whim, she felt compelled to test deeper waters.

"Ghost stories," she said.

"So this person you're going to see, she what, saw a ghost?" Sam asked.

"Yeah, something like that," said Mira, and grabbed the conversation's steering wheel once again. "Are you sure this is okay? You're not going to get in trouble at work, are you?"

Sam shook his head. "No, it'll be fine. But if anyone asks, I've got really bad food poisoning."

"Lovely."

"Be as graphic as you like, but make sure you use all the right terminology."

"I'll bear that in mind," Mira laughed, and felt fully at ease again. Between the terror and the lies and the *urges*, he somehow always managed to pull her back to that place so naturally. "Quite the bad boy rock star today, aren't you?"

"Oh what a tangled web we weave," he quoted. "When first we practice to deceive."

That quotation had been one of their private jokes for years until the day it had stopped being funny. Its sudden reappearance unsettled Mira, and she scrambled for a way to clear her head. The MP3 player hooked up to the car's radio caught her eye.

"Can we have some music?" she asked.

"Okay, but you remember the rules; driver has power of veto or crashing will ensue."

Mira flicked through the cascade of cover images, when the sight of a ballerina's feet, standing en pointe in red shoes, brought a smile to her face. She selected a track.

"Kate Bush?" said Sam, with an air of disbelief as the music began. "When did that start?"

"Holly, this writer, she's really into her, just obsessively," Mira explained. "I thought I'd give it a try."

"Cool, I'm glad someone else is contributing to your musical education," Sam teased. "It was getting really lonely out here, you know. Maybe we should meet, come up with a plan."

"Great," said Mira, with a nervous frisson. A buzzing came from her pocket, and she fished out her phone. She tapped the screen and was rewarded with a piercing shout.

"Mira! It's me, it's Holly. Wow. Sorry, bit excited – never actually rung anyone on this before. How're you doing, is it going alright?"

"Hi Holly," Mira replied. "Yeah, we're good, we're just on our..."

"Wait! Shush! I can hear summat!" Holly cut her off. "Oh my... are you listening to Kate? Good girl! Turn it up!"

Mira worked the volume control but when she took up the phone again, she found Holly had lapsed into a silence that continued for some time.

"You're dancing in a public place, aren't you?" Mira said eventually.

"Of course I am!" Holly cackled. "You know me so well already!"

"Did you want something?" Mira asked.

"Yes. I wanted to ask, how do you send those like letter things on these?"

"Are you asking me how to text someone?" Mira replied.

Sam suppressed a laugh.

"Well, yeah, I guess, if you want to get technical."

"I don't know – what kind of phone do you have?" Mira asked.

"There are different kinds?"

"I'm sure you'll figure it out. Bye, Holly," said Mira, then turned to Sam. "My new friend."

"Funny peculiar?" he said.

Mira nodded as they both exploded into laughter. The car continued its journey far from the city and its demons.

Far away, Holly stood by the banks of the River Ouse, smiling at the small clamshell phone in her hand, when she realised, to her surprise, that she had been seen. She looked up from the phone at a little girl, some four years old, who stood with mouth agape, clearly awestruck at the impromptu dance recital. Holly winked at the child and returned to the matter at hand. After intensive study of the markings on the phone's tiny buttons, vague memories of having once flicked through a manual years ago kicked in. She composed a message with an air of serious concentration.

mira chaudhri look after her when I cant

She was about to send her message when a look of irritation crossed her face. She stomped back and forth along the river bank for a while grumbling, then turned to face the child.

"I'm not saying it," she said determinedly. "I won't. You can't make me."

The girl stared nonplussed, then galumphed away in the direction of a call from her oblivious mother. Holly let out a wordless groan of irritation and added a post-script to her communiqué.

thank you for everything you do for me

Her message dispatched, Holly walked down to the river's edge, and produced five smooth, white pebbles from her coat pocket, which she flung one by one into the still water. She then settled herself on a nearby bench and waited. She sat for a few minutes, tapping her fingers in an occupied manner against the wood, before she was disturbed from her deep thoughts by a loud hissing noise. A fat grey goose stood at her feet, its neck stretching upwards with its head cocked to one side as it regarded her.

"It isn't one in the morning, you know." The goose spoke in a deep, lightly accented voice. "And I'm fairly certain it isn't May either."

"We both know you made that up to keep away time wasters," Holly replied.

"You only came to us two days ago, and then you changed your mind about what you wanted us to do for you at the last minute. Some of my family would consider that time wasting, yes?" The goose flapped its wings as it remonstrated.

"Yeah, but I didn't ask for much, did I?" Holly said defensively.

"I just wanted a couple of little favours. It's not like I asked for me crops to grow or victory in me next battle."

"Would you like victory in your next battle?" asked the goose.

"Yes, obviously, but I'll manage on me own, thanks."

"So what can we do for you today?" the goose asked.

"I need to find..." Holly began and then shook her head. "No, I'm not doing this. Come on, talk to me properly, this is just daft. Can I have a person please?"

"You don't like the goose?"

"I don't have a problem with the goose, I'm just not sitting here talking to it, it's... silly!" Holly shouted at the bemused waterfowl. "I'm not a fairytale princess who sings to all her little animal friends, alright? I'm gonna count to three, and then I want to see a human face. One... two...."

The goose flapped its wings and let out an aggressive hiss.

"Three," said Holly.

A tall man in an elegant suit the exact colour of the goose's feathers was now seated beside her. Everything about him from his neat brogues to his dappled cream tie was immaculate, save for his hair, which was a long rope-like mass of salt and pepper dreadlocks with pieces of wood and stone and other flotsam and jetsam sewn into them. His smooth, handsome face had a barely perceptible greenish tint and glistened slightly in the sun. But it also had a broad smile, and she couldn't help but return it.

"Better?" he asked.

"More like it," Holly said with a nod. "Abandinus."

"Mountain," he responded. "What are you looking for?"

"Bloke came through your way a few years back. Name of Derek Fennell," Holly said. "I need to know what happened to him."

"We know of him," Abandinus said. "As you say, he came to our domain, and passed through. I believe your sister attended to his spirit."

"Might have known," Holy sighed. "Bugger it."

Abandinus shook his head and waved a hand languidly through the air.

"Oh no. Nothing untoward. She fulfilled her obligations exactly as her order instructed and found a place for him." He peered into the distance and pointed a long, thin finger. "He haunts the north bank, upstream from here. Near the fountainhead, I believe."

"So he's just a regular ghost?" Holly asked, confused at this development. "Nothing weird?"

"Well, he's not exactly happy," Abandinus said, the smile never leaving his lips. "He died violently, of course, and there was much anger in his soul before that. That's probably why your sister was sent for him. So, he is something of a tormented spirit, but…"

"Got it, dogs bark at nothing when he's around, but he doesn't do any harm." Holly considered this piece of information. "Is that it?"

A look of concern crossed Abandinus' face as he studied his hands. "Lately, my family have noticed him moving beyond his normal pattern. We can feel him far from our waters and we taste the blood on him. I had thought he was merely starting to remember his old life, but now you are here, I think he really is a wanderer. And I think he is killing your people, yes?"

"Looks that way," Holly sighed. "Don't suppose you know what he's up to next?"

Abandinus closed his eyes. "It will be tonight. He has been thinking about it for the past day. He thinks about the path that rises from the river, where your people built their great gate."

"Micklegate Bar? Are you sure?"

"Yes," Abandinus said firmly. "And he is angry, very angry."

"Well, bloody sodding pumpernickel," scowled Holly. "Did he leave you anything, when he drowned? Anything you might still have?"

Abandinus rose to his feet without a word and strolled to the water's edge. He bent down on one knee and lowered his hand into the river. A moment later, he turned and stood, and fished something from his jacket pocket, which dripped as he held it, but left no mark on his suit. It was a round discus shape encrusted with mud. Abandinus' thin fingers felt along the top for a moment, then the object sprang open with a spray of droplets. Beneath the mud was a portable CD player, and inside, the shattered fragments of a disc encrusted with black mould. Holly took one shard, and thanked Abandinus with a smile.

"Mountain," he said, his concern visible in the eyes that looked deeply into her own. "You seem weary."

"It's been a busy week. And this has all taken a bit more work than I were expecting. I made a new friend, though. So that were good."

"You rose out of a great cataclysm," he said in a voice heavy with experience. "We remember those days. And now, there is so much turmoil among the spirits. I think soon it will happen again, yes?"

"I don't know." Holly gazed into the distance where the buildings of her city clustered around the peaceful riverbank. "But I think summat is coming. Summat awful. Been feeling it in me bones for a while now. Might just be going barmy, mind, least that's what everyone tells me."

"When the darkness came, the river suffered." Abandinus' face grew stony as the bitter memory filled his mind. "I would not see that happen again. If the city brings forth the darkness again, I would drown it and all who dwell there before allowing such horror. Know this, Mountain."

"Hold on," said Holly nervously. "Did we just become enemies?"

"No, not yet," Abandinus replied. "But you should know that a time will come when I must choose between my people and yours. When that day comes, I will not choose yours."

"But we're still mates until then?" Holly asked.

"If you like." The warm smile returned to his face.

"Okay, seems fair." Holly smiled as she turned to go. "Thanks for the mixtape. And I must come night-swimming again if I get the chance. I won't keep you. Lots to do today."

"What will you do now?" Abandinus asked.

"Well, first off," Holly mused, "I think I'd better get hold of someone who's dying."

CHAPTER 25

"The worst?" asked Sam.

"The very worst," said Mira, leaning back to feel the sun on her face. Howden was enjoying a beautiful day, and she had decided to make the most of it. There was time before she was due to meet Susan MacMillan, and it couldn't hurt to waste some at her leisure. So, for now, they sat together beneath a stand of trees that smelled of the end of summer and felt a thousand miles away from anything bad.

"Okay, when we were kids, there was this wall," Sam began. "Near where we lived. It was all that was left of some old building. And it's about so high and so wide." He gestured vaguely upwards, then brought his hands together to a few inches.

"It's probably smaller than you remember," said Mira, shaking her head at the image.

"Maybe. I'll have to go back and check one day." Sam continued his tale. "Anyway, the thing we all used to do was to get up on top of the wall and run along the top as far as we could get without falling off. Which did not go down well with anyone's parents."

"Very idyllic," Mira teased, and leaned in closer to him than she normally would as the warmth of the day washed over them. She felt the new surface of their relationship finally firming under her feet, and gave her long-dormant flirting muscles a gentle stretch. "This is textbook childhood, you know that?"

"I try," he replied. "But Abi wanted to do it too, and there was no way I was going to let her. She was five and…"

"A girl?" Mira challenged him, half-jokingly.

"I never said that," Sam responded quickly, then admitted, "I may have said it at the time. But Abi's Abi, even then, so she's not going to take no for an answer, and one day when I'm not looking, she gets up on the wall."

"Good for her." Mira enjoyed the mental image of tiny Abi standing triumphantly on high.

"Not really," said Sam. "She made it all of three steps, then fell off and broke her arm."

"Ouch."

"And then when our parents got to the hospital," Sam continued. "She told them I pushed her off."

"Sorry. That is awful!" Mira couldn't stop herself laughing. Without thinking, her head flopped downwards to nearly rest on his shoulder, but she swiftly gathered herself and sat upright. Sam didn't seem to have noticed. Her fingers rearranged the material of her dress, something else she wasn't sure that he had noticed.

"She was five," said Sam. "She just thought she'd be in less trouble if it was someone else's fault."

"I bet you didn't say that at the time."

"Well, no. I was pissed off at her for ages. And there were reprisals. My Little Pony may have got turned into supermarket lasagne." He grinned at her, and she wanted to just enjoy the sharing of memories, but she had a reason for this line of questioning and decided to approach it more directly.

"Have you ever told her you hate her?" she asked delicately, not sure if she was intruding on private matters. But if the suggestion of familial conflict had bothered him in any way, he showed no trace of it.

"Loads of times. We both have. I may have said it yesterday while disposing of a bowl of sick."

"But have you ever meant it?" she pressed on.

"No," he shook his head, then considered the matter for a moment. "And yes. You mean everything when you're a kid, don't you?"

"But then you grow up," said Mira, almost to herself as thick clouds drifted across the sun. "Unless you don't."

"Don't what?" asked Sam. "What's this all about?"

"Oh, my friend, she and her sister… they don't get on," Mira explained. "I mean, really don't get on, haven't for years. I guess I'm just trying to understand. Can you imagine what that would be like? If Abi just hated you, really hated you? And was never going to stop?"

"I don't know. I mean Abi and I have fought more times than I can remember, but that's because we know we can always take it back. It's like a pressure valve. Sometimes I think it would be healthier if I could yell at everyone when they piss me off, the way I do at her."

Mira was taken slightly aback by how casual he was and wondered how often he wanted to yell at her, but felt too nervous to broach the question.

"But if it was real?" she asked.

"If she really wanted to," he said calmly, "then I can't imagine anyone who could hurt me more."

Mira held back a shudder. The glee with which Erin had taunted Holly overwhelmed her; it scared her far more than the threats or the violence. The sheer desire to cause pain to someone she should have loved was terrifying, but when she compared it to the open and genuine feeling that lay beneath the surface of Sam and Abi's often spiky relationship, it felt sad and hollow. Mira stood up quickly, and looked around her, trying to glean some sense of her surroundings.

"I should get going. It's nearly time, and I'm not entirely sure where this house is."

Sam rose to follow her, and his presence suddenly made Mira uneasy. After invoking her fears, she felt a pressing need to put as much distance between him and them as she could.

"Maybe you should wait for me here. She's expecting me to be alone, it might make her uncomfortable if I turn up mob-handed. She's been through a lot."

"It's fine – I'll wait outside," Sam replied, keeping pace as she moved away a few steps. "I'll just make sure you get there. In case you walk into something on the way."

"Am I ever going to live this down?" Mira laughed, and felt the sun piercing the clouds. Just for a moment, everything was well with the world again. "I just didn't see the pillar, that's all."

"Mira, they're enormous. And they just painted them bright red."

"You know, my head *really* hurt yesterday," she jokingly pleaded. "Do I get any sympathy from my friends?"

In truth, Sam had immediately fussed over her in the protective manner that came over him when he could see she was in a bad place. Then she'd told him her story, and he couldn't help but laugh at her, which had been far more therapeutic than his concern. For a moment, she'd been able to find her own foolishness amusing as well, until she remembered that the heartwarming tale of ditzy Mira was a fabrication concealing a knife to her throat.

"Okay, come on, then," she conceded. "And you can tell me more adorable childhood stories as we go."

"So your friend, she believes in all the old spooky stories?" Sam asked as they walked down a row of terraced cottages that had been identical once. But each had since slid further into disrepair than its neighbour.

"Uh, yes, yes she does," Mira said, and reached for the opportunity that had been presented. "I don't know, talking to her, it makes you think. I mean, have you ever wondered? We do live in a place where a lot of funny things are supposed to have happened."

Sam took a second to ponder this lurch into the paranormal. "Do you remember when Nathan dragged us round that light and sound exhibit at the Railway Museum last year?"

Mira grimaced. "God, that was dull. How on Earth does anyone combine punk rock and trainspotting as interests?"

"He has layers," Sam replied. "But anyway, he told me that after he got home from the pub later that night, he was looking at his photos of the trains, and he swore that in the smoke on one picture he could see a man and a woman, dressed up all Victorian. He hadn't seen them at the time, but suddenly there they were on his phone. He could make out their faces so clearly, but like they were made of smoke. The next day, he goes to show someone – and they're gone. The picture had vanished from his phone."

"Do you think he saw something?" Mira asked.

"No, I think he got drunk and deleted the picture by accident."

"Hmm. I guess that does sound more likely."

"Has she got you believing too?" Sam asked as they rounded a corner. "I've never seen you as being up for this sort of thing."

"I don't know," Mira said, and realised she was losing count of the number of lies she was telling. "I suppose after... what happened, I just feel, you know, a bit..."

Sam stopped dead in his tracks and turned to face her, all quiet compassion as he completely misinterpreted her mood.

"Mira, it wasn't your fault. There wasn't anything you could have done differently."

"No, I know that, that's not what I mean, it's just..." Mira's head quaked with all the things she wanted to say, but knew she mustn't, or couldn't, or didn't know how to. "What happened, it... made me look at things. Differently, I mean. I'm still trying to get my head around a lot of this. I'm sorry, I'm not really explaining myself very well, but I'm not sure what I think, what I feel any more, I just... There are things I'm seeing differently now. Does that make any sense at all? Because I can shut up instead."

"Twenty-seven," said Sam.

Mira looked at him, baffled.

He pointed to the number on the nearest door. "This is it, right?"

"Oh, yes, right, that's why we're here." Mira tried to shake off her mixed emotions and focus on the job at hand. "This probably won't take long."

"Call me if you need me," Sam said. "I'll just be across the street."

Mira felt him retreating as she looked at the door of number 27, bottle-green paint peeling away to reveal soft, old wood. The simple, white plastic letters attached by dark screws. The closed, faded curtains within the single mould-framed downstairs window. Even though Holly wasn't here, Mira could feel herself stepping into her world and feeling strong there. She raised her hand and knocked.

CHAPTER 26

"So," said Susan MacMillan pointedly, with a sharp puff on her e-cigarette. "What have you got to tell me?"

Mira shifted in her seat, as her eyes roamed the small, cluttered front room. Boxes and piles of papers were stacked on a table and across the faded blue carpet, while empty pill bottles lurked among them. The photocopied face of Peter MacMillan stared up from each stack, and none of the images made him look like someone you would want to find. There was a sense of neglect to the dusty environment, which Mira guessed had taken root three months ago.

"Well," said Mira. "I work for a local historian…"

"Yes, you said," Susan cut her off. "What do you have to tell me about Peter?"

"Well, I, that is, the historian I work for, *with*, I mean with, she…"

"Why didn't she come herself?" Susan asked, with a lingering puff and a hard stare.

"She can't get away at the moment," Mira apologised. "She's got a lot on."

"Good for her," Susan said. "I used to have a lot on sometimes. Not so much now. Now it's one thing. Which brings us to you and what you've got to say for yourself."

Mira reminded herself that Susan had been through a lot. She'd come here expecting a broken woman, had intended to be sympathetic to Susan's loss, to be gentle and avoid causing further pain. But Susan wasn't broken, she was hard and solid and intimidating. Her son's absence had given her life a terrible, unwavering focus.

"Well, the hist… that is, we are researching the death of Peter's father, and that led us to…"

"In other words," said Susan with an oddly aggressive calm. "This is about what I can do for you."

Mira felt self-conscious about having been found out so soon in the conversation. "We've been trying…"

"Do you know where my son is?" Susan's voice remained even and stern, her eyes studied Mira for even the slightest glimmer of a lie.

"No," Mira admitted.

"You want to know about Derek for your bloody vulture book, and you let me think you could help me just so you could get your foot in the door," she said, with no trace of accusation in her voice, just statement of fact.

"I'm sorry." Mira struggled to look Susan in the eye. "This is hard to explain…"

"Oh, I'm sure it is, but who gives a toss?" Susan said. "You want to know about Derek. Derek was a bastard. I'm glad to be rid of him. I'm glad my son never knew him. And yes, I'm glad he's dead. You might want to write all this down."

Mira gazed at her momentarily dumbfounded, before thinking to rummage in her bag for a notepad.

"Oh, don't look so bloody gormless," Susan said, with the hint of a joyless smile. "I haven't had a lot of visitors lately. It's amazing how quickly people stop being 'oh so sorry, if there's anything I can do'. I expect when it's a kid, you get a few months' worth, but when your son's that creepy bloke everyone laughs at then it's a bit too much effort for people to pretend it's any sort of loss."

"Peter never knew his father," said Mira, deciding that was a good place to start.

"I made damn sure of that," she said. "I got out from under him as soon as I twigged I was pregnant. I bloody well wasn't going to subject a child to that. Of course, Peter didn't see it that way. Have you still got your parents?"

"Um, yes, yes, I do," Mira replied, and realised she had never

186

really considered the possibility of answering that question differently before. "I... I don't speak to them as often as I should."

"No," Susan said, as if forming a judgment. "Not having a dad, it didn't sit well when he was a kid. Everyone had a dad. But not him. So your parents are still around. Have you got grandparents?"

"No," said Mira, accepting that this conversation was going to be about give and take. She would let Susan talk around Peter, until she could bring them back to Derek. "I only really remember my grandmother – we were very close. My dad's parents died before I was born, and my mum's dad, he passed away when I was a baby. I've seen pictures of him holding me. I can see my mum in him."

"You see, you can explain death," Susan said. "Like, I bet you asked your mum where grandad was, and you can answer that because he's dead and you've gotta learn that one sooner or later. But if someone's just not there, that's a harder one, especially if why's a bad place. Maybe I should have said he was dead, but lies get complicated. Well, you know that. You lied to get in here. I expect you're lying to that lad on the other side of the street. Oh, don't look so shocked, of course he's with you. Have a look at this."

Susan navigated through the clutter and picked up a shoebox from behind a colony of larger boxes, coughing as she did. As she rummaged through it, one of the pill bottles fell from the shelf and landed softly on a pile of flyers, which promptly toppled over. She held out a piece of crumpled, yellowing paper with flashes of bright colour on it, and Mira could immediately guess what she was about to see. The iconography of a thousand childhoods stared up from the page. It was a crude drawing in crayon, a house and three figures in a line of decreasing size. Daddy and Mummy and Peter. Daddy was huge. He towered over the tiny figures of his smiling family, his head as high as the roof of the house.

"Yeah, I know," Susan said. "All kids draw that. Peter drew hundreds of 'em, and they all bloody hurt. Like I'm not enough. Or like he's bringing that man into our house to hurt us both. Sometimes I just had to burn one. God, that was satisfying. Like bloody voodoo."

187

"But Derek did die," Mira said, as she added voodoo to her list of things that might turn out to be real. "When Peter was twelve."

"That should have been a relief," Susan said. "And it was for a bit, I thought it was all done with. Then there was that whole thing with the news story, I assume that's what's brought you here. God, I was livid. And terrified, you know? What seeing that would have done to him…"

Mira flinched as the box Susan had produced the drawing from fell from its precarious position on the stack, letting crumpled papers spill across the carpet.

"Did Peter see it?" she asked. "Did he ever find out?"

"I don't know," Susan said with another puff that was followed by a bout of coughing. "We never talked about it. But I did wonder. He was different for a while after that. Sullen. But he never said when I asked, and I didn't dare come out with it in case he didn't know and then I'd have to tell him. And after a while, well, I did have other thoughts, you know. But you don't like to think your kid is capable of something like that, not even to someone who had it coming…."

Her gaze drifted into the distance and the protective veneer of anger ebbed away. "I don't know why I'm telling you all this. Suppose I just never had the chance to talk to anyone. You seem like a good girl, so I'm asking you… don't tell your boss any of this. Don't let her put it in her book. I love my son, you know. I miss him and I want him back. But more than once in his life, he's frightened me. There are days when I wish they'd just fish him out of the river, and I hate myself on those days. But if he ever does come back, I know I have to ask him what he did, and I can't, I just can't…"

She took another drag on her e-cigarette and coughed hard, her shoulders jerking as her head lowered.

Mira stood up and moved towards her, placing a comforting hand on her arm.

"I'm sorry. If there's anything I can do…" she began pointlessly, when Susan's head whipped around. Her eyes were wild and blazing and she let out a terrible screech as *something* emerged from her mouth. A gleaming tendril just like the Hangman's lashed from her throat, wrapping three times around Mira's waist. She screamed as she was lifted off the ground and flung into the nearest pile of boxes. Mira looked up to see Susan floating into the air as if held aloft by an invisible hand around her throat. The tentacle thrashed about in the air in front of her as two more crept from the corners of her mouth, followed by trails of frothy spittle and flecks of red. Through Susan's choking cough and the ear-splitting noise of the Hangman's song, louder and harsher than ever before, Mira could hear new crackled and gurgled words.

"You..." Mira made out through the nightmarish cacophony. "YOU. MADE. HIM. DO. THIS. TO. ME."

Then one of the tendrils arced out across the room, came back in a circle and wrapped itself around Susan's throat. Her limbs jerked and her groaning, grating breath grew harder and faster then suddenly stopped. The tentacles zipped back into her mouth as if pulled by some unseen force and her body dropped back into her chair with a thud.

Mira sat frozen in terror on the floor of the suddenly silent room, surrounded by reams of tattered paper. Peter MacMillan's face glared angrily at her a hundred times over. The eerie quiet was shattered as the front door was forced open and a tall figure burst into the room. Mira let out a panicked cry as she scrambled on all fours away from the man who loomed over her before she realised who it was. Sam dropped to his knees and whispered reassuring words that Mira could barely make out. He wrapped his arms around her and pulled her in close, but all she could see was the broken woman sitting lifelessly in the chair.

CHAPTER 27

Susan MacMillan was not the only person to die that afternoon. In the A&E ward of York Hospital, a doctor solemnly acknowledged that his best efforts had not been enough. Forms were signed and a nurse was dispatched to pass on the terrible news. But they were both unaware of a third person by the bedside. A pale-faced blond man in large, round spectacles and a cream suit gazed down at the injured face of the body in the bed, then wistfully glanced out of the window. He strolled away, unnoticed by anyone, his bare feet padding softly on the smooth floor.

As he headed down the hospital's corridors, a thought pricked uncomfortably at the back of his head, ruffling his unflappable demeanour by a fragment of a degree. He felt very aware that he was being observed. It was a sensation he rarely experienced, and it unsettled him. He plucked the glasses which never needed cleaning from his face and nevertheless polished them with a soft white cloth he produced from a jacket pocket. As he looked up, he finally noticed the source of his unease. At the far end of the crowded corridor stood a woman in a deep purple coat with a rats' nest of red-brown curls, who was staring pointedly at him.

"Norman," shouted Holly over the bustle of the room, drawing nobody's attention. "We need to talk." She raised a hand and pointed directly at the ceiling.

Norman nodded and casually opened a locked door marked 'No Access'. On the other side was a stairwell, and he began his journey upwards.

Norman stepped out onto the flat roof and crunched his way across the sharp stone chippings that covered the surface, feeling no ill effects despite his unprotected feet. He looked around, felt comfortable that he was alone and waited for the woman in purple to join him. After a moment, he felt a touch on his left temple, as two fingers were placed there. Out of the corner of his eye, he saw her beside him, her arm outstretched miming the shape of a gun.

"Stand and deliver, your money or your life," she said.

Norman sighed and turned to face her. "That has never been funny."

Holly shrugged and thrust her hands deep into her coat pockets as they walked side by side to the edge of the roof and looked out across the city.

"Erin was at Rowntree Wharf last night," Holly said.

"She was," Norman admitted. "But nothing untoward occurred. We sent her to…"

"I don't care about that," Holly cut him off. "She doesn't go there again. Not ever. Do you understand?"

"That's a little unorthodox," Norman replied, appearing confused by the request. "It's not as if we have individual jurisdictions or anything like that…"

"Not ever," Holly repeated, louder and firmer than before. "I have people there. I will not have them harmed. Are we clear?"

Norman slipped off his glasses and once again pointlessly polished the pristine lenses. "I will see what we can do, of course. And I'm sorry, I know this must still be hard for you. Even after all this time, she retains so much of her mortal life, far more than the rest of us. I can only assure you again that most of the time she does remain at peace. But these old feelings always resurface eventually. They seem to be strongest during your periods of activity."

Holly scowled at him. "Yeah, I make her worse. Tell me summat I don't know."

"We try to help her during these unsettled periods, but there is only so much we can do." Norman carefully replaced his glasses, checking that they were as level as possible on his face. A wry smile formed on the edge of his lips. "Were I mortal, I might observe that we are not her parents."

"No, we're not," said Holly. "But maybe I should've been. Before somebody else took over."

"Ah," said Norman, then let the vowel sound float in the air between them. "I'm afraid we still do not subscribe to your theory..."

Holly let out a grim laugh. "My theory. Holly's crazy conspiracy theory. Woe is come to bloody Troy!"

"If, as you suggest," Norman said with the air of a weary teacher trying to explain a simple concept for the hundredth time, "a third party was behind her... misdeeds, it is quite impossible that we would not be aware of it. I'm sorry I cannot provide a more specific frame of reference. It is hard for an outsider to fully appreciate our state of being. For her to keep a secret from us, and for so long, simply couldn't happen. We know each other in a way nobody else ever could know another..."

"She's my sister!" Holly shouted, cutting through the dispassionate lecture with her fury. "And I know when she's lying, because I were there the day she learned how."

"I am sorry," Norman said, suddenly uncomfortable at the emotional turn of the conversation.

"No, you're not," Holly replied.

"As far as we can tell," Norman continued, clinging to his serene composure like a life ring. "She does these things purely to amuse herself. Although, in studying occasions like the current situation, where she creates an abomination, we have come to realise that perhaps she does so in the hope that you will be obliged to awaken and deal with it. You might say she misses you."

He gave her what was intended as a placating smile.

"Oh, poor little thing – is that supposed to make it alright?" Holly snapped, her voice thick with disgust. "People have died, Norman. I don't care how much she loves me."

"Unfortunately, it's hard for me to value the distinction between life and death, given my situation," Norman said. "It is merely another state of being to us."

"Oh, really? Well answer me this – who comes for the people

she kills? The people her pets kill? Because it's not you lot. Where do they go? What state of being are they in?" Holly pressed her point home, gesticulating wildly as she did. "You say she can't keep secrets from you, but four people have died! When I talked to you the other day, you hadn't even noticed anything funny! You're asleep at the wheel, Norman! Where are they now? Do you even know?"

Norman shrugged. "We're not infallible. Sometimes we miss people. You know that better than most. I'm…"

"Please, if you tell me you're sorry one more time I swear to God I will push you off this roof."

"That would be somewhat futile," said Norman. "And we know where the people she kills go. She deals with them herself."

"So she makes monsters that you can't keep dibs on instead," said Holly. "Or sets up little tin gods like Scraggles to cut you out of the loop. Don't tell me you weren't happy I broke up his bloody parlour game."

Norman gazed at his bare feet in vague embarrassment. "That was… for the best. Hubert Scraggles' situation was something that should never have come to pass."

They stood not looking at each other, gazing out across the city that each in their own way had chosen to look after, and silently contemplated the impasse between them.

"So, at a rough guess," Holly asked, "how many times have we had this same conversation?"

"Fifty-seven," Norman replied with absolute precision.

"Fifty-seven. You'd think we'd have an answer by now."

"She is what she is," Norman said calmly. "I try to be philosophical…"

"When the hangman comes to call." Holly fixed him with a cruel, icy stare.

Norman looked back at her, his expression pained.

"That was uncalled for," he said, his voice rising ever so slightly for the first time in the conversation. "I have told you, I don't wish to be…"

"Reminded of watching a man hang for summat you did?"

Holly said with a ruthless ease. "Watching the bloke with the noose take a pair of boots that should've been yours? Oh, I know you don't. Hangman, Hangman, slack your line, slack it just a while. Why is he the Hangman, Norman? I mean, never mind all the strangling and that, she gave this one a name and everyone knows it. Why the Hangman? Do you know what I think? I think it's because of you. I think she's having a laugh at your expense. The poacher turned gamekeeper turned prize naffhead who thinks she's a good girl at heart."

"You're trying to make me angry," Norman observed.

"Of course I am, why do you think I opened with that stupid joke? I know it's not funny, it's bloody horrible. I know it hurts when you see that bloke's face, or think about what you did when you were human. I know."

"So why do it?"

"Because I've tried everything else, fifty-seven times apparently!" shouted Holly. "Every time we come back to this, I go off on one and you just stand there all zen and we get nowhere! I've had enough! We have been so bloody indulgent with that girl! We've let her get away with murder! Literally! Well, I am done with…"

Holly grimaced and swayed woozily from side to side. "No… no, not now…" Her legs gave way momentarily and she fell, but recovered quickly enough to lean away from the edge and to get her hands and left knee under her. Her fingers clawed through the stones as Norman came to kneel beside her.

"I won't lose someone else to her, I won't. Not again. I can't, I can't…"

"Watch her kill again." Norman completed the sentence with a gentle whisper, and was rewarded with a scowl.

"Don't be insightful, Norman, I'm in no mood."

"How long has this latest hunt lasted?" Norman asked. "Just over a week, and you can barely stand. It's not my place to interfere, but perhaps it would be easier for you to simply focus on the task at hand. Like we do. The things Erin does are cruel, we understand that, but they are insignificant. An acceptable flaw in the system. And, ultimately, she is not your problem to solve. Perhaps you should try not to think of her as your sister."

Holly thrust out her hand and seized Norman's wrist in a tight grip. She used his arm for leverage as she pulled herself to her feet.

"But I am focused on the task at hand. The Hangman only exists because of Erin, and Erin only exists because of you. And don't ever call what she does insignificant. She's enjoyed that advantage over you for far too long."

"What are you suggesting?" asked Norman, squirming. Even though he knew he could not be harmed, the edge of the roof still felt uncomfortably close.

"It's really very simple." Holly squared up to the man and met his gaze with a fierce, unblinking stare. "Erin's power comes from you lot. If you can't control her, then you're a problem. And my job is to solve problems."

Norman tried to recover his normal air of detached calm. "Even if you could move against us, I don't believe that you would. Without our guiding presence, the spirit world in this city would fall into anarchy."

"Erin's found every loophole in your precious guiding presence, so it seems to me there's not much left to lose. And don't tell me what I can't do. I figured out how to bring down Scraggles, and I'm sure I can do the same to you if I have to. That's the thing about me and my sister. We always find a way."

She broke eye contact to look across the city. "You know I don't want to do it like this. You do keep things in order, and I am glad of it. I always have been. But things are changing around here and you're not and that worries me. Sort it out, Norman, or I'm gonna have to, and you won't like that. Or *he* will, whoever he is, and you'll like that even less. As will everyone else." And with that she strode away.

"Holly, please," called Norman, using the name she had chosen for the first time in their exchange. The word stopped her in her tracks and she turned back to face him. "Don't see us as your enemies. Our system is imperfect but it is necessary. The things you suggest are dangerous. Please, you are courting chaos."

"Chaos can sing under me window any time he likes," said Holly, then pointed to her chest with both thumbs. "But if he touches these without asking, I'll rip his knackers off."

CHAPTER 28

Mira shivered as she sat alone in the interview room. Sam had called the police right away. Of course he had, that's what a normal person does. She'd had to think fast once she'd recovered enough of her wits to come up with a story that she hoped made sense. Susan had suddenly started choking, she'd said. It all happened so fast, she'd said. I don't know what happened, she'd said. Please can I go home, she'd said. The answer had been no. Someone was coming. Someone who wanted to talk to her about a related case. So she'd been left to wait alone.

She had no idea how much time had passed. There was no clock in the featureless grey room, and her phone was in her bag, which was with Sam, wherever he was. And so she was alone with her thoughts with nothing to distract her, which was the last place she wanted to be.

The room was cold, and she rubbed her bare arms anxiously. Her coat was even further afield than her bag, sitting in the back of the car in anticipation of a sunny day. She'd plucked the long-neglected summer dress from the back end of the wardrobe this morning on a whim, delighting in the ludicrous thought that Sam might suddenly see her in a different light. But in these stark surroundings and grim circumstances, it just made her feel silly and juvenile, trying to look pretty while people died.

Of all the things she had seen in the past week, Susan's death had been the worst. Seeing the bodies of the Hangman's victims and the spirits of Scraggles' had been frightening, but not like this. Even seeing someone die wasn't new – she'd held her grandmother's hand at the end and yesterday there had been the old man Erin had shown her. But this was different, this was *murder*.

That the killing was supernatural did not change the ugliness of the fact that it shouldn't have happened, not to anyone, but it had, and she'd watched and there hadn't been anything she could do to stop it. Confronting the Hangman at the Minster had made her feel powerful, but that was gone now. She knew that later she would be angry, and it would help, but right now she could only feel weak and helpless in the face of it all. She wanted to cry and really, really wished she didn't.

She flinched as the door creaked open, and saw a familiar face, but not one that was comforting to see. It was the detective who had questioned her before, whose partner had died on Saturday night. Caroline smiled hollowly as she sat opposite Mira and went through the motions of switching on the tape recorder and stating her name for the record.

"Hello, Ms Chaudhri," Caroline began. "I don't know if you remember me – I interviewed you about the death of Christopher Morley."

Mira nodded as the only possible reason for Caroline's presence raced through her mind. The detective reached into a pocket and produced a grainy, black and white picture, describing for the tape's benefit what she had placed on the table. The image was nothing but static, except in the upper left corner, where a figure could be clearly seen. A figure whose face was instantly identifiable.

"This was taken from CCTV footage of the night that G... that DS Gregory Unwin was murdered. Is this you?" She tapped at the corner of the frame. "Is there anything you'd like to tell me?"

Mira swallowed hard and shook her head. She didn't want to cry, so didn't dare speak.

"I've had a look at the body of Ms MacMillan," Caroline continued, her voice flat, even and authoritative. Any need to be approachable had clearly evaporated. "A pathologist will need to do a thorough examination, but the marks on her throat are very similar to those we found on the bodies of Michael Jamieson, Sandra Fisher, Christopher Morley and DS Gregory Unwin. You appear to have been present at the deaths of the last two, and now Ms MacMillan as well, so I must ask you again. Is there anything you want to tell me?"

"I'm not the Hang..." Mira blurted out then panicked as she realised what she had said. "Man."

"The Hangman?" Caroline looked at her quizzically. "Why do you call him that? I don't think the press have quite decided on a nickname yet. Last I heard they were trying to think of something Viking-y, on account of... on account of DS Unwin dying outside the Jorvik Centre. Why do you call him the Hangman, Mira?"

Mira didn't respond, so Caroline pressed on to another point. She pushed the photograph across the table and ran a finger across the edge of the static.

"Do you see this area, just next to you?" Caroline asked. "There's someone else there. Obviously, we can't identify them due to the poor quality of the image, but we know that someone was with you that night. Who was there with you, Mira?"

Mira clutched her arms hard to her sides and didn't speak.

"When we talked to you before, you mentioned an intruder in the shop where you work. A woman with red hair." Caroline tapped the picture twice. "Is this her? Who is she, Mira?"

Mira remained silent. She turned her head, unable to meet the detective's gaze. Her hair flopped away from her face, exposing the bruises on her forehead and around her eye.

"How did you get those marks on your face?" Caroline asked. When she didn't receive an answer, she took a moment to study Mira's terrified expression.

"Mira, I don't think you're the killer," she said, clearly deciding it was time to play the good cop. "And I know it isn't your friend, Mr Nesbitt. But I think you know who it is. Tell me who did this, Mira. Tell me why she's doing this."

"It's not her, you don't... it's not her," Mira stammered.

"Is someone threatening you?" Caroline asked, leaning across the table and lowering her voice. "It's okay, Mira. We can protect you. Just give me a name. Help us to stop her, and we will make sure she never hurts you again, I promise. Just tell me who did this, Mira."

"You wouldn't believe me," Mira whispered hoarsely.

"I think you'd be very surprised what I'm willing to believe. Just talk to me, Mira."

Caroline's eyes were kind and imploring, and Mira was sick of lies, sick of isolating herself behind one deception or another. She let it all fall away and asked Caroline the question. The only question that mattered.

"Do you believe in ghosts?"

Caroline's face twitched for a second, and she sat back hard in her chair. She paused, carefully choosing her response. When it came, it was clinically professional.

"Mira, I want to help you, I really do. But there's nothing I can do for you if you're not straight with me."

"Can I go now?" Mira asked, giving up completely.

"You're not being charged with anything. You're free to leave. Your friend is waiting out front. But I want you to think very carefully about this. If you tell us what you know, I give you my word we will do everything we can to keep you safe. But if you don't help us, you could be charged as an accessory to five murders. Do you understand?"

Mira nodded. "I just want to go home."

Caroline produced a pen and notepad from a pocket and scribbled a number down. "If you need to talk, if there's anything you want to tell me, call this number. I'd advise you to do so."

Mira took the piece of paper and left the bare room as fast as she could, desperate to escape. Caroline switched off the tape and sat alone for a moment. Her right thumb ran under the scar on her cheek, while the fingers of her left hand moved across the blizzard of black and white on the photograph. She shook her head suddenly and sharply.

"Stupid."

CHAPTER 29

"Bugger it," said Albert Graymalkin, as a fragment of glass slipped from his fingers onto the surface of his workbench. He spun around on his stool and removed the jeweller's lens from beneath a bushy eyebrow to glare at Holly. "Can you at least try and look after these things?"

"Sorry," said Holly sheepishly. She stood in the corner of the small, cluttered workroom at the back of Graymalkin's shop. The bare plaster walls were lined with shelves on which strange objects competed for space with battered boxes of various materials. The room was lit by a single strip light in the ceiling and the lamp on Graymalkin's bench, where he was studying the tendicula and grumbling fiercely as he did.

"This is twice in one week!" he moaned. "I should never have let you have this after you broke my umbrapersequor!"

"I said I were sorry," Holly protested. "Anyway, you told me the river spirits were good for running one of those off of."

Graymalkin extracted a fragment of glass from the smaller lantern with a pair of tweezers. "Yeah, but not if you're using it on a ghost that drowned! I didn't think you'd be daft enough to try that!"

"I didn't know he'd drowned. It's not like I get time to check their biographies before I fight these things! Look, can you fix it? I need it tonight."

Graymalkin moved a set of steps across the room, and clambered up to rummage in a wooden box.

"I think I've got some spare panels for it here. Should only take a few hours. Don't see why I should, mind."

Holly shook her head. "Sometimes I think you want the world to end."

Graymalkin stepped down, bringing the box with him, and carefully removed a series of flat objects bound in bubble wrap.

"The world isn't going to end, Holly," he sighed.

"Don't you start. I spoke to Coffin Norman today, and he reckons I've gone daft too," she said. "But Abandinus, he thinks everything's coming up apocalypse."

Graymalkin snorted derisively. "I wouldn't credit anything either of those buggers said. Now, are you going to trouble me for anything else? I'm a busy man."

Holly did not reply, but a gleeful smirk crept across her face. She strolled across the room, crouched down by the workbench and slapped her left hand onto the surface, then wiggled her fingers to show off the ring.

"You'll be wanting the rest of it, then?" Graymalkin said, unimpressed. "I've got it back here somewhere. I'll see if I can dig it out. Can't see what good it's going to do you with this one, mind."

"Au contraire," Holly said, picking up the smaller tendicula lantern and turning it between her fingers. "I were having a look at the book, and it says that if you've got a memento mori, these things can be used for a transition ritual. Is that true?"

"Yes, it is," Graymalkin said. "And I suppose you've managed to get hold of one, have you?"

"It just so happens," said Holly, looking ever more pleased with herself. "That I have."

"Oh, good," said Graymalkin with a forced smile that he immediately withdrew. "You'll need two."

The sun was going down by the time Mira and Sam slouched exhaustedly into the flat. Sam had asked Mira if she was alright as soon as they had been reunited, because even though it was a stupid question it needed to be asked. Then they had driven home without talking, neither sure what to say. Mira had been able to see her friend's mind at work all through the journey, trying to second guess how she was feeling, to judge what she might need. Even though Sam remained unaware of the cause of the deaths Mira had witnessed, their very existence was a barrier. She had experienced something he was not equipped to deal with, and it gnawed at him. She could see the helplessness all over his face, and how much he hated it. The urge to feel guilty about presenting him with a problem he could not solve bubbled up within her, and so they had lapsed into ugly, self-critical silence.

Mira slumped on the sofa in a dejected heap, while Sam stood at a distance, contemplating the political implications of putting the kettle on. She shook her head as the first syllable of the question formed on his lips. He crossed to the armchair, thought better of it, and sat down on the sofa beside her instead.

"Remember when we finally found out about Emma and Dominic?" he asked after a lengthy silence. The non-sequitur was enough for Mira to finally meet his eyes.

"Everywhere we looked, we realised it had been staring us in the face," Sam continued. "Do you remember those nights where we'd be picking over every little thing they'd done that we didn't understand or that bothered us and realising they were enormous bloody great clues. How did we not notice? But the weird thing was everything kind of made sense, just in an awful, depressing way. At least we didn't have all these nagging warning signs of *something* to worry about anymore. Just the big denouement."

Mira felt utterly at a loss as to where he was going with this. She wasn't sure digging up the past was the best way to take her mind off the ugly present, but was prepared to take what he was offering.

"Well, I feel like I'm waiting for your denouement," he said. "The thing that's so bad, that it makes everything that was already bad make sense. Do you know what I mean?"

Oh. Mira nodded, and the guilt at everything she was keeping from him writhed in her gut.

"Mira, three people have died around you this week," he said softly. "Last night, you went out and came back with those bruises on your face."

"I walked…"

"And then there's this weird new friend I've not met," Sam pressed on, gently but seriously. "I don't know who she is, but the police seemed really interested in her."

"Sam, I can't…"

"I'm just worried about you, that's all."

"Sam, I can't explain it. There are things I can't, I don't know how to…"

"Mira." He silenced her with a hand sliding over hers. "I don't need you to explain anything to me. I mean, if you're in some kind of trouble, I'd like to know, but that's up to you. You don't have to tell me everything. I just want to know how to make things better. Because I don't think a cheesy joke and a shared sense of betrayal is going to hack it this time."

Mira laughed sadly at the shared memory. "No, I guess not."

Sam's hand was still on top of Mira's, warm, heavy, guitar-callouses catching her knuckles slightly.

"You know," she said, "back then I was a bit surprised we didn't jump into bed – to spite them."

Mira was shocked at herself. She didn't know where that had come from, but it was true at least, and she felt slightly better offering that small honesty. A smile ghosted Sam's face.

"I don't think that would have helped."

"Would it…" Mira began, but then decided she was done trying to express herself in sentences. She leant in and kissed him. Sam inhaled sharply and jerked back a touch.

"Oh," he said, a beehive of emotions blurring across his face. "Mira, I…"

"Sam, it's fine," Mira said, finding her old strength returning. "I'm not in shock. I'm not going mad. I've just figured some things out, that's all. So, um, that's my denouement."

"Sometimes I thought…" he said breathlessly. "But it always seemed…"

"I know," she said. "Well, actually, more sort of hoped until a moment ago, but I know now."

They looked at each other in silence. Both could see a great weight lifting from the other, but neither knew what to do with their newfound freedom. Mira smiled nervously, as they both allowed themselves to laugh at the situation.

"I think this is the bit where you kiss me back," Mira volunteered. "Or possibly where I go to my room and start packing."

"I'm good with the first one," he said, pulling her towards him as he did.

Holly strolled up the steps leading in to Rowntree Wharf, an easy happiness to her demeanour in spite of everything that was at stake. It was not a mood that lasted all the way to the door, however, as she stopped sharply and turned around.

"Okay, what is it?" she shouted to no one. "Come on, I know you're there."

No response came from the empty river.

"Look, if you've got summat to say, come out and say it. I'm done playing silly buggers."

There was still nothing.

"Fine, be like that," she grumped and opened the door. "I've had it up to here, you mardy cow."

Holly slammed the door hard and was gone. Silence descended on the river for a moment, before Erin's head poked out from beneath the stairway. Smiling to herself, she hopscotched her way up the steps to the door, and gave it a push. It did not open. Erin glared at the door and pushed again, but it was still firmly locked. Frustrated, she rattled it fiercely and received nothing for her efforts. She stared up at the building in disbelief, and then sloped dejectedly into the gathering dusk.

THE DAY HE DIED

Peter MacMillan felt the hot tea searing down his throat as he gulped the last dregs back impatiently. He stuffed the thermos into the end pocket of his school bag and hugged his thin jacket tighter against the cold night air. Three times he had stood on the bridge, hoping to catch a glimpse of the man he had sought all his life. He gazed into the darkness, waiting to see the familiar figure on his regular walk home.

The first time that Peter had seen Derek Fennell, he had been with a friend. Raucous laughter and friendly insults had been traded back and forth before they parted.

The second time, there was a woman. Peter had watched with uncertain feelings as they had stopped and kissed on the bridge, his discomfort rising as he watched Derek clutching at her body. She had let out a scream that made Peter jump with terror, fearing discovery or something worse. But it had been followed by a burst of drunken giggling as she swatted Derek with her handbag and bemoaned the coldness of the hand that had crept beneath her skirt.

Tonight, he was alone.

Derek strolled out of the distance, a cigarette poised between his lips. He wore a battered motorcycle jacket of black leather and a set of headphones dangled around his neck. To Peter, he looked impossibly glamorous. There was no one with him, no one else to be seen. Peter took his courage in his hands.

"Excuse me," he squeaked. "Are... are you Derek Fennell?"

Derek stopped and turned to face the unexpected interruption. "Who wants to know?"

"I'm... you... you're my dad." Peter forced the words out

excitedly. "I'm… Susan MacMillan. She's my mum. I'm your son. You're my dad."

Derek took a moment to regard the gangly, eager youth before him, before choosing the most appropriate response he could think of.

"Piss off."

Derek continued on his way, but Peter was not to be deterred and galumphed after his father.

"'I'm your son. I know who you are," he shouted into the night, the volume of his declaration making Derek more and more visibly uncomfortable. "My mum didn't want me to be here, she doesn't know, she never told me who you are, but I found my birth certificate and I figured it all out, and I found out where…"

"Alright, alright," said Derek, sighing through a plume of smoke as he turned to face the boy. "You're Susan's kid?"

Peter nodded vigorously.

"What do you want?" Derek asked.

Peter looked thrown by the question. "You're… you're my dad."

"Yeah, yeah. Look, how much?"

Peter felt a strange feeling in his stomach. This was not going the way he had imagined it would, and he had imagined the conversation thoroughly on several occasions. None of his pre-prepared words fit with the reality of the situation.

"I don't… What do you mean? I just… I'm your…"

"Oh, for God's sake." Derek rolled his eyes, and flicked his cigarette into the river. He grabbed the boy by his shoulders and pressed him against the bridge's railing. With one hand, he grabbed Peter's school tie and pulled hard.

"I'm not your dad, alright?" he snarled in the boy's face, who coughed at the scent of the man's acrid, smoky breath. "You don't come near me again. I don't want you, I don't want your mother, I don't want your happy bleeding families, do you get it? And if I see you again, you might just go off this bridge. D'you want that?"

Peter shook his head as tears filled his eyes. Derek released him, and turned away.

"Go home," he said. Peter collapsed in a heap by the side of the bridge, snuffling.

"Please..." he keened. "I just wanted to see you. You're my dad, and I want you... Please please please..."

Hope swelled in Peter as Derek stopped to look back, and held up a hand gesturing for silence. He then slipped the headphones over his ears and reached inside his jacket. A muffled tune leached into the night air and Derek, smiling at the boy, mouthed the words 'not listening' before turning away.

Peter rose awkwardly to his feet, tears and snot dripping down his contorted face. He grabbed the thermos from his pack and ran after his father. Catching up with him in the middle of the bridge, Peter swung the flask through the air. He landed a glancing blow on Derek's shoulder which made his father stagger back towards the parapet. Peter pushed hard and Derek was gone, his startled face slipping down into the darkness below. Peter looked around, saw he was alone, then ran, as fast as he could and not stopping.

CHAPTER 30

Mira couldn't sleep. She lay in Sam's bed, her head rested against his shoulder, and felt the gentle rise and fall of his breathing while her eyes drifted open and shut in the darkness.

So you've slept with Sam, she thought. *That's a thing that you've done. A good thing?*

Mira kicked the thought around her head, but wasn't sure she knew how to turn it into an opinion. It was certainly a thing she'd thought about doing. Once or twice. Maybe more than that. Okay, a lot more than that. But there had always been a voice in her head pointing out the not terribly specific reasons why this wouldn't be a good idea, and she'd always felt that voice was worth listening to. Until tonight.

Mira had always had a love-hate relationship with change, quick to become bored and slow to do anything about it. But this place, this man, had been the most stable things she had, and that mattered. And now, in a moment of madness she'd tipped over the table and change had happened. For the better? Maybe. Or maybe she'd end up losing something she'd come to rely on just when she needed it the most. Of course, Mira's life hadn't been what you might call dramatic for a while. Last week, she could probably have afforded to sacrifice a little safety to liven things up.

But that was last week. Before Holly Trinity had blown into her life like a hurricane. Before she'd watched someone die. Before she'd become a murder suspect. Before everything and more besides. She began to wonder if she could afford another big change. The safety of how things had been was going to be far more vital if she was to continue helping Holly. Somewhere to retreat to when things got too weird.

Do you have to help Holly?

She wasn't exactly obligated, it was true. But the weariness she was used to seeing in her new friend's eyes made walking away a hard thought to contemplate. Holly *needed* her, she had no one else and maybe never would, that was all too clear. And Mira had to admit that despite herself, she also wanted to be there. Holly's world was irresistible in its strangeness. Terrifying, infuriating and likely to get her killed at any moment, but to know it was there and turn her back on it – she couldn't bring herself to do that.

Could she have both? If things were changing anyway, why not change everything at once? It was a scary thought, but not impossible. She felt proud of herself for even considering it.

Mira Chaudhri, 23, third generation British Indian, history graduate, second-hand bookseller, wanted to vote Green but chickened out and went for Labour, monster hunter... girlfriend?

But things were going to get complicated. *Well, obviously.* They were already complicated. She was lying in bed with her supposedly platonic best friend, and you didn't need long-leggedy beasties for that to turn into a mess. Things were already going bump in the night, the supernatural just added more twists to the knot.

It *had* been a while.

And Erin knows where we live. She's been in our home. He's met her and has no idea what she is, how close he came to death. To Death, in fact, or so it seems.

You could always try telling him the truth.

Mira thought of the night when Sam and a group of his friends had marathoned their way through the Spider-Man movies. She'd spent most of the second film practically screaming at the screen, "For God's sake, just tell her you're a superhero!" It was less amusing now. How do you begin to explain something like this and not look like you're out of your mind? Mira had always known that ghosts don't exist, and that everyone knew that, really; it's just that some people would prefer that they did. But now Mira knew it was the other way around, and didn't have the luxury of believing or not believing – these things were a fact. But how do you explain to someone that everything they understood about the world was wrong? And if she didn't, what was she supposed to pretend Holly and she got up to together? Badminton? One day she was going to come home badly hurt, or not at all.

But all these things paled before the thought that scared her the most. The time when there could be no hand to hold.

Whatever happened next, she was going to have to introduce Sam to Holly, and that blotted out all her other worries for the time being. Monsters and murder were one thing, but just Holly being Holly would be enough to freak most people out. She'd have to come up with a plan and make sure Holly stuck to it. Otherwise, they might just wake up one morning to see her sitting at the end of their bed like an expectant child, waiting for Mira to leap up and go on an adventure.

Mira opened her eyes fully. Holly *was* sitting at the end of the bed. Mira jolted upright with a cry of shock, rousing Sam from his slumber.

"Who the hell..." he began, muzzily.

"It's okay, don't panic. This is... my new friend." Mira tried to sound reassuring.

"Hi," Holly held out a hand and flashed a beaming smile. "I'm Holly. You must not be Mira's boyfriend." Mira pulled the duvet tighter around herself and cringed.

"There's some things we need to chat about," Holly said as she stood, apparently grasping that she wasn't wanted. "I'll just be in the living room. I'll stick the kettle on, come and join me when you're done with... whatever you're doing."

She left the room, and Mira flopped angrily back onto the pillow.

"So, this friend of yours," Sam said, feeling around for the most important point. "Did you give her a key?"

"No, she just... does things like that." Mira realised even the lower foothills of Mount Holly were going to be a hard trek. "I should see what she wants. It's probably important. Or she just wants a cup of tea. I don't know. Is it stating the obvious to say this is really not how I wanted you to meet her?"

"Don't worry about it. Do you want me to come with you? Or I could hide in the wardrobe, if that would be better. What do you need?"

"My clothes, some coffee and a very strict set of social ground rules, in that order."

CHAPTER 31

Mira dressed hurriedly, and then left Sam's bedroom with a deep breath. She entered the living room to see Holly buzzing with excitement, a delighted grin plastered across her face. As soon as Mira had closed the door behind her, she sprang from the sofa with arms spread wide, but was stopped in her tracks by a forcefully pointed finger.

"No," said Mira. "No hugs. Hugs are for people who respect boundaries."

"Oh, fine," said Holly as she flopped back down. "Nice dress, by the way. Bit rumpled, mind."

"Enough, Holly." Mira noted Holly's sturdy-looking jeans and T-shirt and concluded that only one of them was dressed for the occasion.

"Oh, I'm only teasing, I'm just happy for you is all. Didn't I tell you it'd be alright? You see, everything's gone according to plan."

"There was no plan today," Mira sighed and sat down next to Holly. "And even if there was, nothing went according to it."

"Oh, really, because the knickers on the bedroom floor are what I'd wear if I had a plan..."

"She died, Holly." The words were softly spoken, but still sliced through Holly's cloud of optimistic glee. Mira looked to the door, feeling very aware of Sam in the next room, and lowered her voice further as she got into specifics. "It killed her. Somehow it followed me there, and it killed her."

"Oh God, Mira, are you...?" Holly began, her energy suddenly blown away in a gust of guilt and frustration. "No, of course you're not, bloody stupid question. You were supposed to be, though, you were supposed to be far away from all this."

"I know, it's not your fault." Mira sat back and rubbed her face roughly with both hands. "It was just... there was nothing I could do. It was so horrible and I just couldn't stop it. And then the police questioned me. Wanted to know all about you."

"Don't worry about that," said Holly. "They'll never find me."

"That's not the point! They've found me!" Mira snapped, angry at Holly's failure to understand. "I don't get to disappear! I have to live here, I've got an address, a phone, a national bloody insurance number! And I'm there whenever their serial killer attacks someone! They know I'm hiding something, Holly, and that's not going to go away! They're going to keep looking for a killer even if we stop the Hangman, and the first place they're going to look is right here!"

Holly studied her fingers thoughtfully, as if an answer might present itself between them. In the face of the modern world and its rules, she was rendered unusually speechless.

"So I come back here, and since my life is a complete disaster anyway, I hurl myself at Sam, because why the hell not?" Mira hissed, nervously keeping her voice as low as possible. "May as well wreck everything before they lock me up. God, I'm an idiot. I don't know what I was thinking. And yes, you were right, he does like me too. He'd be better off if he didn't though, because I'm a self-pitying, lying psychopath, who's probably going to prison for something a completely different psychopath did. What a mess."

"So..." Holly rolled a question around her mouth but failed to think better of it. "How was it?"

"Um... yes. Kind of... great, actually." Mira gave in trying not to mirror Holly's smile for a fleeting moment, before a stern resolve came over her as she turned her attention to the business at hand. "It's Derek. It spoke and I'm pretty sure it's Derek. I think Peter killed him. That is, Susan thought that Peter might have killed him."

"Yeah, that fits. Look, maybe..."

Mira saw Holly's thought and stamped down hard on it. "No," she said, coldly and calmly. "What I saw today... that doesn't happen. Not to anyone else. Not ever. Which means you have to stop it. And that means I have to help you. Now tell me you have a plan."

"I have a bit of a plan," Holly admitted. "I know where to find it and I think I know where we went wrong before. But time is not being friendly. It's going to kill again, tonight. Somewhere around Micklegate Bar, I can't narrow it down more than that. Tomorrow, we'll be a step ahead. But tonight, someone needs our help and I have no idea who."

"Micklegate Bar." Mira was lost in thought for a moment, when she heard a door creak open. She leapt to her feet to see Sam stood in the bedroom doorway, looking untidy and concerned in hastily thrown on clothes. Mira panicked as she wondered how much he might have overheard and which bits were the worst.

"Is everything alright?" he asked. "Sorry, I heard shouting, do you need anything…"

"No, no, everything's fine. I'm just… we're both having funny days. Don't worry. I might need to pop out in a bit, but it's all good, don't panic, everything's… good." She stumbled forward in his direction and quickly kissed him, it seeming like the thing to do. Her mind swiftly circled round its list of priorities, and she kissed him a second time, longer and more passionately, her fingers running through the unruly mess of his fresh-out-of-bed hair. She smiled reassuringly at his uncertain expression, but then noticed it was drifting back and forth over her shoulder.

"Hello, again," said Holly with a small wave.

Mira made an embarrassed noise at the spectacle of her own impulsiveness.

"I should get changed," she squeaked, while trying to avoid looking at either of them too closely. She scurried from the living room to the sanctuary of her own tiny bedroom, while Holly lounged back on the sofa, fixing Sam with a wicked grin.

"Good on you, fella," she said. "Just do right by her, or I will have to kill you."

"Holly, get in here!" Mira shouted from her room.

Mira slipped into a T-shirt and jeans in record time, then pulled her file on Derek from its hiding place under the bed. No matter how hard she concentrated on the matter at hand, the solitude of the enclosed space left her trapped with her thoughts. She felt the confidence of the kiss evaporating in the face of the future. It tasted cruel now, like a promise she couldn't keep. She flicked purposefully through the papers as Holly slipped into the doorway and lurked.

"I knew it," Mira said. "Derek's last known address is 53 Nunnery Lane, just around the corner from Micklegate Bar. Holly, he's going home."

"Okay, that's good," Holly responded. "Look, this might be a long shot, but when we get there, keep an eye out for anything that looks like it might have been there in Derek's time. I need summat connected to him, summat personal."

"Something personal... hang on." Inspiration propelled Mira to her feet and she pushed past Holly out of the room, heading to where her jacket hung on the wall. She rifled through the pockets, and returned clutching a crumpled piece of paper, which she handed over. Holly unfolded it and looked at the smiling faces of the crayon family.

"Peter drew that," Mira said. "I mean, it's not Derek's, but it's of Derek, and if Peter's somehow mixed up in this – could that work? Derek seems very angry with him."

"Oh yes, yes, this will do very nicely. Owt else?"

Mira looked pleased with herself, a sense of purpose sweeping her worries away. She produced her phone, and gave it a few quick swipes, then proudly held it up for Holly to see.

"Well, I did manage to do this."

"How is breaking the screen supposed to help?" asked Holly.

"No, it's..." Mira began, disappointed at not being immediately appreciated. "Look, it's the song. I can play the song on my phone, maybe we can use that to calm it down."

"You should get your oats more often, you're on fire tonight," Holly grinned. "We just need to go to the Shambles and pick up a few bits. And then we're catching ourselves a monster."

CHAPTER 32

Holly bristled with nervous energy as she rapped on the door of the gift shop she had visited when Mira had followed her around the city. It seemed a lifetime ago.

Mira felt strangely peaceful. She told herself that it was having a job to do that was stopping her overthinking for a change, rather than "getting her oats", as Holly had so tactfully phrased it. Still, she hadn't thought about the police since they left the flat, and she felt more confident in her shifting relationship with Sam. But as soon as she looked at it clearly, she saw the problem. An itch at the back of her mind nagged her, telling her that she was becoming infected by Holly's simple view of the world. Things were not good, not by a long shot, and feeling calm didn't make them so. For now, she was glad of a place to escape to, where she could fight the monster, get the guy and pass go and collect £200 without going to jail. But the big fear was not going away. Not unless…

Someone unlocked the door and pulled it open, but at first Mira saw no one. It was only when she looked down that she saw the small figure of a short-limbed man some four feet in height, clad in dusty overalls. His heavily lined face was a ruddy, bristly mass of beard and bushy eyebrows, and his wiry grey hair was pulled back in a tight ponytail.

"Graymalkin," said Holly by way of introductions. "Mira."

Graymalkin led them into the shop, a low-ceilinged cavern of gaudy, touristy bric-a-brac. Between a rack of tea towels decorated with Yorkshire roses and a shelf of crudely painted porcelain minsters sat the familiar box containing the tendicula.

"Good to go," Graymalkin said, handing it to Holly, who passed it to Mira, who buckled slightly at the weight she had forgotten about. "I had a look at the book, and you're right. Presence of the dead, that's what you'll need for a job like this. Oh, when you used it before, how far apart were the lanterns?"

Holly shrugged and looked at Mira. "I don't know. About what, ten feet?"

Graymalkin thundered as if his mother's good name had been slandered. "Ten feet? Bloody hellfire, woman, you're a menace! Ten feet? No wonder it blew up. You want at least four times that! Ten feet!"

"Alright, alright!" Holly yelled over the griping, then paced the shop floor muttering to herself. "No good in a house then. Forty feet, presence of the dead, forty feet, presence of the dead, forty feet…"

"If you need time to think, can I put this down? It weighs even more than before," Mira interrupted.

"Forty feet, presence of the dead! Yes! On the counter!" Holly yelled with a triumphant gesture. "Gray – Martin-cum-Gregory church, I saw it were having work done a couple of weeks ago. Are they finished yet?"

"Don't think so," Graymalkin replied.

"Grand." Holly crossed to the shop's counter where Mira had dumped the case. She flung open the box and removed the two lanterns, which had been repaired and, Mira noted, even polished. Graymalkin clambered onto a high stool set behind the counter and leaned forward, his round, red nose inches from his prized devices.

"What good are these if we can't use them?" Mira asked. "You're right, there's not going to be a forty-foot gap and a dead body in someone's living room."

Holly crouched down, her eyes level with the boxes. "No, but I know where we can find both those things if we have to. In the meantime, there's summat else these can do."

From one pocket she produced the drawing and placed it beside the smaller lantern, and from another the grimy CD shard she had obtained from Abandinus, which she handed to Mira. Then she reached forward with both hands and gently opened one face of each device, which folded down like miniature drawbridges suspended on tiny delicate chains.

"Right, when I say now, put that in the big box, same time I put the drawing in the littl'un. Then close them up sharpish. Ready? Now!"

They swiftly deposited the items and sealed the lanterns shut. Mira felt more than heard a delicate hissing noise before both objects disappeared with a soft pop. Nothing remained in each box but a cloud of tiny, black particles, while a faint wisp of white smoke emerged from the top of each box.

"A transition field," whispered Graymalkin, impressed. "Well I'll go to buggery."

"What have we just done?" Mira asked.

"We've linked the boxes to our pal Derek," Holly said as she straightened up. "When they're around, he'll be a bit more... physical."

"Is that a good thing?" Mira asked nervously.

"It is if you want to give him a bloody good hiding," Holly said. "Gray, I'll have that other item now please."

Graymalkin nodded and barrelled off into the back of the shop. Mira watched him go, then leaned in close to Holly and whispered.

"So, um... what is he?"

Holly looked perplexed. "He's... Graymalkin. He helps out. In an annoying sort of way."

"Yes but, you know... is he... something else?" Mira pressed on, eyeing the door he had disappeared through. "Like a... a goblin, or a hobbit or something? Are they real too?"

Holly raised an eyebrow over a pointedly neutral expression, then said very slowly, "He's a shopkeeper."

"More specifically, a shopkeeper with achondroplasia," said Graymalkin as he re-entered the room, carrying a long, thin bag of green canvas in his arms. "Where'd you find this one? Bit rude, isn't she?"

"Don't mind her, she's had a trying week, but she's a bit post-coital today so it's looking up."

"*Holly!*" shrieked Mira before turning to Graymalkin, who suppressed a smile at her twofold embarrassment. "I am so sorry... I just, well... I thought..."

"Nowt to bother," grinned Graymalkin, as he handed Holly the bag. "Here you go. Do try and bring it back in one piece, 007."

"One of these days, I'm gonna watch one of those films and then I'll get that joke." Holly undid the drawstring at one end of the bag, and slipped the material down the length of a slim, gleaming sword. She weighed the weapon in her hand for a moment before swinging it in a series of precise arcs.

"What good's a sword going to be?" Mira asked. "If you can hurt it with that thing, then surely you can hurt it with something a bit more... modern? At least so you can keep your distance. Have we got any guns?"

"A couple of flintlocks and a lance flammes," said Graymalkin as if this were the most normal thing in the world to possess. "And a blunderbuss, but the barrel's knackered."

"None of which is any use to us. This, however...." said Holly, spinning the sword in her hand and turning it to face point down. She pointed to the pommel, and Mira noticed a small circular indentation cut into the metal. Holly slipped the ring from her finger, and pressed it gently into the gap. A harsh scraping noise came from the sword, and the ivy pattern of the ring began to appear on the pommel. It continued down the hilt, the crossguard and finally onto the blade itself, as if some invisible instrument was carving into the metal in a series of jagged strokes. When the dark lines had reached the tip, Holly tossed the sword in the air, caught it, and repeated her earlier fencing display – but this time a faint ringing noise echoed as the blade flew through the air.

"You've got a magic sword," Mira said with a bewildered smile.

"I've got a magic sword," Holly replied. "And you thought I was cool before. Cheers, Gray, we need to get cracking. I told you everything'd be alright, Mira. We've got the music to distract it, we've got the tendicula to make it whackable, we've got a big stick to whack it with, and somewhere to take it when all's done. Don't worry, Mira. No one's going to die today."

THREE MONTHS AGO: SLACK YOUR LINE

Peter MacMillan was going to die today.

He stood in the small crenelated parapet surrounding one of the bridge's lamp posts, then hauled himself up onto the wall in faltering steps and stared down into the murky brown water below. His hands trembled and he closed his eyes. His father's face swam before him. Derek's last expression of utter bemusement had imprinted on his memory so vividly in this place, all those years ago. Now it would be gone. Now he could lay the ghost to rest, and for the first time since he broke his childhood upon this spot, he would know peace. All he had to do was take a single step.

"Hullo," said a voice. "Nice day for it."

His eyes snapped open and he saw a girl standing on the parapet beside him, her head covered with a woollen bobble hat. The shock of being disturbed from his thoughts left him off balance, and he instinctively lashed out to grip the nearest arm of the lamp post.

"Don't try and stop me!" he shouted.

The girl shrugged dismissively. "Wouldn't dream of it. Actually, I'm more here to facilitate, if you must know."

Peter could only stare open-mouthed at the girl, who stood proudly on the top of the wall, her hands plunged into her coat pockets while his own clawed for purchase. It was as if she were daring gravity to do its worst.

"Would you like a sweetie?" she asked, producing a paper bag from her pocket. "I've got some here. Thought you might like one, sort of a last treat for the road, you know?"

"No, no I…" Peter gabbled breathlessly, as he rested his forehead on the lamp post's curled arm. "Please, please just leave me alone. I just want to be alone…"

The girl nodded and picked through her bag. She produced a squashy disc clustered with sugary blue dots and eyed it suspiciously.

"Do you like these ones? I don't like these ones. There's always ones you don't want, aren't there? Suppose that's life, really. Sure I can't tempt you? No? Please yourself."

She dropped the sweet from between her fingers and leaned forward to watch it fall.

"Long way down," she said, smiling at the bewildered Peter. "I'll say this for you, you're dramatic. You know, doing it out here. Mind you, I suppose it's got to be here, really, given the circumstances…"

"You don't know anything about me," Peter whispered.

"Oh, is that so?" she replied. "Well, I'm looking for a bloke who topped his dad on this bridge when he was twelve, and I thought it might be you."

Peter gripped the lamp post all the tighter. His eyes flicked from the girl to the waters below. "Who are you?" he asked.

"It's alright, Peter," she said soothingly. "Please, don't be afraid. I'm here to help. One way or another, I'm here to help."

"Help how?"

"I understand, Peter. I know you don't think anyone can, but I do. Families are funny things, aren't they? No matter how much they hurt you, you can't let go. And you don't have to, Peter, I promise you, you don't." She stuffed her bag of sweets in her pocket, and held out her hand. "The people I work for sent me to help you on your way. But you don't have to go if you don't really want to. You think you can't make it right, and that's true, you can't. But I can. If you help me, I promise I can make everything right."

Peter glanced nervously at the river, then at the outstretched hand and sympathetic smile of the strange girl.

"Would you like that sweetie now?"

CHAPTER 33

"It's an easy mistake to make," protested Mira as they marched up the steep incline leading to Micklegate Bar. "I mean, even his name sounds like something out of Harry Potter, and you said you don't know any normal people..."

"I don't." Holly paused outside a church, and looked up at the tower thoughtfully. "He's a business acquaintance. I wouldn't call him normal; he made a bloody great magical arsenal in his spare time. I wouldn't call him a goblin either, mind, certainly not in his own shop."

Mira took the opportunity to drop the box to the floor, as Holly continued to size up the building. She ducked down an alley beside the church grounds, came back looking as if she had found what she wanted, and pressed on. The pause had given Mira time to think of the things she still didn't particularly want to focus on.

"Holly..." She started to tug on the thread she had found as they reached the looming arch of the gate tower at the far end of the street. "When this is all over, what happens? To you, I mean?"

"Back to the church, back to sleep until the next problem crops up. Which if you lot are in luck, won't be for a very long time. But I suspect I shall be calling on you before long. You can tell me you're gonna miss me, if that's where this is heading."

"I was more thinking, maybe, you could take me with you."

The request stopped Holly dead in her tracks. She turned to face Mira, suddenly all concern.

"I mean, let's be realistic," Mira began, trying to assemble the ideas that had buzzed in her head all night and make them into a reasoned argument. "What happens to me when you're gone?

I'm the only clue the police have to finding their killer, and we both know there won't be any more. So they come after me again, and I can't say anything, because what is there to say that anyone would believe? They're going to decide that the simplest answer is that I killed those people. They already think I'm covering up for whoever did, and that's bad enough. Even if I'm not going to prison, I'm going to have people thinking I might be a serial killer for the rest of my life. Do you know what I've been thinking about on this walk? What my first tabloid headline will be. I don't want that to be my future."

Mira steadied herself as she pressed on, talking into the night as she struggled to look at Holly in case she faltered.

"All those stories about you, and people like you. The herder dies after telling his tale. I get it now. Because you can't go back. You've gone somewhere you weren't meant to be, it's like... I don't know, you're incompatible somehow. They die because they don't belong in the world they knew anymore."

"The people I knew died because she killed them," said Holly, the pain behind the words barely perceptible. "They weren't doomed. They were resented."

"The kings in the stories have knights and retainers and you've got no one," Mira pleaded. "Please, Holly. I may not die after telling my tale, but my life is done with. There's nowhere else to go."

"What about Sam?"

"Oh, Sam," Mira sighed. "Sam was a mistake. I love Sam, and maybe he loves me too for some stupid reason, but he doesn't deserve all this. I'd just drag him down with me. The same for everyone else I care about. But if I can go with you, just disappear..."

Mira had tried to keep cold and dispassionate, tried to feel like she was making a logical case, but it was no use. Holly took her hand, and looked up to the imposing gatehouse, with its crenelated towers and bright heraldry.

"Time were I couldn't cross this gate," said Holly, then turned away to point into the distance beyond the walls with her sword.

The lights of the south end of the city stretched on ahead in the glittering night. "Now I've got this lot to look after an' all. There's a fantastic little Italian café just up that way. I had to exorcise a poltergeist from their stock-room once. Paid meself in ice cream. I never would have dared to dream all this back at the start."

She turned her eyes back to Mira, a sad smile on her face. "You can't come with me, Mira. I'm sorry. Nobody knows how to do whatever it was they did to make me like this. I can protect you from my world, but I can't protect you from your own."

"What do I do?" Mira asked.

"I don't know, Mira, I can't tell you that," Holly replied. "I get that you're scared, and I think maybe you got out of the habit of that. But you stood your ground against the Hangman and Scraggles and my little sister on her worst day. Whatever happens next, just be that Mira, okay? 'Cause she's mickle."

Mira nodded and they resumed walking. They had reached Nunnery Lane now, and Mira noted the house numbers with trepidation as they drew ever closer to the end of the journey.

"You're wrong, you know," she said. "If there's one thing I've been a lot since we met, it's scared."

"Didn't stop you though, did it?"

"I suppose not," said Mira, then noticed Holly suddenly tense. She spun on her heel and thrust her sword out, the tip standing inches from Caroline's face.

"And neither will she," Holly said. "Whoever the scut you are."

"Hello Ms Chaudhri," said Caroline, ignoring both Holly and the weapon which Mira urged her to lower. "And this must be the fabled intruder in the book shop."

"You've noticed me. Not many people do that," Holly said. "You were following us. Why?"

"Did you think this was low profile?" Caroline said, producing her warrant card from the pocket of her raincoat. "DI Caroline James, North Yorkshire police. And yes, Mira, I've been following you since you left Howden. Now, I have a few questions I would like to ask, but right now, I'm thinking I'll start with that."

Caroline reached up and placed a finger on the tip of Holly's blade. Instinctively, she pulled the sword back.

"Oh, right. That," Holly said, suddenly on the defensive. "I'm Mira's fencing teacher?"

"Please," said Caroline with the thinnest of thin smiles. "Don't be a smart arse with me."

"Okay, can I go and be a smart arse somewhere else then? Only I don't think you and me are gonna get on."

"Holly, please don't make this worse," whispered Mira.

"Holly, is it?" If Caroline was remotely worried about facing down an armed murder suspect, nothing showed on her face. "Well, Holly, perhaps you'd like to explain…"

"Yes." Holly cut her off short, adopting a chatty tone that was aggressive in its forced geniality. "Yes, I love explaining things to people, you know, but only them's that wants to listen. There's not many that do these days. Do you want to listen? Because if you don't, I don't see much point in all this."

"Holly, please stop…" Mira began.

"You were ready to throw your whole life away because of her, so, no, I am not stopping!" Holly snapped, and for a moment, there was something of Erin's fury in her voice as she squared up to Caroline. "She did nothing! Do you understand? Nothing. She is not your killer. You wanna find out whodunit? You follow me, right now. I'll introduce you."

Caroline did not flinch, but as she opened her mouth to speak, a crash and a muffled scream came from inside the house.

"Bang on time," said Holly.

Caroline reacted faster than either of them and reached the door first, banging heavily on the wood. The sound of more cries and something thrashing around inside reverberated into the street. Caroline rattled the doorknob, then put her shoulder to the frame.

"Give me strength," said Holly, as she roughly pushed Caroline aside and opened the door. "Mira, get out the small lantern and switch it on. Only the small one. That'll activate the transition field, but not the trap. It'll only blow up on us if we use both of them in here."

Caroline stared as Mira unbuckled the case, produced the smaller of the boxes and activated it, then swiftly followed Holly into the house. The three of them made their way through the dark hallway, lit only by the lights from outside streaming through the open door. The screaming had stopped, but they could still hear something moving around, crashing and buffeting. The wall to their left shook and a picture dropped from its hook to smash loudly on the floor. Holly pointed to the nearest door, and looked at Mira and Caroline's anxious faces.

"Ready?" she said, then registered the unspoken no. "Well, it'll have to do."

Holly flung the door open and raised her sword as she sprang into the room, followed by Mira waving the lantern. Caroline could only stare open-mouthed in shock at what she was seeing. The Hangman was huge. It had grown since its last manifestation and its massive bulk practically filled the small living room. It had smashed the light fitting in the ceiling, and the room was now illuminated only by the faint glow from the lantern and the eerie gleam of the creature's writhing tentacles as they slapped violently against the walls, leaving piles of broken furniture. In the midst of the wreckage, a grey-haired woman was crying in terror, clutching the limp body of a man.

"Derek!" shouted Holly, and the creature's body shifted impossibly, whatever internal structure it had rearranging itself to face them. The great cowl now loomed over her. "That's enough of that!"

Holly took a swipe at the thing with her sword, but it expanded itself upwards and outwards, lashing two tentacles in her direction. She ducked as one swiped across the wall, then spun aside as another smashed into the floor to the sound of splintering boards. The Hangman twitched awkwardly and turned to regard Mira, its surface appearing to get harder and thicker. For the first time, Mira could see something beneath its hood. Eyes were visible in the darkness and she peered closer to see. A grinding, choking noise emerged as a barely human face lunged out to snap a wide mouth at her. Mira realised with horror that she was seeing Peter's drawing made flesh, a great round, noseless head with cracked, waxy skin and unblinking, uneven eyes of solid pale blue. The thin red line of its mouth cracked open to reveal a gaping, shadowy maw with the irregular nubs of rounded teeth.

The Hangman seemed to be folding in on itself, and the cowl and tentacles were replaced with a vaguely human shape, all in the same bright colours, looking as if its bulky form were carved from plastic. Its blue arms culminated in hard and heavy pink globes, each with five thick pointed appendages sticking out at various angles. Holly struck it across the shoulder with a ringing blow from her sword and it roared shrilly, then retaliated, striking her with a clumpy fist and sending her flying across the room.

"Mira!" gasped Holly, as she clambered to her feet. "Play the song!"

Mira looked to Caroline, whose face was contorted in terror at the unnatural creature before her, and thrust the lantern into her hand. Caroline gathered herself quickly and seemed to understand. She held it aloft as Mira pulled out her phone, while Holly dodged another heavy blow that smashed through the wall. Mira stabbed the screen with her thumb and held the phone in the monster's direction. A tinny burst of energetically chirpy singing erupted from the phone.

"Shit, wrong track!" Mira shouted, as she scrambled in search of the right one.

"*Mira!*"

Mira found the right song and as the Lyke-Wake Dirge started playing, the crayon man stopped, its arm raised ready to pummel Holly into the ground. Its childlike form rolled back on itself and the more familiar hooded shape of the Hangman emerged, seemingly immobilised as it haltingly joined in the song. Holly had her opening, and she took it, thrusting her sword into the depths of the creature's cloak. The Hangman squealed with rage, its tentacles lashing madly around the room. One arm shot forward in Mira's direction, striking the phone and shattering it into a rain of tiny plastic chunks. Mira backed away as it rose up to fill the space, while Holly stared intently at the Hangman's midriff, around where her blade had struck.

"Oh, that's where you ended up," she said and punched forward with her empty hand. Her arm disappeared into the creature up to the shoulder. It struck desperately at her with its tentacles, and she tried to fend off the blows with her sword. With a roar of effort, she pulled her arm free in a sweeping arc. The Hangman's body bulged, stretched and snapped back into place as Holly's umbrella was torn from its innards, glistening with viscous fluid. The Hangman's movements became ever more frantic, its singing rising to a piercing shriek as its body shrank away and finally disappeared. For a moment everything in the house was silent, a peace rudely shattered as the umbrella burst open, the arms bent outwards and the awning a sticky mess of torn rags. Then everyone was talking at once.

"This is... D... DI James... I... I need uniform officers and, and... an ambulance to Fif... Fifty-three Nunnery Lane..."

"Me umbrella."

"It's alright, he's breathing, I don't think he's too badly hurt."

"It actually *ate* me umbrella."

"Is that it? Did you kill it?"

"How do you eat an umbrella?"

"Please, is he going to be alright?"

"It's alright, madam... I'm... I'm a police... police officer. Help is... Help is on the way..."

That was as far as Caroline got comforting the house's owner before she doubled over and vomited on the floor inches from where they were sitting. It did the trick however, as the distressed woman's tears came to an abrupt halt. Her unconscious husband shifted slightly and let out a groan. Caroline gasped and looked up at the smiling faces of Holly and Mira.

"It'll pass," they both said at once.

"Please..." said the woman, wiping her tear-stained face. "You called that thing Derek. He's dead, he's been dead for years..."

She resumed wailing. Caroline tried her best to be consoling, as Holly put the pieces together.

"He lived here with her. First Susan, now her – he's remembering. Not just places, but people. Oh scut, I hate it when that happens. It always goes domestic."

"What now?" Mira asked. "I don't suppose that finished it off."

"No, he's just gone to ground," Holly replied. "But I know where he goes. A little bird told me. He'll be resting, so if we get there right away..."

"Gotcha, kill the monster in its lair while it sleeps." Mira completed the thought. "How Dracula."

"Oh yeah, we're doing all the classics tonight," Holly said. "Let's get gone."

They headed out of the house, walking straight past where Caroline was trying to comfort the woman. Mira caught her eye as she paused to retrieve the tendicula. As they marched down the street, the sound of footsteps followed close behind. Caroline was running to catch them up.

"Wait!" Caroline shouted. "What was that thing?"

Holly simply kept walking, but Mira turned back to face her and seized the chance to tell the truth without fear.

"That was your killer, DI James," said Mira, her voice steady. "It killed your friend. It killed Susan MacMillan, and Chris Morley, and the others. And it will kill again. Please let us stop it."

"Let you stop it?" said Caroline, incredulously. "Why you? Who are you?"

"We don't have time for this, Mira!" shouted Holly from further down the street.

"Well, she is the King in the Mountain, the immortal protector of the city," Mira said. "And I work in a book shop. Goodnight, DI James."

She ran to catch up with Holly, but Caroline kept pace, striding along beside them.

"She's not coming!" snapped Holly.

"I'm not letting you two out of my sight," Caroline insisted. "So, either I come with you, or you come with me."

Holly sighed irritably and gave thin air a swipe with her sword. "Fine. Mira, look after her."

"She catches murderers for a living. Can she look after me?"

"Fair point," said Holly, and seemed to weigh up their relative merits. "Both of you try not to die. Come on, we need to get to the river. To the Fountainhead."

CHAPTER 34

Pikeing Well squatted on the bank of the River Ouse. The building was a square block of bricks that had been pale once, but were now grimy from centuries of burst banks. Facing the river was an archway with a padlocked gate of rusted black metal. In the dim light, there seemed to be nothing but emptiness behind it.

Mira was very familiar with Pikeing Well. In her first year of university, a boorish fellow student had drunkenly regaled a group of their friends with its grisly story. It was an ancient prison cell, and condemned criminals would be left there to wait until the rain came and the river rose, flooding the chamber and drowning them all. It was beginning to rain now as they approached it.

Of course, that story was nonsense and Mira had said so to anyone who would listen. The well was less than three hundred years old for starters. It had been a fountain and a natural spring, at least until someone discovered the water was unsafe to drink. The ominous gates were a modern addition in the interests of health and safety. No one had really listened. She'd explained that it was a popular destination for skinny dipping and prostitution in Victorian times, but even then, the facts had never been salacious enough to gather followers, and the drowning prisoners were still doing the rounds when she graduated.

Holly casually pulled the padlock open, and disappeared into the shadows. Caroline flashed Mira a look of impressed confusion. She had picked up the basics of the situation very quickly, but the specifics still intrigued her.

"How does she do that?" she asked.

"Holly can open any locked door in the city. So she can protect whoever's on the other…"· Mira paused her explanation to laugh at herself. "Sorry. It's just… so that's what that feels like."

Mira and Caroline hopped down to the sunken floor of the muddy, dripping interior, which sat a foot below the street level and was scattered with leaves and debris. The roof was a smooth, low arch coated in brilliant green moss, while in the centre of the floor was a small depression about a metre square. Holly handed Mira her sword and pulled out a torch, laying it beside her as her hands splashed about in the small patch of standing water, flinging aside damp leaves as she looked for something. Mira noted that Holly was muttering under her breath, her face knotted in concentration.

"That usually means something weird is going to happen," she whispered to Caroline.

"Erin's sealed it with a password," Holly finally said. "You say the right words, it'll open."

"Like the Mines of Moria," said Mira.

"I knew this was going to get geeky," sighed Caroline. "I'm guessing whoever this Erin is, they're not going to make it easy for us…"

"Love to Dad," Holly declaimed to the water, and the pool suddenly became a shower of droplets which fell away from them as the surface they had collected on disappeared into nothing. A patter of splashing noises echoed from below. "She always uses the same one. That's a bad habit these days, isn't it?"

They peered over the edge, into the deep dark of the well below. The torchlight picked out ripples on the water at the bottom, as well as a series of old and rusted metal rungs screwed into the crumbling brickwork. Holly handed the torch to Mira and lowered herself down. An uneasy feeling gripped Mira, which she could sense Holly shared beneath her bravado – Erin had chosen an easy password because she wanted them to go down there.

"There's no more rungs!" Holly shouted up. "I can't see anything, mind. Hang on a minute, I'm gonna do summat a bit daft."

Before Mira could ask what, she saw Holly vanish into the

dark, and realised she had released her grip and dropped into the well. A splash followed, then a loud cry.

"Holly, what happened? Are you alright?" Mira shouted, leaning as far down the well as she dared and scanning the dank bottom with the torch.

"No, I'm not! The water's up to me arse and it's scutting freezing!" came the reply.

Mira leaned back, rolling her eyes. "Okay, but aside from that, have you found anything?"

"Yeah, chuck us the torch down. Then the sword. Blunt end first if you don't mind."

Mira dropped both items into the well. There was no splash, so Holly had clearly caught each in turn. Mira could just make out her face by the light.

"There's a tunnel in this wall," Holly shouted up, "right under the last rung and above the water line. I'm gonna have a look. You follow me down."

Mira clambered into the hole, keeping an eye on the light from below. She felt the weight of the tendicula case nestled in her lower back pulling at her shoulders, threatening to drag her to the depths. When her feet reached the last rung, she heard Holly's voice echoing around her.

"On your left there's some outcroppings. Use those to climb down." The torchlight revealed the stubby edges of bricks protruding from the wall. "Climb down those until you can hang onto the bottom rung, then swing yourself over and I'll grab you."

Mira looked down and saw the light shining on a short lip of orange bricks jutting out an inch into the well some way below her. As she climbed down, she saw that beneath the ladder was an oval opening, the width of the wall and just high enough for Holly to crouch in. Mira stretched out her arm to grab the bottom rung, and pulled herself around to bring both feet onto the ledge. Holly grabbed her by the waist and pulled her through the hole in the wall.

They were standing in a smooth tunnel, little more than four feet in length, with a cold light filtering in from the other end. Water dripped from the walls and low ceiling. Holly retrieved her torch and sword from where she had laid them on the floor and the light illuminated the unnaturally bright green mould covering every surface. Caroline followed them down, Holly repeating her instructions and Mira pulling her into the tunnel with them. Carefully, they made their way in the direction of the light.

One by one, they stepped out into a small, round, low-ceilinged chamber. The river water pooled around their ankles, with takeaway packaging of various brands bobbing on the surface. The floor beneath their feet felt rounded and uneven, as if this were a natural cavern rather than a man-made space. A troll cave, Mira thought. Everything looked green, but not from the mould. The dripping stone walls were illuminated solely by the eerie verdant light that came from the thing which lay on a cylindrical plinth of dark brick in the middle of the room.

It resembled a jellyfish, about a foot across, its soft, pulsating surface lit from within by a sickly glow. A series of egg-shaped growths clustered around the side of the shape that faced them, and an overpowering smell of decay rose from its rubbery body.

"What the hell is that?" said Caroline, grimacing with disgust.

"It's Derek Fennell," Holly said as she walked around the podium. "This is it. This is where it sleeps. Oh scut, this is bad, very bad."

"What's wrong?" asked Mira. Something was making her feel uneasy as well, and she wasn't sure what it was.

"I saw someone try to do this once, ages ago," Holly said, circling the thing at a short distance. "Count the pods."

"There's five..." said Mira, studying the sacs hanging off the thing's flesh and noting with distaste the sticky residue coating the plinth and glistening in the cold light. "Five victims."

"Where do they go?" Holly whispered, more to herself than Mira and Caroline as she strode around the room. "The spirits of the victims. Norman doesn't know, the Death Collectors don't know, nobody knows. It's because they don't go anywhere. They're right here. It's a harvester."

"A what?" said Mira. Her anxiety wasn't going away. She looked around the room, hoping yet not hoping to see what she was nervous about.

"There were this bloke once, fancied himself a warlock." Holly continued her slightly distracted ramble. "Jumped-up little fustilarian, he was. But he knew about this, tried to do this. Couldn't pull it off. This is old magic, really old, like prehistoric, nobody could do this back then, never mind now."

"Do what, Holly?" Mira placed a hand on her friend's shoulder, tried to pull her back to the here and now.

Holly placed her sword and torch on either side of the shape, and leant in to regard it closely. Its luminescence shone on her face from below, for all the world like she was about to tell a ghost story by torchlight.

"You make a harvester by binding a ghost, an angry one, to a site, and you make it obey you," she began. "And then you send it out to kill people. Randoms, people you don't like, whatever. But it's set up to kill a certain number. And when it's done, the pods hatch and you get a new harvester for each victim. And they go out and kill their quota, and when they're done they make little harvesters of their own. And so on, and so on. You could wipe a city from the face of the Earth with one of these. Back in the Civil War, both sides knew about this and they both wanted the secret. I made damn sure neither lot cracked it. Getting the ghost to play ball's hard enough, you need summat that gives you a really strong hold over it."

"And now Erin's figured it out," whispered Mira. "A weaponised ghost."

"Sort of. I don't think she's got it working properly." Holly scooped up her torch to shine a light across the thing's flesh. "Harvesters aren't supposed to know about their human lives. They just do as they're told. But Derek's started remembering. He didn't remember his life when he were a ghost, why's he doing it now? He went after his exes. Does it just remember who he hates? I wonder what the others'll remember from the spirits they've grown out of. Who will they want to kill?"

236

"Greg had quite a list," Caroline added, nervously drawing closer to the thing.

"What about Chris?" asked Holly, returning the torch to the plinth and poking the secretion with a finger. "Did he have any enemies?"

"I don't think so, he always seemed nice enough," said Mira. "I mean, you wouldn't want to get him started on politics..."

She stopped as she considered the ramifications of Chris' staunchly-held views in this context.

"Exactly," said Holly, then began chuckling to herself. She backed away from the thing, the grin spreading across her face looking far more unsettling than usual in the eerie light. "Oh, Abandinus, you clever little goose! You sensed it! Right under your beak, it was! I knew it, I knew summat were coming! It's the end of the world as we know it!"

She kicked out, sending a spray of water and a polystyrene box flying across the chamber.

"Well, I'm glad you're so happy about our impending doom," said Caroline testily. "How many people does this thing need to kill before it multiplies?"

"I don't know," said Holly, as she tore a strip from a pizza box and began using it as an improvised ruler, comparing the size of the sacs to the main body of the creature. She suddenly stopped and looked up, with an uncertain expression on her face. "Although I've got a nasty feeling the Hangman has six arms for a reason."

Mira was only half-listening. Her eyes were fixed on the surface of the water. The thing that had been staring her in the face suddenly swam into focus.

"Holly, does Erin need to eat?"

"You what?" said Holly with a bemused look, and continued studying the creature.

"Being what she is, does she still need to eat?" Mira pressed on. "Not just those sweets, but actual food. Does she need it?"

"No, she's invulnerable with a 15-year-old's metabolism. She don't need to eat."

"So who ate all these takeaways?" said Caroline, following Mira's thought.

"There's someone down here with us," Mira whispered what they were all now thinking, in the mistaken belief that it might be helpful. Holly grabbed her sword and began scanning the walls with her torch. The light caught a movement, and for the first time they noticed a deep recess in one wall. Something was hiding in the shadows.

"This is the police, come out slowly," Caroline called out, slipping automatically into familiar territory as a figure shambled out of the darkness, then tumbled to land on all fours in the water. A shaggy head of black hair rose up, and Holly's torch picked out a grimy, bearded face that Mira immediately recognised.

"Peter?" she said softly, gesturing to Holly to lower the sword as she drew closer and crouched down to bring her face level with his. "Peter, is that you?"

"You're not supposed to be here," he slurred. "Not supposed to be here."

"You need a strong hold over the ghost," said Holly. "And she had his killer and his son."

"How long have you been here?" Mira asked as she gently helped him to his feet.

"She said she'd make it right," Peter croaked. "But you're not supposed to be here…"

"She told you she could bring your dad back, didn't she?" said Holly.

Mira studied her friend's face closely, saw the pain she was trying to fight back.

"She offered you the one thing life hardly ever gives us. A chance to take it all back." Her eyes flicked momentarily to Mira as she spoke.

"She wants to help," he said through a wobbly smile. "She understands…"

"I'm sure she does," said Holly. "A man trapped forever in the worst moment of his childhood. How could she resist? But she's not bringing him back, Peter. She's making summat worse. She just needed you to wish really hard."

"I did it, I shouldn't have, but…" He shook his head frantically, his thin frame shuddering with the effort. "She said she'd make it right…"

"I know, Peter. And I know you regret what you did. I can tell," Holly said. "But it happened. You've gotta find a way to make peace with that, 'cause there's no takesy-backsies."

"We need to get him out of here," said Mira. "But what do we do about that thing?"

Holly returned to the plinth, and laid down her implements again, ruffling her hair as she wrestled with the problem.

"It's not ready to spawn yet, so if we get Derek's spirit out of the physical body, the rest of it should just die on its own. We can use the tendicula, but like Gray said, we need the presence of the dead to make it work."

"Wait, I know this," Mira said. "Pikeing Well was sealed off because the water was unsafe to drink, because it was draining through the surrounding cemeteries!"

Her voice rose with triumph as she made her revelation, earning a surprised stare from Holly.

"Colossal nerd, remember?" she added.

Holly grinned and ran to the nearest wall. She placed both hands on the slick surface, closed her eyes and whispered inaudibly. When she had finished her inspection, she spun around, her face blazing with triumph.

"Yes, that's it!" she shouted. "That's how this whole set-up works! She's drawing power from the graves to feed the blob, so we can turn it around to run the tendicula off and yank Derek out! The trace is faint, but if we're lucky, it might just be enough. If not, we need to get this thing out of here. Mira, take the big lantern and go about thirty feet upstream, then switch it on. I'll work the other end from here."

Mira supported the case with one arm as she grappled with the clasps, when suddenly Peter tore it away from her and hurled it across the chamber.

"No!" he shouted hoarsely, as he charged around the room. "You're ruining it!"

Caroline reached for his arm to restrain him, but his movements were frenzied and he broke free from her grasp, sending her toppling over to land on her back in the water. Peter swayed awkwardly around the room, pounding at his temples with his hands, the fingers extending out to rake the sides of his face with filthy nails.

"You're not supposed to be here!" he wailed. "Miss! Miss! Miiiiss!"

He turned and blundered in the direction of the tunnel, and ran straight into Erin. Mira wondered how long she had been there, calmly watching them fumble in the dark. Holly snatched up her sword, but what happened next came too fast for any of them. They heard a faint slapping and popping noise and saw Peter's body jerk back as a gasp erupted from his throat. No one saw the knife but they all sensed it was there. Erin reached out with her free hand to stroke Peter's matted hair.

"I'm sorry, Peter, you've been a good boy, but Daddy doesn't need you anymore."

She placed her hand on his forehead and pushed, sending him sprawling on the ground. Mira immediately ran to his side. He was still breathing. She hauled him up out of the water and pressed a hand to the wound. Caroline had risen to her feet, ready to run at the intruder, but Holly gestured at her to stop.

"Oh, have you got another one? That's nice," said Erin, gesturing with the dripping knife.

"Drop the knife, I am a police officer..." Caroline began through gritted teeth.

"So was Greg Unwin, and he's getting mulched behind you so excuse me if that doesn't impress me much." Erin's flat monotone rose to a piercing yell that reverberated off the round walls.

"Enough of this, Erin. I want to know what you're playing at," Holly demanded.

"It's a bit of a laugh is all," Erin replied with a shrug. "I just like to see that look on your face."

"I don't believe you," Holly said. "That thing could kill everyone in this city, and that is too big for you. Now tell me what's going on!"

"Could it? Wow. That's quite impressive actually," Erin said, her face all little-me innocence. "Anyway, much as I'd like to stay and chat, I think you might have more important things to be getting on with. Hangman, Hangman, slack your line, slack it just a while, I think I see my sister coming, riding many a mile…"

"Erin, stop this!" Holly shouted, as the distant sound of the dirge began to echo off the walls.

"Sister, sister, sister, I bought no gold, for to pay the Hangman's fee…" Erin continued her own song, her furious eyes glowing and her face looking like nothing human as the green light bathed her.

"This isn't you!"

"But I come to see you swingin', swingin' high from this hangman's tree," she finished. "Time's up."

Holly, Mira and Caroline all turned to the plinth. The shape was writhing and pulsing. Cracks were appearing in its skin and viscous fluid was pouring out. Holly turned back to Erin, who let out a high-pitched giggle and pointed to her sister's face.

"Aw, that's the look I was talking about. Anyway, gotta run, but good luck slaying that monster." She raised two thumbs and flashed a gleeful smile. "Go team."

And with that, she disappeared into the well.

"What do we do now?" said Mira, dragging Peter over to the edge of the room, where the water was shallowest. He murmured softly as his arm batted at the stone wall. "We can still go through with your plan, right?"

"No, we don't have time. Can't risk it not working. We need to make it follow us, lead it somewhere we know we can fight it. Mira, grab the case, and follow me." She took the torch from the plinth and tossed it to Caroline. "You, copper, stay here, look after him. Don't worry, you'll be safe. Just make sure his hand's alright."

"What's wrong with his hand?" asked Caroline as she took

over tending Peter's wound from Mira, who splashed across the room to retrieve the case.

"Yeah, sorry about this," replied Holly, and swung her sword over Caroline's head to strike at the wall. Peter let out a shriek of agony as Holly snatched up the little finger she had neatly severed, returned to the plinth and plunged the digit into one of the cracks in the creature's skin.

"Follow the hand that killed you, you bastard," snarled Holly, and then charged after her sister, the sticky finger clutched in her palm.

Mira exchanged a concerned glance with Caroline before following her. Holly was already halfway up the ladder by the time she reached the well, climbing one-handed with the sword, like she was storming a castle. Mira adjusted the strap of the tendicula case, and gingerly stepped across to the first outcropping.

As Caroline moved Peter's right hand to tightly grip his injured left, a roaring and gurgling noise filled the dank chamber. The shape swelled up, then shrank away to nothing like a balloon deflating. Its light was extinguished and there was just a shadow that roared past Caroline and Peter in pursuit of the others, plunging the room into pitch dark aside from their small pool of torchlight. With one hand pressed to Peter's chest, Caroline scrabbled for her phone with the other, her fingers moving automatically to make the call.

"This is DI James. I need an ambulance... Yes, another one. At Pikeing Well immediately. This is an emergency. We're actually in the well. You'll need... whatever you use. I don't know, just bring it, alright? A winch, a ladder, Skippy the Bush Kangaroo, just get here now."

She hung up but kept the light alive as they huddled in the wet darkness together. Caroline could feel the cold water around her getting warmer as, despite her best efforts, Peter's blood flowed away.

"You're the police?" he asked, the effort to speak clearly straining him.

"It's alright," she said. "Help is on its way."

"No, you have to listen to me," he said through ragged breaths. "I killed him…"

"Stay calm. The ambulance is coming."

"No, you don't understand, I killed him," Peter squealed, tears forming in his sunken eyes. "I killed him, I killed him, I killed him…"

"Look," said Caroline conspiratorially. "I don't need to know about this. You were just a kid. I'm sure you didn't mean to hurt anyone. Just try and stay calm."

"Please…"

Caroline gazed down at his tormented face, and suddenly realised what it was he wanted from her. Something only she could give him.

"Peter MacMillan," she began softly. "I am arresting you on suspicion of the murder of Derek Fennell. You do not have to say anything, but it may harm your defence if you do not mention when questioned something you later rely on in court. Anything you do say may be given in evidence. Do you understand?"

"Thank you," he whispered with a sad smile, then his eyes closed and he was no more.

CHAPTER 35

The church of St Martin-cum-Gregory, which had caught Holly's attention earlier that night, was hollow. From outside, it appeared like so many of the old churches that dotted the city, but the central hall stood completely empty, a facade of its former purpose. It had not been put to religious use for many years now. There were no pews, little imagery of faith, just an open arena of grey stone, lined by rows of icy white columns and arches, surrounded by great leaded windows letting a faint light filter in. Even the tower was an empty shell, with no internal wall dividing it from the church, or stairs to ascend – just open space rising to a small, square patch of ceiling. As the rain beat down hard on the metal roof, the ghost of the church reverberated with the impact.

The door banged open heavily and two figures stormed in out of the rain. Old as it was, the church was not without modern additions, and a light switch was quickly found, illuminating the dark hall from fixtures set around the ceiling. Holly shook droplets from her wild hair.

"Why does it always start chucking it down when a monster's eaten your umbrella?" she griped. "Give us the small lantern."

Mira opened the tendicula case and handed the smaller one to Holly, who laid down her sword on the floor, then activated the device, the high-pitched *thrum* bouncing off the stone walls. She ran to the dark wooden pulpit, one of the few remaining religious accoutrements, placed the lantern inside, and returned to Mira.

"I'm waiting for you to ask me why we're here," Holly said.

"I assume because of these." Mira poked one of the slabs in the floor with her foot. There was a name and date inscribed into the stone, and several more had similar inscriptions. "We need the presence of the dead to power the trap, so bodies buried under the church floor. Clever. We take the other lantern down the street so it's far enough away, then trap it."

Holly shook her head as she took off her coat, grabbing a handful of small items from her pocket as she did so, one of which she tossed to Mira. It was a small clamshell phone of crimson plastic.

"There are two numbers saved in that phone," said Holly. "Anything happens to me, you ring the one that isn't yours. They'll know what to do."

"Wait, what are you talking about? What's going to…" Mira stopped startled, as Holly thrust a rummaging hand under her own T-shirt. It took a moment to realise what she was doing, and Mira did not like the answer when she figured it out.

"Did you just put Peter's finger in your bra? That's officially disgusting."

"Wouldn't be the first to get down there," Holly said with a final decisive adjustment. The last item she held was a hair bobble, and she began forcing her unruly curls away from her face and into a tight ponytail. "Anyway, you can't take the tendicula away from the church. Too far from the graves, it won't work."

"Great, so it's got to be near the church to get the power, and far away to not blow up on us. That's impossible!" said Mira, before she noticed that Holly was looking over her head. She turned around and stared in horror into the upper reaches of the tower.

"You can't be serious! How are we supposed to get up there? There's no stairs!"

"We don't," said Holly grimly, picking up the sword. "You do. There's repairs being done on the outside of the tower, so there's scaffolding out the back. Climb up to the top with the big one, and switch it on when you get to the roof. He's following the finger so he's focused on me – on my left pap, to be precise. I'll hold him here."

She swung the sword in a few wide sweeps, but suddenly fell off balance. A wave of nausea came over her, and she pitched forward, dropping the sword to the floor. Mira caught her by the shoulders and steadied her.

"You can't do this, look at you," Mira said. "Holly, this is a really stupid plan."

Holly swallowed a ragged breath, as a distant singing came from the street, and eerie light flickered through the windows. She straightened up, placing a hand on Mira's cheek briefly as she did.

"Yeah, I know. But it's the only one we've got."

They turned to look, and the Hangman was already in the hall with them. It floated ominously on the far side of the church, its tentacles crawling like snakes across the floor. Holly scooped up her sword and forced back her pain and exhaustion. She strode towards it, and whispered something under her breath, so quietly Mira couldn't hear it.

"Holly, don't."

"Pick a song," Holly said as she drew closer to the creature. "And run."

"But you'll die!" shouted Mira.

"I haven't yet," she growled, and leapt forward. The Hangman swung a tentacle, but she dove under it to strike a glancing blow across its body. She was still speaking, but louder now, and this time Mira could hear the words. She wasn't whispering, she was singing, proudly and defiantly.

Mira raced for the door, clutching the case, but the Hangman swung a tentacle across the room and caught her ankle, the cold wet flesh constricting tightly against her leg and burning her skin. Mira clung hard to the door handle as she strained to pull herself free, when suddenly Holly was standing between her and the creature. Her blade slashed through the tendril, sparks striking from the stone floor as the blade scraped across it. The end around Mira's leg shrivelled and faded to nothing. Holly sang out, louder and stronger than ever.

Mira dived through the door and into the storm. The Hangman retracted its arm, the other limbs cradling it. It shrank back for a moment, shuddering as if shocked by its sudden vulnerability. Holly danced forward, swinging her sword and bringing 'The Sensual World' with her.

CHAPTER 36

Mira circled the church in the driving rain, struggling for balance as the mud churned treacherously around her feet. Coming around the far side of the building, she saw a ramshackle structure of metal poles and wooden flooring panels rising alongside the height of the tower. It looked particularly rickety next to the solid blockiness of the church itself. But there was nothing for it. Today was going to be all about climbing. She slipped the shoulder strap of the case over her head, reached out to grasp the chilly metal of the nearest horizontal bar, and headed upwards.

The Hangman's arms sliced through the air from above, and each blow was followed immediately by another as the tendrils moved in circular arcs. Holly leapt from side to side as each arm slapped into the floor with a plume of stone dust before rolling back for the next strike. It was moving too fast, its arms too numerous and swift and its body safely guarded behind them. Holly watched and waited for her opening. As the wounded arm struck the ground, the next came down a fraction slower, and she parried the blow, then spun to slice across the creature's body. Its shoulders swelled and the tentacles writhed in a frenzied display.

"Oh, good one, Holly," she whispered to herself. "Make it cross, why don't you."

The rain was beating into Mira's face and the wind grew stronger the higher she went. The bars of the scaffolding felt like ice beneath her numbing fingers.

Pick a song, Holly had said. Fine. Kate Bush worked for her. As she clambered up to the next level, she gave a faltering stab at the chorus of 'Running Up That Hill' with the little strength she could muster.

Suddenly, her foot slipped against the slick metal bar beneath it. Her hands gripped desperately as she hung suspended in space. Looking down to her dangling feet, she saw the dark ground spinning beneath her. She kicked out towards the scaffold for firmer footing and found it, getting wooden boards beneath her and grabbing for one of the corner poles tightly.

"Problems, problems, definitely problems…"

The Hangman lashed out wildly and caught Holly across the right shoulder, sending her sword spinning across the church to land with a clang on the far side of the room. But it did not take the opportunity for a killer blow. It simply loomed over her, its body swelling and billowing. Holly fancied that it knew she could not hurt it without her weapon and was enjoying her helplessness. For the first time, she had a sense of the kind of man Derek Fennell had been. She looked around the church for something, anything to fend it off with.

She caught sight of a structural support, a horizontal metal bar that stretched between the top ends of two of the arches, high above her head. That would do nicely.

Holly circled slowly, and the Hangman mirrored her, placing itself in the centre of the room, directly between her and where her sword lay. It was being clever. It was also doing exactly what she wanted. Holly dashed away from it and was immediately pursued. As she drew closer to the arches, she leapt into the air. Her hands grabbed the bar and with a roar of effort, she swung her entire body up and around it in one smooth circle, then released her grip to send herself flying over the Hangman. The creature almost comically slammed to a halt before it struck the wall, while Holly landed on her feet, skidding across the floor to where her sword lay. She grabbed it, ran forward and plunged the blade into the creature's body up to the hilt. The singing rose to a shriek as she withdrew the weapon, and the Hangman rearranged its form, the head sinking into the underside of its body, before a new cowl rose up at what had been its back to face its attacker. A tentacle whip-cracked into the floor between Holly's feet, but she did not flinch.

Mira could see the crenelated top of the tower at last. The scaffold didn't quite reach to the very peak, so she stretched over the buttress to pull herself up when a hand gripped her wrist tightly. She was hauled over the short wall, then tossed hard to the slick, flat roof. Small as she was, Erin looked enormous from Mira's prone position, standing against the night sky with eyes blazing maniacally.

"So before we get started, I've just got to ask," she said casually. "Do you like my new hat?"

Holly's head swam and her muscles ached as she batted aside strike after strike of the Hangman's tendrils. When the creature paused, she charged forward, her own blows connecting even quicker as she lashed out at the amorphous shape. She remembered her promise to the city she loved and didn't give the thing that would harm it another opening.

Whatever happens, I'll keep you safe...

"Whatever happens," Erin said. "I'll keep you safe. We'll make it through this. I'm not going to leave you, I promise. Every night, whenever the monsters came, she made me feel so brave. I bet she said the exact same words to you, didn't she? Second-hand promises and broken ones at that."

Mira's frozen fingers fumbled with the slippery clasps of the case, while Erin looked to the sky, letting the rain cascade over her face.

"Please, Erin, let me stop this!"

"Seriously, that's what you're going with? Stupid puppy." Erin grabbed her by her collar, dragged her to her feet, and swung her across the small space on the top of the tower. Mira slammed into the buttress, her head snapping forward to look over the edge. The ground was barely visible in the dark and the rain.

"Do you think she cares?" Erin shouted over the whistling wind. "Do you honestly think she gives a toss about you? About any of us? You climbed all this way, you put your life on the line again and again and again. You actually believed her when she said she'd look after you, and you know what? She'll forget you! That's what she does, it's what she always does! She will crawl back to her hole in the earth and abandon you! Why can't you people ever understand? It's just her and me! It's supposed to be just her and me!"

Mira turned back to face the livid girl, shaking her head in disbelief.

"Oh my God." she said, a hollow laugh in her throat. "Oh my God, you... you... *fucking child!*"

"You don't understand..."

"Don't I?" said Mira. "Because it sounds like you killed all those people just because you've got a strop on at your big sister!"

"She left us!" shrieked Erin. "She made a promise, and when we needed her, she left us, because it were more fun to play the big hero than care what happened to her family! And she will do the same to you because that's what she is!"

"Or she'll die!" Mira replied, grabbing Erin, pinning her arms to her sides and slamming her into the buttress on the opposite side of the tower. "She is fighting your monster down there when she can barely stand! That's what she is! Now let me stop this!"

Erin rolled her eyes, her furious expression giving way to an amused smirk.

"Stupid puppy. Stupid, stupid puppy. She's down there fighting a monster I created. However will she get out of that one? Stupid. It's not going to kill her. Why d'you think it didn't kill her the day we met? 'Cause it answers to me. She's not going to die, you are. She'll just get to feel really bad about it for, ooh, forever."

Mira's grip slackened for an instant, long enough for Erin to crook a leg between her feet and bring her crashing over backwards onto the hard lead surface. Through the rain, she could see the knife glinting in Erin's hands.

Erin crouched down, resting a knee on Mira's midriff to pin her as she leaned in close.

"There's only one kind of person she doesn't forget, and that's the ones who don't come back," Erin said, as she rested the flat of her blade against Mira's face. "I like to know that she cares. I think what happens to you is going to make her care a lot."

Holly didn't see the tendril as it streaked across from her left, and before she could move, it had wrapped around her throat. Her vision blurred as it constricted, burning cold against her skin. She pulled her arm upwards in a sweeping arc in front of her, the sword slicing through where she hoped the tentacle stretched, and was rewarded as the flesh choking her curled up and vanished. She took in a great gasp of air.

"Two down, four to go. I don't think you're even trying, Derek," she rasped.

The Hangman's cowl rose up, and out of the darkness underneath sprang the great clumping, waxy arm of its crayon form. The hammer blow sent Holly sprawling to the floor.

"Don't tease the monster," she moaned to herself. "One day I'll remember that one."

"You know I probably shouldn't be doing this," grinned Erin, her voice trembling with manic glee. "But I don't think anyone'll notice you in all the kerfuffle."

It was taking all of Mira's strength to hold her arm back as the knife pressed closer and closer to her eye.

"Five people are dead because you don't want to share," Mira spat. "Killing me won't make that any less pathetic."

"Four actually. You can't count Peter," Erin said with a pedantic air, and Mira saw it. The glimmer of a clue that Erin had let slip.

"You don't know about Susan."

"Who the bloody Hell is Susan?" said Erin, relaxing her grip. She looked genuinely baffled.

Mira pushed on, joining the dots like her life depended on it.

"You don't, do you?" she said, with an exhausted laugh. "Of

251

course, you don't. You're like Holly, you only exist in the city! But the Hangman doesn't, it can leave whenever it wants to! It was in Howden this afternoon. It killed Peter's mother! And you don't know!"

"You're lying." Erin waggled the knife shakily as she backed away, her face clouded by worry at the train of thought Mira had set her on.

"You were in the well," Mira continued, rising to her feet as she pressed her momentary advantage. "How many pods were there?"

"I... I..."

"How many?" screamed Mira.

Erin looked terrified. Her malevolence had been swept into the storm and she was every inch the child she appeared to be.

"It doesn't obey you. Not anymore. It's Derek now. It does what Derek wants. You can't control it, Erin, so your sister is going to die!"

The tentacle shot forward like a harpoon and punched a hole through Holly's right shoulder. Her head snapped back with the shock of the blow. The sword fell from her useless arm and she dropped to her knees. A cry of pain escaped her lips as the Hangman wrenched its arm clear, sending a spray of her blood across the flagstones.

"To brig o' dread," the Hangman hissed to itself. "Thou com'st at last..."

Mira grappled with the box while Erin stood dumbfounded. She pulled the lantern free, placing it firmly on the roof. As she reached for the control with shuddering fingers, she caught a flash of movement out of the corner of her eye and just managed to grab hold of Erin's wrist as she thrust the knife forward.

"No!" roared Erin, the tears in her eyes mingling with the driving rain. "You don't get to save her! I'm gonna save her! You're gonna die and I'm gonna save her!"

Erin's hands were shaking, her grip less strong than it had been.

As the blade descended, Mira pushed against her wrist, straining with all the strength she had left to twist it round, to drive the point of the weapon anywhere that was away from herself. She felt a grinding sensation as it plunged through something soft, and in between something hard. Erin pulled back and Mira saw the knife protruding from the dragon on her T-shirt, a growing red stain drowning the image and a look of profound irritation on her face.

"How many sodding times!" she shouted, jumping up and down as she spoke. "Indestructible! How hard is that to remember! Inde-sodding-structible!"

"You'd better hope so," said Mira, scooping up the leather case and swinging it with exhausted arms to hit Erin in the face. The blow knocked her back and sent her tumbling over the edge of the tower. Mira slumped to her knees, crawled forward, and peered over to the ground far below. She could just make out Erin, her body impaled on the metal railings surrounding the edge of the church grounds.

"I really don't like her," Mira sighed.

The Hangman's arms were all around Holly now, binding her tightly as they pulled her off the ground. It took a tremendous effort of will for Holly to use her right arm to push aside the tentacles, and pain flared through her whole body every time she did. There was no stopping her left, however, which pulled and tore at the writhing mass of damp flesh until glowing ichor dripped on the church floor. The Hangman rose into the air and took her with it, shaking her like a ragdoll. Finally, it swung her round and hurled her in the direction of the great window on the tower wall.

"Oh scut," said Holly as the wall rose up to meet her. She pulled her knees up to her chest and wrapped her left arm around her head, forming her body into a tight ball before it tore through the lead and glass, fragments slicing at her as she came to land with a crash in the mud outside.

When she looked up, she saw the face of her sister. Erin's

body was painfully stretched across the spikes of the railings and her head was turned at an impossible angle, a thin trickle of blood leaking from the corner of a wry smile. A sound of shattering glass erupted from behind Holly, and she flopped over to see the Hangman leap into the gap in the broken window, its huge bulk framed by the ornate opening like some terrible living gargoyle. Its arms crawled like glowing ivy across the tower and sent a rain of glass fragments scattering to the ground. Holly tried to stand, but couldn't. Pain and exhaustion flooded over her, her strength ebbing away as her blood mingled with the rain and mud.

The Hangman began to twitch uncontrollably. Its body swelled and contracted, while its arms beat violently against the stone walls. The tune of its singing degenerated into a piercing shriek of torment. The cowled head stretched forward as if trying to get away but it couldn't. It was as if the creature was being sucked back into the church by something inside, something too powerful to resist. The great distorted child's drawing face rose from its body and roared one last time before it was gone in an instant, its body pulling into itself and disappearing through the broken window with a booming rush of air. A moment later, there was a sound like thunder, and a circle of brilliant white light exploded out from the top of the tower. And then there was silence.

Holly collapsed back against the railings, her breathing slow and shallow. Her eyes fluttered closed briefly, but she was roused by a faint tapping on the side of her head. She turned to see Erin's dangling arm, the fingers right beside her face. The girl twisted her broken neck further round to regard her, and spat out a mouthful of blood.

"Bloody hell, sis, look at the state of us," she gurgled.

Holly gave a tired and grim laugh.

"You want to watch you don't bleed to death down there," Erin added, a faint note of concern just detectible beneath her inappropriately casual tone. "This is a bit different, getting impaled and all, but I think I'll walk away from it. Sorry to disappoint."

"Don't say that," snapped Holly, the exclamation draining her further as her breathing slowed to a wheeze. "I don't want that, you know I don't want that."

"No?"

"No," Holly said firmly. "I just… Sometimes I wish you'd forget me."

Erin wriggled as she tried to free herself from the spikes piercing her body. "You don't ask much, do you?"

"Erin, shut up and listen, please." Holly looked away from her sister to stare at the great broken hole in the side of the tower. "I can't remember our names. Our real names, the ones mother and father gave us, I don't know them anymore. I don't know if you know, don't suppose you'd say if you did. And most of the time, it don't bother me, 'cause I get to be Holly Trinity instead, but when you're around it just gets me. 'Cause I can't remember me name or yours, but I remember every single time we've hurt each other."

Erin remained still and silent, as she listened to her sister's lament. Holly's voice grew quieter and more distant as she spoke.

"Norman says I should stop thinking of you as me sister, but I can't. So you have to. Because all this, it's no good for either of us. I need you to forget me, please just forget me."

"Maybe I will," said Erin, for once devoid of mockery.

Holly's eyes had drifted closed, but she heard a series of wet popping noises as Erin pulled herself free from the spikes.

"You stuck a rocket up Norman's arse today. He'll come down hard, no doubt. They'll want to stop me being me again, so yeah, maybe I'll forget. But just for a bit. You know how I get."

There was a dull thud and a splash. Holly opened her eyes to see her sister crouching before her.

"I made me choice," whispered Holly. "I put this whole place first, before you, and I thought you'd understand. I don't know how to fix all this…"

"Just say what you usually say when you get all maudlin." Erin's voice was gentle and almost sincere. "Tell me you left because you thought it were the right thing to do. Tell me you only ever wanted what were best for me. Tell me you love me. And then tell me you're sorry."

"I… do…" said Holly, as her head drooped forward. "And I am, I'm sorry…"

Erin nodded and leaned closer, her small hands cupping the sides of Holly's head, and stroking her face with tiny, delicate fingers. She leaned forward and gently kissed her on the forehead, then held her sister's head against her own for a moment as Holly drifted into unconsciousness. A hand slid down, and Erin pushed her left thumb into the oozing wound in Holly's shoulder. Holly's head whipped back and she cried out, her eyes snapping open to see the cold, hard face of what her sister had become.

"Good," it said.

CHAPTER 37

Mira blinked, then blinked again to banish the spots from her vision. It was still raining. Her skin tingled with an electrical charge and her ears rang slightly. She sat up on the roof, leant up against the buttress of the tower, and peered intently through the rain at the box. The glass was dark now as if stained with soot. When she had activated it, she hadn't been sure what would happen, and for a moment nothing had. Then there had been a flash of blinding light and a rush of wind that had knocked her from her feet.

Was it over?

She shuffled forward to where the box lay and picked it up. It was even heavier than before. Through clearer patches in the black glass, she could see *something* moving. Over the wind and the rain, she could just make out a thin, deteriorating refrain of the Lyke-Wake Dirge, which faded and died.

It was over.

Mira slumped back against the wall with a short burst of breathless laughter. But her feeling of triumph was immediately undermined by a nagging voice in her head. *What do we do now?* The answers that came were frightening and exciting, but one soon blotted out the others with its urgency. Holly. Where was Holly?

Caroline drove aimlessly around the city. Her immediate responsibilities had all been dealt with – Peter's body had been taken away and her colleagues had been updated on what she felt able to tell them. But she felt the need to find her way back to Holly and Mira, to help in whatever way she could. So she drove until she saw something. She had a feeling that whatever it was, she would not be able to miss it. A flash of light in her rear-view mirror proved her right.

Mira clambered shakily down the last few levels of the scaffolding. The prospect of falling had pushed aside other concerns, aided by the weight of the case and her cold and uncertain limbs. She jumped down the last level and ran across the wet churchyard. Holly lay on the ground beside the fence, not moving. Erin's body was nowhere to be seen. Mira raced over to her friend and dropped to her knees beside her. Blood was running from a wound in her shoulder and several smaller cuts across her body. She didn't seem to be breathing. Mira tried to remember that this was the third time she had seen Holly like this. *Yes, but she wasn't bleeding to death then, was she?* came the voice of fear. Mira pulled off her rain-soaked jacket and pressed it to the wound as if she knew what she was doing. She knew with mounting dread that Erin must have survived the fall. She waited anxiously for approaching footsteps and a knife plunged into her back. Instead, a car pulled into the cobbled street alongside the church, and Caroline ran to meet her.

"Where's Erin?" shouted Mira hoarsely. "Did you see her?"

Caroline shook her head, and pulled her phone from a pocket. "This is DI James, we need an ambulance... yes, a third one, at Martin-cum..."

"Wait!" said Mira, suddenly reminded of something. "Look after her! She told me what to do!"

Mira dug the tiny red phone from the pocket of the blood-soaked jacket, then left Caroline to look after Holly. The phone had survived the struggle on the roof intact. As promised, there were two numbers stored, so she rang the unfamiliar one. After only three rings someone answered.

"Oh my word, this is you. Sorry, I meant to say, Hail the King..." came a voice she recognised.

"Angie?" said Mira.

"Oh... is this that nice girl we met the other day? Yes, it is, isn't it? How are you, dear?"

"We're at a church on Micklegate. Please, we need your help, Holly's hurt, I don't know if she's..."

"Alright dear, don't upset yourself. Can you get her to Holy Trinity or do you want us to come to you?"

"We've got a car," Mira said. "I think we can..."

"Right you are. We'll get down there now and get things ready. And don't you worry, dear. Everything will be fine."

Mira snapped the phone shut and turned to Caroline. "We need to get her to Goodramgate, to the old church."

Caroline accepted the vague instruction without question, and together, they lifted Holly up and carried her over to the car.

"Wait, we should... I need to get her things." Mira left Caroline to prop Holly up, waving the detective's objection aside as she ran back to the church. Somehow, she felt sure that leaving the sword and the lantern behind was a bad move, that they needed to be kept safe. Mira stumbled through the door and snatched up Holly's coat, then slipped it on for convenience. The thick material felt warm and comforting. She took up the sword and retrieved the other half of the tendicula from the pulpit. It had developed the same smoky stain as its larger twin. She tried not to think about the splashes of blood on the stone floor.

Mira raced outside to where Caroline was parked with the engine running and leapt into the back seat beside Holly, whose head came to rest against her shoulder. They drove away at speed, the lights of the dark city glittering against the rain-spotted windows. Briefly during the silent journey, Holly's eyes opened a little, but only once.

"We did it, Holly. It's over. You're nearly home, just hang on, okay?" Mira whispered, trying her best not to sound afraid. She caught a glimpse of Caroline's eyes in the mirror, and saw no hope in them. She tightened her grip on Holly's pierced shoulder, while clutching her limp fingers in the other hand.

"You haven't died yet," she whispered. "Not yet."

Soon they had pulled up outside Holy Trinity, where a figure stood by the gate, sheltering under an umbrella. When Mira stepped out of the car, she saw it was Chloe, who took Holly's belongings from her as she and Caroline carried the unconscious woman into the church. Inside, all of the candles were lit, bringing small patches of warmth to the cold grey surroundings. Angie stood by the trapdoor.

"Quickly now. Mira, can you and Chloe carry her down to the coop?" she said, her voice urgent and business-like. She placed a firm hand on Caroline's arm. "Sorry, dear, you'll have to wait up here."

"What do you mean? What's going on?" Caroline said, appearing slightly put out but relinquishing her hold on Holly to Chloe nonetheless.

"She doesn't know you, dear," said Angie kindly. "Maybe one day she will, but not today."

Angie climbed into the crypt, followed by Chloe, who took hold of Holly's ankles and indicated to Mira to lower her down. Between them they carried her down the steps, and when they reached the door of the Hen Hole, Angie placed a hand on Mira's shoulder.

"We'll take it from here, love. Don't you worry," she said with a reassuring smile, as Chloe took Holly up under her arms and dragged her inside. "You should see to your friend. You'd better take this though. You look like you could both do with it."

From the pocket of her bulky raincoat, she produced a small thermos and pressed it into Mira's chilled fingers. She squeezed her empty hand and smiled more broadly than before, then followed her granddaughter into the chamber and closed the door behind her.

When Mira returned to the church, she saw Caroline seated at the end of a simple wooden bench. She was about to speak when the sight of her folded hands and bowed head silenced her. After a moment, Caroline looked up from her thoughts.

"Sorry, didn't mean to disturb you," said Mira in a respectful whisper, and raised the flask for Caroline to see. "Angie wishes us tea."

She came and sat beside the detective, and poured out a

steaming capful, which they passed back and forth between them, bursts of heat suffusing their cold bodies as they drank.

"It's okay. Old habits, I guess. Being somewhere like this." Caroline seemed to relax in Mira's presence for the first time. "Are you religious at all?"

"Not so much. Dabbled when I was a kid, though. Used to love going to the temple with my Grandma," Mira replied. "I think my parents were secretly very happy when boys became more interesting."

They sat side by side in the candlelight, in quiet contemplation. Mira pulled Holly's coat tighter around herself to shut out the cold, then shivered all the more when she saw the dark patch where Holly's blood had run during the journey. She glanced sideways at Caroline's face, trying to get a handle on someone who had been an obstacle in her life a few hours previously. She could sense something at work and had a notion what it might be. She also needed a distraction, so decided to pry.

"When we met tonight," Mira said, "Holly was surprised you noticed us. Because nobody does, if you can believe that. I thought it was just because you were following me, but it's something else, isn't it? I don't want to intrude, it's just... I know how hard it is when you can't share these things."

Caroline nodded her understanding. "A few years ago, there was this case. A couple died in their home – you don't want to know the details. I know people always say that, but you *really* don't want to know the details. We could never figure it out. How the killer got in, where he went, how he... did what he did. Nothing made sense. They just binned it in the end. Unsolved. But I couldn't get it out of my head, there was something... not right, and I had to know. I kept going over it, trying to find the one thing that made sense of it all."

"Did you find it?" asked Mira, as Caroline passed the cup into her shaking hands.

"Sort of," Caroline replied, touching her scarred cheek. "They found me wandering the streets, and I had this. No idea where it came from. I took the hint and dropped it. But then I came here and this whole city feels a bit like that house where they died. Not in a bad way, just like there's something out of the corner of my eye that I can't see. After a while, you start looking harder. I've been looking for what I saw tonight for a very long time. And now I've seen it, I feel like I just got given another one of these."

She squinted as she studied Mira's face closely.

"Yours barely shows," she said and took another sip of tea, then licked her lips thoughtfully. "Is there whisky in this?"

"I bloody well hope so," said Mira, and they laughed together for a moment.

Caroline sank a hand into her coat pocket, and held something miniscule out to Mira. A sim card for a mobile phone rested between her thumb and forefinger.

"I picked that up off the floor in Nunnery Lane when your phone got smashed," Caroline explained. "As far as anyone knows, you were never there tonight."

"But that woman saw me."

"She also saw her dead ex, a giant squid, and the ghost of Frank Sidebottom," Caroline replied matter-of-factly. "I'm not sure she's a reliable witness. Traumatic experience."

"Thank you," said Mira, taking the tiny chip from her hand.

"Don't thank me yet. I have a feeling you won't like what I'm going to say next." Caroline took an ominous moment, then dropped her bombshell. "Peter is dead. He confessed to killing his father and then he died. And we have five victims and no killer."

Mira sprang to her feet, as if the horror of what Caroline was suggesting had physically driven her away.

"You can't! He didn't kill those people!"

"Mira, right now, you are the only suspect in this case. The only way this doesn't follow you for the rest of your life is if somebody else did it."

"So what, we just frame someone for murder instead?" Mira looked at her aghast, but Caroline remained utterly impassive in the face of her outrage.

"We're not talking about sending an innocent man to prison," she said. "Peter's dead. And he has killed a man…"

"He was a kid. He didn't know what he was doing!"

"I know, I know. I think he was still a kid at the end, really," Caroline sighed, her hard exterior cracking ever so slightly. "But he still killed his father and he must have had an inkling what Erin was doing."

"But who do we say killed him?" Mira asked. "Because if you think you can arrest Erin…"

"I did," Caroline said, not blinking. "In self-defence. I'll have to go to counselling, which I'll probably need after tonight anyway, but that'll be the end of it."

A sickening thought overcame Mira. "Oh my God, you've done this before…"

"No, of course I haven't. I'm just trying to work with what we've got!" she snapped as she stood and faced Mira directly.

Mira could see that the suggestion of impropriety had genuinely offended Caroline, but her tone became gentler as she made her case.

"As of this afternoon, Peter has no surviving family, and from what I've seen of his case file, nobody missed him much when he disappeared. He's an easy way out. Look, Mira, I have a meeting with my super tomorrow morning, and it's probably going to end in me being taken off the case. If you want my help, this is it. Tomorrow, you take your chances with whoever they give it to, and they will come after you. I don't like this any more than you do, but we have five dead people whose families need to know it's over. Mira, please let me tell Greg's daughters that it's over."

Mira nodded her assent, and Caroline instantly became every inch the police officer giving a report.

"Good. Then this is what happened," she said. "Peter killed his mother in front of you. He told you he had seen you at the book shop. He told you he killed those people. He told you who was next, and that he would kill you too if you went to the police. You didn't say anything to me because you were scared, but you knew you had to do something. So you tried to warn the next victim. I was following you, caught Peter in the act, pursued him to Pikeing Well, where he attacked me with a knife, and was killed in the struggle. Can you remember all that?"

"Sure," said Mira resentfully. "What's one more lie now I'm so good at it?"

Caroline ignored the remark and continued with her instructions. "Tomorrow you'll come in and make a statement. You will be asked to identify Peter's body. You'll be told how brave you are by people who have no idea how true that is. And then you'll be free to go home. Which, incidentally, I recommend you do, because all this is nuts. You should stay away from her, for your own sake."

She looked Mira in the eye, then cracked a smile. "But since I can see that's not going to happen, you know where I am if you need me, okay?"

"Be careful around the river," Mira said, and Caroline looked puzzled by the advice. "Peter's dead. But what if he isn't gone?"

"Well, if he comes after me, I'll have you two to call on," said Caroline, her gaze suddenly drawn over Mira's shoulder.

Mira turned to see Angie approaching clumsily, rubbing her legs and drawing in deep breaths with each step. Chloe stood further back, the tendicula case slung over her shoulder.

"Is she alright?" Mira blurted out.

"She'll be fine, dear," groaned Angie. "She's sleeping. Oh, my knees."

"Can I see her?"

"No, dear. I mean she's *sleeping*, gone back, you know? Until next time." Angie sighed and gave her most motherly smile. "Ooh, what a night. We'd all best get home, Chloe's got school in the morning, and I've got to see about exorcising that thing. I dare say you two must be exhausted. Could you let me have that coat back, dear? It'll want to go in the drycleaning."

Mira slipped Holly's coat off and handed it to the old woman, who folded it carefully over one arm.

"Oh, thank you, dear," she said, letting a trace of irritation creep into her jollity. "The fuss she kicks up if this old thing isn't there when she wakes up. You'd not believe the notes she used to leave me, all that effing and jeffing…"

"It's been down a well and she's bled all over it," Mira admitted. "Hope it's not a lost cause."

Angie's gaze flicked around the church and she leaned in as if imparting a great secret.

"Don't tell her, but a couple of times, I couldn't get it cleaned up, so I just bought a new one. She's never noticed the difference."

Mira laughed softly, but the thought was not a comforting one.

CHAPTER 38

Sam had been dozing off on the sofa when he became dimly aware of the sound of the flat door opening and closing quietly. He finally woke to hear wordless groans and mumbles just audible on the other side of the living room door. When he opened it, a rain-dampened Mira was revealed in the process of peeling a grimy sock from her left foot. The ends of her trousers were caked in mud, as were the shoes that had been discarded in corners of the vestibule. She snapped upright with a start, the sock clasped in her hand.

"Hi," she said, silently wishing she was holding something that smelled better. "I... got caught in the rain."

"I tried texting you. Is everything alright?" he asked.

"Yeah, I lost my phone. And my coat as well. Not having a good night." She shook her head, then realised a second too late what she had just said. "Sorry, no, did have a good night, bits of it were very good with... but then not so much with..."

She gestured from him to the door, and tried to read something on his gently amused face.

"I'm sorry I ran out on you," she sighed. "That was probably really harsh, wasn't it? It's just Holly had a... family thing, and it was really urgent and she needed help, but it's done now and I'm back. And everything's okay, we can... pick up where we left off? I mean, not exactly where we left off, but we can talk or... or we can forget. You know, just go back to normal. Or... you know what, I'm exhausted. I have no idea what I'm saying anymore. I'm just going to go to bed, and in the morning, or probably the afternoon actually, we can talk or forget or... um, yes. Good night."

She reached for the door handle of the box room, but then Sam placed his hand over hers. She turned to look up at his face and saw the kindness that had always been there.

"Mira. You don't have to sleep in there. I mean, if you didn't want to."

"You know," said Mira, narrowing her eyes. "It wouldn't kill you to interrupt when I start gabbling."

"I like it when you gabble," he said with a smile. "I always have."

Mira shared his laughter as she collapsed up against him, their arms wrapping tightly around each other. His body felt hot against her own chilly frame, and she relaxed into the comforting warmth as hands gently caressed her shoulder and back. Even so, she could not feel entirely at ease. There was a weight that needed to be lifted. She knew tomorrow she would have to lie, so tonight, she would not. Not to this man, and not to herself. She knew she couldn't say all of it, but she said what she could, and every word was true.

"Sam, I…" she began. "I know who killed Chris. And that woman today. I saw him."

"What do you mean?" He pulled back from her, a worried look entering his eyes.

"I saw him, when he killed them both. I thought he might kill me too, I was so scared…"

"Oh my God, Mira," Sam said, all shocked unease, as if the killer might leap out on them at any moment. "Look, we need to talk to the police again…"

"It's okay, I did that tonight," she said soothingly. "I spoke to that detective again. They know who he is, it's all over now…"

"Why didn't you tell me?" he said, the sharpness of the accusation taking Mira by surprise after so much unquestioning support.

"I know, I should have," she admitted. "You knew something was wrong, and you gave me a hundred chances to say what. But I was too scared to talk to anyone. I thought something might happen to you if I did, I just couldn't. But it's over now. He's gone and I don't have to be afraid of him anymore. So it's okay. Is it okay?"

Sam remained silent. Mira stared intently at his face and could see him starting to slip away from her. She could sense what was worrying him, and raced to smother his fear.

"Sam, please believe me, what happened tonight, that wasn't me trying to distract you from all this. That was something I've wanted for a very long time. And I am not exaggerating when I say that this has been the strangest week of my life. So much has happened and I've not been ready for any of it, and I just couldn't see my way out. Please say something."

It took Sam a moment to give her what she wanted, but it seemed to last for hours.

"When did you get so brave?"

Mira winced at the word. "I don't know. People have been saying that to me a lot today. It'd be nice if I could feel good about it. But I just feel like I've been clinging on for dear life."

"That's kind of how I've felt for a while now," he admitted. "Then suddenly I didn't have to."

Mira raised an eyebrow as she scrutinised his demeanour. "You seem oddly calm."

"Well, that's good, because I'm trying very hard not to freak out," he admitted. "Mira, I'm not going to say this is all normal, it's not, you've got mixed up in things I could never understand."

Mira dodged his gaze, trying not to give anything away.

"But like I said, I'd rather know," Sam continued. "I just wanted to know what was going on with you. Obviously, it's your choice what you tell me, but if you trust me, I can try and help."

"You have no idea how much you have already."

"I can carry on doing that," he said. "Just tell me what you need."

Mira felt the weight of the world slipping away. She dove forward and clung to him, sinking deeper into the warmth of his arms.

"I need…" she began, but stumbled for words as she rested her head against his shoulder. "I need to be safe somewhere, and

I want it to be here, with you. And whatever happens out there, I just want to come back here and be safe with you."

"Okay," he said.

They kissed and everything slipped away, while everything else came rushing back.

"And I want to take this other sock off right now."

Elsewhere in the city, a small boy was gently dreaming. He lay curled up in his bed, his fingers twitching unconsciously as his mind wandered elsewhere. Caroline watched her son from the doorway. Kicking off her shoes, she tiptoed silently across the room and sat down on the bed beside him. He did not wake but rolled over to lie close to her as she sat still and silent, with her eyes open in the darkness.

As the sun rose the next day, Erin waited on the bridge once again. She had run, which was pointless but felt appropriate. But now her time was passing. She did not watch the dawn; her eyes were fixed on the ground and her own boots. Silently, a pair of bare feet glided across the tarmac to stand alongside them. She felt a gentle hand on her shoulder and looked up with sad eyes.

A great flapping and squawking reverberated around the bedroom, and Sam sprang awake. He had become used to its absence, but now the familiar noise was coming from outside the window. The geese were on the river for the first time in a week, beating the water with their wings and uttering their rasping cries at one another.

"And I was just beginning to miss them," grumbled Sam, but Mira did not respond. She lay on her side, deep in a peaceful and dreamless sleep. He lay back down beside her, and wrapped an arm gently across her midriff. She did not stir. It was safe here.

CHAPTER 39

George Arthur Lankin gazed at the tiny, moist creature that squirmed before him, its body slick with its own filth. With a disapproving tut, he reached for the spray bottle at his feet and squirted the leaf. The lily beetle obligingly dropped to the floor.

"There," he said with gentle satisfaction.

Looking up, he saw the girl standing at the gate of the allotment, her hands dug deep in her pockets and a sheepish expression on her pale face. He rose to his feet and gestured for her to come in, then unlocked the door of his small shed. The cluttered interior was washed over with amber sunlight streaming through grimy windows. A table sat against one wall and on it, a large set of drawers made of dark wood. He pulled one open, then picked up a brass scoop and a paper bag from a shoe box that lay alongside it. As Erin entered and flopped into a lawn chair in the corner, he filled the bag with sweets from the drawer, and handed it to her. She poked through the contents purposefully, before looking to him in disappointment.

"There's no red ones," she whined.

"I don't recall authorising the killing of Mira Chaudhri," Lankin replied casually.

"I just thought, you know, you might be okay with it. You don't like her having help," Erin said.

"In the past," said Lankin, "I have asked you to remove certain people who became too close to your sister. That does not give you carte-blanche to judge who I wish to be rid of."

"No, sir," said Erin nervously.

"Your sister's new friend interests me. I wish to see how things develop. It may come to pass that this relationship will be of use to me in the future. So unless I say so, you will take no further action against her."

"Yes, sir."

"I will not have you defying my wishes for the sake of a family squabble."

"No, sir."

"Nor will I have you sulk." He crouched down to her and held out his open hand. A piece of bright red liquorice sat in his palm. Erin beamed back at him, as she scooped up the sweet and thrust it hungrily into her mouth.

"The Hangman was a marvellous creation," said Lankin with a fond smile. "Do you know, I've not seen a Harvester at work since the Fall of Rome. You really have done very well."

"It's not much good to us now," Erin replied.

"Patience. It's all grist for the mill," Lankin said. "And perhaps it is a little too soon for such drastic measures. We've come a long way, you and I, and this city. Soon, the end of all things will be at hand."

He rose to his feet, and extended a hand to the girl.

"But not just yet. For now, there is work to be done. Come along, you can make yourself useful and give an old man a hand with his azaleas."

CHAPTER 40

The sun shone through the dusty windows of the second-hand book shop across from the Minster, where a now thoroughly bored Mira Chaudhri was trying her best not to nod off.

Life had gone back to normal. Sort of. Some things, one thing in particular, were not normal as she had come to know them. In fact, she could safely say they were better, very much so, if a little scary at times. But there were no more monsters to fight, no mysteries to solve, no spectres to confront. Just her, a book shop and a different sort of adventure.

And there was no more Holly.

Of course, Mira had been told that Holly would be gone when her work was done, but she'd also been told that she would come back. That had been the whole point in offering her help, that there would always be something else. But after a few days, it seemed she was gone for good, and Mira's life felt small. The day they'd first met, Mira's life had already been feeling small. But now just when she should be happy, it was as if everything was shrinking. The sensible part of her brain reminded her that she was not the guardian of the city, that she was lucky to still be alive, and her chances of seeing thirty were drastically improved by Holly's absence. The Hangman still haunted her dreams and he did not need company in there.

The silly part of her brain felt like there was a really great party going on down the street to which she wasn't invited.

She ticked herself off for thinking that way. It felt ungrateful now that things were going so well with Sam. She'd done her bit, been rewarded, and Holly was enjoying a well-earned sleep that would last for decades if the city was fortunate. It's not like Holly was just going to be standing in front of her one day, waiting to go on another adventure.

She opened her eyes. Holly resolutely refused to be standing in front of her.

Instead, a clattering came from upstairs, and Tony entered the room, half-falling down the last few steps. His hair was somewhat askew, his eyes were ringed and there was a noticeable stain of baby vomit on the shoulder of his jumper. But on the whole, he seemed happy.

"Do you think anyone would mind if I had a nap in art history?" he asked.

"I can't speak for the customers, so on your own head be it," she joked, surrendering their one and only chair. "I can pop out for coffee, if that's any use."

"You are a life-saver," he sighed, slumping into the chair. "It's caught up with me all of a sudden. I miss sleep. Sleep was good. And I was doing so well this morning. I even got her to buy a book."

"Who?" said Mira, as she slipped into her recently acquired new jacket.

"The Red Queen," mumbled Tony, not noticing her startled reaction. "She came in while you were out at lunch, and I was all ready for another epic browse, but when I spoke to her, she knew what she wanted, and actually paid for it. I think parenthood's improving my salesmanship. Mira? Mira, are you alright?"

Mira wasn't listening. Her eyes were fixed on a piece of paper pinned to the notice board, where Peter MacMillan had once glowered at them. The scrawling message on it read *Rowntree Park, 8 o'clock tonight. Might be dangerous.*

At one end of Rowntree Park stood a simple bandstand. It was nothing more than a raised circle of concrete surrounded by a natural bowl of grass, ringed with hedges and beyond that a circular line of trees. The park was closed and deserted, except for one solitary figure, who stood in the middle of the stage as if about to deliver an aria. Her purple coat was as good as new

273

and her sword sat at her left hip. Her right hand rested on an umbrella, the handle carved into the head of a duck with an iridescent green surface. The amber eyes caught what light there was and sparkled.

"Did you pick a song yet?" she called out into the night.

"How did...?" began Mira, who had approached the bandstand from behind, she had assumed unnoticed. "Quite liking 'Hounds of Love' at the moment."

Holly turned to face her with a broad smile.

"Yeah, that fits." She tilted her head and took a moment to regard Mira closely before forming her diagnosis. "You look happy."

"I am, yes," Mira said, as she hopped up onto the stage. "It's good to see you up and about."

"So how long have I been gone?" Holly asked. "I know it's the same year, but I'm a bit fuzzy besides. Last thing I remember, I were in a hell of a state. Were we in a car? I remember a car. Then this morning happened. I'd say I'd missed you, if it's been long enough to say that, but I just sort of skipped the bit in between. And it might have been yesterday for all I know. I'd sound a bit clingy if I said I missed you from yesterday."

"It's been three weeks," Mira said, happily letting the familiar stream of consciousness wash over her. "And you can say you missed me if you like. A 'thank you, Mira, for saving my life' wouldn't go amiss either."

"Thank you, Mira, for saving my life," Holly repeated in a childlike monotone. "I were sorry I missed you at the shop this morning, really. Did you see I bought a book? Thought I probably should. Actually, I think I'm in it. It's always a bit weird when that happens. You up for more thrilling escapades?"

"I'm here," said Mira, as she turned to the one nagging thought undermining her excitement. "Just tell me your sister isn't going to turn up."

"No, nowt to do with her. Just a common or garden boggat this time, ordinary day at the office. Still, it might kill me, or at least drool on me coat, so I'll be glad of the help," she said cheerily, before deciding to engage with the question that was hanging in the air. "I think one way or another she's been sent to her room. Serves her right, the mardy cow."

Mira didn't entirely believe the remonstration. There was sadness in Holly's demeanour, but another wave of energy quickly washed it away. She tossed her umbrella to Mira with a smile. "Here, you'll need this. Graymalkin knocked it up for me. When this thing rears its ugly head, just point the brolly at it, then press the duck's eye."

Mira held the umbrella at arms' length. She didn't entirely like the way the duck was looking at her.

"What does it do?" she asked.

"It's complicated. I don't really have time to explain, but you'll figure it out," Holly replied. "So, three weeks with Sam, how's that working out?"

"You don't have time to explain the magic umbrella," Mira said slowly. "But we've got time to talk about my love life."

"This is all the time I get, do you think I'm gonna waste it on summat as boring as brolly instructions?" Holly replied. "I'd rather catch up with you, then improvise when it gets here."

Her explanation was interrupted by a rustling in the bushes along the edge of the amphitheatre. A low groaning and grumbling could be heard. Holly drew her sword, while Mira raised the mysterious umbrella.

"It's in the trees," whispered Holly.

"It's coming," Mira replied on cue, and was greeted with a Cheshire cat grin.

The creature burst out of the undergrowth with a mighty bellow, and they ran forward to meet it. What happened next took it completely by surprise.

Find out more at www.bensawyerauthor.wordpress.com